Art Learning Situations
For Elementary Education

Warren Anderson

University of Arizona

WADSWORTH PUBLISHING COMPANY, INC., BELMONT, CALIFORNIA

DEDICATION

To Karl, Brian, Linnea,
other children,
and their teachers

L.C. Cat. Card No.: 65-22642
Printed in the United States of America

PHOTOLITHOPRINTED by MALLOY LITHOGRAPHING, INC.
ANN ARBOR, MICHIGAN

Contents

Contents

Art Learning Situations

Introduction

In the elementary schools many classroom teachers are at least partly responsible for the development of children's aesthetic and artistic potentialities. This book is intended to help teachers to cope with that responsibility.

In order to help a teacher focus on several aspects of this responsibility sixteen objectives for art learning have been introduced. These objectives, mostly derived from the author's experiences in art and education, are value judgments as to what is of worth in art learning. There is considerable current consensus that they are worthy objectives. As value judgments, however, these objectives are subject to further scrutiny and possible modification by anyone who would choose to employ them.

Each of the sixteen objectives, with the exception of one, is followed by a set of related art learning situations, which can be developed in a classroom. Most of these involve an open-ended kind of problem solving. Moreover, each situation within a set is intended to make the objective to which it relates become as "real" as possible in practice. For example, an art learning situation related to the objective "Recognition of a range of art expression from pictorial to pure" relates *mainly* to that objective rather than to any of the other fifteen. Of course, all modes of activity in art relate to one another. But by focusing on one specifically stated objective from the over-all sea of artistic endeavor, the teacher can plan for more concentrated learning. In essence, these objectives and related learning situations serve as guidelines, not dicta.

It is hoped that this objective-related learning situation approach will increase the scope of an art curriculum and leave less to chance. The ability to make more adequate evaluations should also be considerably enhanced by operating from a platform of well-articulated objectives. Chance, questionable scope, and fictitious sequence will no doubt still remain, but to a lesser degree.

Each set of art learning situations, related to a specific singular objective, is further developed in an assumed order of complexity. The first situation in each set is the least complex, the last the most complex. In relation to unique groups, however, this order of complexity might not always obtain. Careful observation on the part of a teacher will help determine where a group best responds along the gamut of complexity implied in the suggested situations. Conceivably, some fourth grade classes might respond well to most of the situations numbered from four through seven that have been developed in relation to the objectives. Other fourth grade classes, on the basis of many differences and experiences might in general better respond to clusters of situations immediately before and after those just designated. Accordingly, it is not possible to equate these art learning situations with a specific grade level. And always there will be individuals within a group who differ in levels of response according to capacity, ability, inclination, and background. A forthcoming discussion of evaluation will consider these problems.

For purposes of further organization the sixteen objectives (and related art learning situations) have been allotted to the following three areas of emphasis in art education: Area One, *Visual Perceptual Learning* (which contains

1

seven objectives); Area Two, *Developing Art-Related Behavior* (containing four objectives); and *Visual Organizational Learning* (with five objectives).

Area One pertains chiefly to looking at and thinking about art, *Area Two* has to do with possible ways of behaving differently as a result of experiences in Areas One and Three, and *Area Three* involves the actual handling of art media while conceptualizing en route. All of these areas interact; none occurs in isolation. It is only as a means for organization that these areas of emphasis have been designated.

Further clarification of the three areas of emphasis and the sixteen objectives allotted therein follows shortly. Some bits of procedural advice regarding the implementation and eval-

uation of the art learning situations also precede the main body of this publication.

It is intended that these objectives and situations should serve as a point of departure for a classroom teacher. At the conclusion of each set of situations a blank page has been provided for the purpose of developing a new situation related to the current objective. With the foregoing in mind, this publication can serve as a structure that will enable a teacher to *deduce* and to a degree predict what learning is likely to occur in art while the learners make *inductive* discoveries. The main body then contains several ideas, by way of suggestion, that are intended to help the teacher make the objectives come to life in a well-organized, purposeful art program.

ART LEARNING SITUATIONS

A Basis for Art Learning

There is much that children can learn in and about art. Many classroom teachers are aware of the learning possibility and of their own responsibility in relation to it. But how does the teacher decide *what* should be learned? And by what means can he help the child learn? These questions, of course, are asked about all phases of education; they are not confined to the role of the visual arts in elementary curriculum.

The visual arts, however, present a unique problem with regard to what should be learned. Because our society is not art-oriented, the teacher cannot look to society as a source for very many objectives that would help identify what is of worth in art learning. Nor can he expect young children to establish many of the objectives. As a consequence, determining what is of worth in learning is reduced to the problem of making several value judgments. These value judgments could culminate in a set of objectives which, in turn, could serve as one kind of basis for art learning. It is the intent of this publication to provide such a basis.

The sixteen objectives introduced in this book have been successfully implemented in a variety of classrooms and schools. Many viewpoints have been considered. Because these objectives are derived from value judgments, however, they are subject to further scrutiny, continual reexamination, and possible modification by the reader.

These value judgments, restated as art learning objectives, contribute to a structure that is intended to be of some help in organizing an art curriculum. The presence of objectives (these sixteen or modifications thereof) can do

much to provide scope for an art program that might otherwise be based upon a limited number of aimless activities. In addition to increasing scope by providing some direction, objectives may enable a teacher to predict what learning in art is likely to occur; less is left to chance.

Well-articulated objectives lead to the structuring of situations conducive to art learning. Accordingly, the main body of this book consists of fifteen sets of art learning situations that relate to all but one of the stated objectives. These situations are presented as *guidelines*, not as dicta. Moreover, neither the objectives nor the related situations are offered as a panacea. They are offered instead as a possible way of learning something in and about the visual arts. Most of the situations involve an open-ended kind of art problem solving. Each set of situations is developed in an assumed ascending order of complexity (to be tested by the teacher in reference to a unique group). Each situation relates chiefly to a single objective. By focusing on *one* aspect of art at a time in reference to the total structure of objectives, the teacher can work toward a more concentrated learning activity. He is encouraged to nibble rather than to gulp. So, within the over-all scope provided by the sixteen objectives at least a little depth can be reached in relation to each.

The sixteen objectives are further organized in three areas of emphasis in art learning. Seven objectives are allotted to Area One, which is referred to as *Visual Perceptual Learning*. This area is concerned mainly with looking at and thinking about art and the visual environment.

THREE AREAS OF EMPHASIS	SIXTEEN ART LEARNING OBJECTIVES	IMPLEMENTATION
	Development of a vocabulary for the visual arts	(Chap. Three) ⟶
	Recognition of the visual as nonverbal communication	(Four) ⟶
	Ability to make comparisons of art forms	(Five) ⟶
Area One VISUAL PERCEPTUAL LEARNING	Understanding of the varying past and present roles of artists	(Six) ⟶
	Recognition of a range of art expression from pictorial to pure	(Seven) ⟶
	Awareness of visual relationships between art and nature	(Eight) ⟶
	Awareness of visual relationships between art and manmade objects	(Nine) ⟶
	Cultivation of a capacity for aesthetic response	(Ten) ⟶
Area Two DEVELOPING ART-RELATED BEHAVIOR	Examination of opinions and values as a basis for art judgment	(Eleven) ⟶
	Utilization of intuition in developing resourcefulness and imagination	(Twelve) ⟶
	Individuality as well as intelligent conformity	(Thirteen) ⟶
	Ability to arrange the visual components of art in various ways	(Fourteen) ⟶
Area Three VISUAL ORGANIZATIONAL LEARNING	Familiarity with a variety of art media and processes	(Fifteen) ⟶
	Frequent experimentation with one particular art medium	(Sixteen) ⟶
	Expression through art of ideas, attitudes, and feelings	(Seventeen) ⟶
	Production of evidence of sensitivity toward form in art	(Eighteen) ⟶

Figure 1. The Interrelation of Three Areas of Emphasis and Sixteen Objectives in Art Learning

More objectives and related art learning situations are assigned to this area than to the others because most children, when they become adults, will do more perceiving of art than creating of art.

Area Two comprises four objectives that are concerned with *Developing Art-Related Behavior*. This kind of behavior is assumed to grow out of, and in turn reinforce, experiences in Areas One and Three.

Area Three comprises five objectives that are concerned with *Visual Organizational Learning*. The objectives and the related situations involve the handling of art media in a variety of compositional, expressive, and skill-attainment problems.

As the vertical arrows at the left of Figure 1 indicate, all of the areas of emphasis and the objectives within them are interrelated. For example, a child investigating the potential of watercolors in relation to the objective "Frequent experimentation with one particular art medium" (Area Three, Visual Organizational Learning) is also perceiving and possibly thinking about other watercolor paintings he has seen (Area One, Visual Perceptual Learning). No doubt he is also relying on his resourcefulness and imagination (Area Two, Developing Art-Related Behavior). In fulfilling the objective, however, the *emphasis* would be on the attainment of skill and knowledge with regard to some of the uses of watercolors. Accordingly, the horizontal arrows to the right of Figure 1 re-emphasize that the objectives serve as bases from which many art learning situations can be (and have been) implemented. Further clarification of each of the three areas of emphasis and the sixteen art learning objectives follows.

Area One: Visual Perceptual Learning

Learning to see is of major importance in art education. Even though there is little actual handling of art materials in this area of emphasis there can be considerable activity in a classroom because perception is not a passive affair. Perceptual activity might be more inward than outward. Because of this lack of apparent overt activity, visual learning in elementary art education is often neglected in favor of working with art materials (which is emphasized in part of Area Three). The objectives and the related art learning situations in Area One go beyond the working-with-materials approach

and lead toward a kind of "visual literacy."

With the goal of visual literacy in mind, the teacher can use the art learning situations to help children become more aware of the visible world. When vocabulary is stressed, words become vehicles for concepts that can enhance visual percepts and vice versa. Area One also emphasizes recognition of many visual aspects of the environment as nonverbal kinds of communication consisting of both intended and unintended symbology. These nonverbal kinds of communication often serve as raw material for future drawings and paintings to be executed in Area Three, Visual Organizational Learning.

Visual literacy involves the development of an ability to perceive various art forms. One objective is the ability to make comparisons, on an elementary level, of what one form of art, such as poetry, does that another form, such as painting, cannot do. While one set of art learning situations compares what these various art forms can and cannot express, another set attempts to build concepts about the varying past and present roles of artists, roles frequently as misunderstood as the works of art emanating from them. Visual perceptual learning in these instances involves exchanging stereotypes for valid concepts about art and artists.

In Area One children can have an opportunity to become familiar with a wide range of painting styles from "pictorial" *naturalism* to "pure" *nonobjectivity*. Other objectives and situations pertain to seeing visual relationships between art and the environment. A brief summation of each of these seven specific objectives in Area One follows.

OBJECTIVE: Development of a Vocabulary for the Visual Arts

This is the only objective of the sixteen for which a set of related art learning situations has not been developed. A list of art terms has been compiled instead. These terms appear in *italics* throughout the art learning situations. This objective, then, will be met implicitly in every situation.

The acquisition of an art vocabulary is intended to lead to the formation of more adequate concepts about the visual arts. Concepts sharpen and direct perceptions. This is not to say that words alone will develop a child's

5

visual sensitivity. There is an evasive point at which the visual properties of whatever one is looking at become assertive in their own expressive way. If the visual experience could always be reduced to word description, there would be no need for art. But words about art can give additional meaning to art. The verbal and the visual work in concert.

OBJECTIVE: Recognition of the Visual as Nonverbal Communication

This objective represents an effort to attain equilibrium between verbal and nonverbal communication. The goal here is to become more aware of a variety of symbology, intended and unintended, that appears in our surroundings. These kinds of visual symbology constitute the raw data of some art forms.

In the situations related to this objective, children have opportunity to "read colors" in order to determine many shades of meaning in them. The situations include looking at a bent nail or at the varying shapes of plants and animals as special kinds of communication. Windows communicate something about the over-all character of a building. Certain objects and events are associated with nations. The "arrangement" on the teacher's desk communicates something at a nonverbal level (intentionally or not).

Children, before they learn words, are by necessity particularly sensitive to nonverbal communication. This sensitivity should not be allowed to dwindle.

OBJECTIVE: Ability to Make Comparisons of Art Forms

Children are sometimes asked to paint while listening to music. The assumption is that the two art forms can somehow be equated. Actually, music and art share, at the very core, some basic principles, such as *rhythm* and *variety*. Music as a *form*, however, is audible and moves through time; a painting is confined to a space and is silent. This objective, then, involves the comparison of various art forms with regard to similarities and differences. For example, in what ways can a seascape be treated by music? By painting? By photography? Comparison of the *visual* art forms with other art forms, including poetry, drama, and dance, might replace misconceptions with adequate

concepts. Here again, a concept could be helpful in directing a perception, in this instance a beginning realization of the function of form in art, another kind of visual literacy.

OBJECTIVE: Understanding of the Varying Past and Present Roles of Artists

Early in the elementary grades most children encounter a unit of study devoted to "community helpers." Throughout the curriculum the functions of many occupational groups are identified in reference to society. The roles of merchants and bankers and other familiar figures are often understood through incidental learning. Somehow though, in our culture, the artist emerges as a *stereotype*, a stereotype too obvious to comment on here. Since many artists behave in highly individualistic ways, their roles are more likely to be misunderstood, especially in a complex culture. To understand the roles of artists, children can discuss industrial designers, sculptors, painters, craftsmen, and architects, in terms of their varying positions in the past and present—all in an effort to replace stereotypes with concepts.

OBJECTIVE: Recognition of a Range of Art Expression from Pictorial to Pure

There are as many styles of art expression as there are artists. The situations that grow out of this objective, however, identify eleven major stylistic differences out of many that have evolved in painting. Painters who typify these styles are specified. The differences among several painters *within* a style of expression, say surrealism, will become more apparent when reproductions of their works are examined.

Children can be taught to make discernments among many styles of art. Moreover, they should be able to comprehend the varying rationales of the painters, which often account for the corresponding visual differences. They might also learn that one style of painting is not "better" than another. Judgments (discussed in Area Two, Developing Art-Related Behavior) are made in reference to an individual painting regardless of whether it is cubistic, expressionistic, or impressionistic. It is essential to realize that stylistic differences in art expression do exist.

OBJECTIVE: Awareness of Visual Relationships between Art and Nature

Since art is a product of human expression, nature itself is not art. Very often nature, in terms of the visible appearance of things, erroneously becomes the "norm" for art. Nature and art do have many affinities. The *elements* of art—line, shape, color, and texture—all appear in nature. The *principles* of art—balance, rhythm, dominance, proportion, transition, variety, and unity—all derive from nature. These very principles that artists over many centuries have derived from nature for application to their art at times become mere abstractions with no meaning outside a studio or classroom. The intention here is to make this objective "real" by taking the perception outside the classroom and applying these conceptual elements and principles of art to a more acute view of natural surroundings. Many artists, among them Paul Cézanne, have erected formal concepts from which to view nature. However, in the application of this objective to classroom situations such perceptions need not culminate in a painting. Just the act of perceiving the surroundings more acutely might be sufficient. If the teacher emphasizes relationships, the children's perceptions might become apparent in their paintings. Conversely, many actual scenes in nature might be viewed according to the varying interpretations of painters ranging from the atmospheric compositions of the French impressionists and the rotund Midwestern landscapes of Thomas Hart Benton, to the segments of California revealed in wide brushstrokes by Richard Diebenkorn. Nature and art are mutually supportive but not identical.

OBJECTIVE: Awareness of Visual Relationships between Art and Manmade Objects

The immediately preceding objective emphasized visual perceptual learning in reference to the *natural* environment. Almost all objects exclusive of those found in nature may be referred to as objects of the *cultural* environment —what man has made. Most of these objects, for better and worse, had their inception on a drawing board or underwent some kind of design process. Most are objects of utility. People tend to value them economically. Utilitarian objects can, however, possess both functional worth and pleasing visual quality.

It is in quest of the recognition of visual qualities in manmade objects that art *principles*, as workable concepts, can once again prove helpful.

Man has always designed. He designed first, perhaps, in response to his physical needs. His products became more logically sound and complex until his intellectual needs were increasingly satisfied. His products, through embellishment and pleasing form, began to offer gratification for emotional needs as well. These needs, which persist in the present era, are further modified by the natural and cultural environments. In other words the designer of a shelter would have to unify it with the terrain and help make a mere house become a home for those who would live in it. As the forthcoming art learning situations reveal, both worthy and unworthy designs are perpetuated by the people who tolerate and consume them.

Area Two: Developing Art-Related Behavior

The assumption underlying Area of Emphasis Two is that the kinds of behavior exemplified therein are possible outgrowths of the art learning situations stressed in Areas One (Visual Perceptual Learning) and Three (Visual Organizational Learning). And, as indicated in Figure 1, these outgrowths of learning are further assumed to reflect into performance in Areas One and Three. However, this possible transfer of learning is not assumed to occur automatically. It is more likely to occur if these art-related behavioral objectives are tentatively identified and if opportunities for learning occur accordingly.

Many of the art learning situations that emanate from the objectives in Area Two involve the use of art media. The products of these media, however, will be de-emphasized in favor of the kinds of behavior that occur while a child is responding to the problem at hand. The behavior and the product cannot actually be separated, but one aspect of the total experience can be singled out for emphasis, observation, and evaluation. More attention will be given the product in response to objectives stated in Area Three.

These art-related behaviors tend to be more general than specific when contrasted to objectives in the other two areas. The objectives in the other two areas of emphasis are more

7

closely related to the visual arts. For example, developing resourcefulness and imagination is important in the *entire* elementary curriculum. And learning in all subjects involves the examination of opinions. Art education *shares* the responsibility for developing these kinds of behavior. Art education, however, does offer some unique possibilities by which these behaviors might be developed.

OBJECTIVE: Cultivation of a Capacity for Aesthetic Response

Many observers from the time of Tocqueville have indicated that American society orients itself more toward practical things than toward ideas or objects that have no apparent use. If these observations are even partially correct, they could account for the ironic fact that capacities for aesthetic response are seldom utilized! An aesthetic response consists in becoming involved with something for what it is *not*—for what it is not in terms of its economic value or use. Many people are able to react in this manner to a sunset. Their response certainly shows the presence of a capacity to respond aesthetically. It might be possible to extend the range of such responses.

An aesthetic experience must be spontaneous. It involves more of an open disinterested attitude than one of purposeful interest. Disinterest, however, is not uninterest. The experience is more felt than thought. Aesthetic response is not limited to natural phenomena or art forms. Manmade objects, though utilitarian, elicit an aesthetic response. Children respond more to the intrinsic visual properties of an object than to its use, as evidenced by the "impractical" things they collect on the way home from school. The intent of this objective is to maintain and extend the capacity for such response.

OBJECTIVE: Examination of Opinions and Values as a Basis for Art Judgment

If children have opportunity to look at a variety of art forms (Area One, Visual Perceptual Learning) and criticize their own work (Area Three, Visual Organizational Learning) they can, in turn, be given opportunity to state opinions about art. This behavioral objective has to do with examining these opinions, identifying beliefs, and extending them to form a basis for art judgment.

Art is perceived and judged from several viewpoints. These viewpoints are representative of different "realities." For example, if one values and judges a painting on the basis of its economic worth and the fame of the artist who executed it, he is responding in terms of a "social reality." By contrast, a response based upon "physical reality" would be concerned with the actual painting itself in terms of the total composition.

In addition to examining four possible "realities" as bases for forming art judgments, the situations related to this behavioral objective will invite children to examine their concepts of beauty and ugliness, subject matter preferences, and favorite styles of painting. Eventually, through these and related efforts, sound judgment could replace bias.

OBJECTIVE: Utilization of Intuition in Developing Resourcefulness and Imagination

Intuition is difficult to verify in experience, yet artists frequently use the term to account for what is otherwise unaccountable in their various ways of working. The production of a work of art seems to demand an intuitive behavior; it involves a reliance on "refined hunches" in lieu of facts; it involves a willingness to dare. It is also likely that this intuition is composed, in part, of concepts about art. Intuition accounts for much of the ingenuity and resourcefulness so evident in the arts. The term "resourcefulness," incidentally, is used here instead of "creativity," because children are for the most part "discovering," in a personal way, many phenomena previously discovered by other people.

In addition to skill, the use of art media and tools demands resourcefulness. Starting something with one intention and switching to another intention en route requires flexibility on the part of a child. The use of a limited amount of material—for example, a half pound of clay—in a limited problem, such as "building something as tall as possible while using the clay as thin as possible," involves the combination of unexpected relations.

Many styles of painting are dependent on imagery. To develop imagination, art learning situations may involve looking at a peculiar door and imagining what is beyond or looking at a photograph of a car in the midst of a

8

desert and painting a picture of where it might have been.

Outcomes of these and other art problems developed akin to this objective can include a variety of adequate solutions. The behavior en route should be stressed, because varying solutions are more likely to occur if children are encouraged to follow hunches. Also, failure, as a result of experimentation, might be considered a kind of success. Conventional success, which by contrast emulates the trite, might be considered a kind of failure!

OBJECTIVE: Intelligent Individuality as Well as Intelligent Conformity

Again, experiences gained in Areas One and Three can be reinforced by situations that relate to a behavioral objective, in this instance, an emphasis on individuality in response to art problems. However, in encouraging unique responses, the teacher should realize that the mere revelation of a child's personality traits by way of an art medium does not by itself constitute a work of art. The objectives stated in relation to all three areas of emphasis are intended to go beyond the limited notion of assumed "self-expression."

Also, since a classroom is somewhat of a microcosm of a larger community, the children must maintain a kind of sensible conformity. Quite often opportunities for cooperative group art problems arise, such as group mobile sculpture, or a modification of existing holiday symbols (that all will be able to understand despite visual changes).

Individuality is asserted in response to singular problems such as interpretive portraiture or designing a personalized house within prescribed limitations of size and materials. Each art problem, whether group or singular, possesses limitations in terms of its demands and the medium to be employed; consequently, another kind of intelligent conformity is in order. Art education, along with the total curriculum, strives for an equilibrium between individuality and conformity to carefully evaluated external demands.

Area Three: Visual Organizational Learning

This area of emphasis concerns the more obvious aspects of art learning in the elementary grades. The objectives within this area stress the importance of developing concepts about art while working with materials. In developing concepts, children should become aware that there are no axioms in contemporary art. Yet there is an implicit order that prevails in objects and paintings that have pleasing visual qualities. A child who has had opportunity to organize compositions and manipulate art media becomes more attuned to these qualities.

"Self-expression" with art materials is insufficient as preparation for sensitive visual response. Moreover, the imbibing of theories apart from the actual organizing is no more effective. It seems, though, that sustained efforts involving the rational and irrational, the known and the felt, are likely to be quite helpful in making a child more visually aware.

The intent in Area Three is not to educate young people to become artists, but rather to educate them to respond effectively to the visual arts. The art learning situations that relate to each objective, though involving the actual use of art media, are mainly directed toward development of responsiveness. There is some need for a positive kind of dilettante in the original meaning of the word, "one who is sincerely fond of the arts." In addition, the school must provide opportunities in elementary education wherein potential professional artists, a distinct minority, may also develop. In the emerging era of cybernetics and automation, artists will become increasingly essential.

OBJECTIVE: Ability to Arrange the Visual Components of Art in Various Ways

Most of the art learning situations that relate to this objective are in the nature of "pure" (nonpictorial) design problems. These problems involve the arrangement of art *elements:* line, shape, color, and texture as things in themselves, separate or combined with one another, in consideration of one or more *principles* of visual order. The principles consist of balance, rhythm, dominance, proportion, transition, and variety, all of which must culminate in a unity. These elements and principles interact in a given space, actual or illusory. It is hoped that this conscious emphasis on the interaction of elements and principles will improve the perception and production of works of art in accordance with some of the other stated objectives.

9

OBJECTIVE: Familiarity with a Variety of Art Media and Processes

Without art *media* there would be no objects of art. Materials serve as means of expression but are not necessarily central to it. The first essential is a person who has something to express and the need to design. The various art media, both two- and three-dimensional, are subservient to this essential. The person must have some knowledge of these media. Variety is important. With some discrimination and competency concerning art materials, a child can select the medium best suited to what he wants to express. Atmospheric landscapes and fluid rhythms might be best interpreted in watercolor, insect forms with cut paper. Although many children need variety in order to maintain interest, they can be encouraged to become less novelty oriented. For some, however, a new medium might give impetus to an expression that might have otherwise remained latent.

Very often a medium can serve as a stimulus to be enjoyed and investigated for its own sake. Accordingly, it is important that children recognize both the limitations and the possibilities of many art materials. These recognitions when coupled with rudimentary skills can be helpful in facilitating more valid visual expressions.

OBJECTIVE: Frequent Experimentation with One Particular Art Medium

If a child has learned something about the properties and limitations of a variety of art media, he will be able to select one that suits his own interests and personality. Whenever possible, within the limited time of the elementary curriculum, a child should have a chance to explore a *favorite* medium to the extent that he can develop greater skills and find satisfaction with it.

This objective serves as an agent of equilibrium to the one immediately preceding; in a way it opposes variety. In the context of this book it is difficult to suggest art learning situations related to only one medium. The medium of personal choice should be just that. But, in order to make this objective meaningful, the rather evasive medium of *watercolor* has been isolated as an example for a more thorough investigation.

OBJECTIVE: Expression through Art of Ideas, Attitudes, and Feelings

The first objective in Area Three stresses conceptualization of the elements and principles of art. The second and third objectives stress learning about some of the various art media. This fourth objective has to do with *content* or expressive qualities of the visual arts. These four objectives are often evident in each art product. To reiterate, *the objectives have been isolated in order to focus upon important single aspects of art learning.* In attending to this current objective, a teacher can still talk to a child about balance and color repetition (principles of composition) in reference to a painting that contains *subject matter* and content. It is also obvious that knowledge about the uses of art media will help a child express himself. In addition to compositional abilities and facility with media, it is of further importance though to consider "what is being said."

To clarify, *subject matter* has to do with what is being stated in art, visually rather than verbally. The *content* has to do with the *expressive* qualities of the subject matter. Twenty paintings about the local community (as subject matter) by as many children could each reveal different ideas, attitudes, and moods (as content). An art form can have content without subject matter; a nonobjective symbol for a world's fair, for example, can have emotional impact on a viewer. Likewise, a child's emotional state can become a part of the content without being the subject matter; a painting composed only of ambiguous lines might depict feelings.

The main emphasis of this objective then will be on how artistically a child is able to *visually* express something. En route the child might also develop more adequate concepts about the many possible meanings of art.

OBJECTIVE: Production of Evidence of Sensitivity toward Form in Art

Form, in art, is that ultimate structure which fulfills and embodies by means of an appropriate medium the expression of an artist. Form is not to be confused with medium. The latter, as indicated, is only a means to the final structure. For example, a *mural* is a form of visual art with unique structural properties (it is sequential and conforms to a wall) which differ from those of a *painting* (which is usually a smaller, singular composition confined by a frame); yet both could be executed by means of the same medium, tempera perhaps. Murals, in other words, are not merely large paintings; they differ in concept, function, and, consequently, structure (form).

In Area One children have opportunity to learn what one form of visual art does as compared to another form among the *literary* or *performing* arts. In the art learning situations related to this final objective in Area Three, children will compare the structural properties of forms solely among the *visual* arts by actually producing several of them. By doing so they might more readily learn what woodcuts can do that paintings cannot do and vice versa. They could become more aware of the structural attributes of a collage as compared to those of subtractive sculpture or a drawing. By producing a variety of visual art forms, children might develop a budding sensitivity toward

which form is most appropriate for whatever they would like to express. As with all of the objectives and situations in Area Three, what they learn here also could increase their visual perceptual awareness of form among the works of art by noted artists introduced in Area One.

The remainder of this book, following Chapter Two, is divided into three sections. Each section corresponds to one of the three areas of emphasis outlined in Figure 1 and described in this chapter. Each area, in turn, contains chapters that relate to the sixteen objectives just described. With the exception of one, each chapter contains art learning situations which are intended to give substance to a specific objective. Suggestions for implementing and evaluating these objective-related art learning situations appear in the following chapter. If a teacher selects two appropriate situations from each chapter, he will be able to present one a week throughout most of the school year.

11

Organizing and Evaluating Art Learning

2

Each art learning situation in the subsequent chapters is intended to involve a group of children working together. Group situations are not intended to replace activities in art that a child might initiate on his own. For that matter, many of these situations could serve as a nucleus or further impetus for self-directed activities. The effectiveness of these situations is greatly dependent upon how well they are developed and further evaluated by a teacher in relation to a unique group.

The way in which a teacher organizes learning is largely an individual matter. It is possible however, to state hypotheses that can be valuable as a means for testing out ideas. A kind of "if-then" thinking occurs—"if I try this, then this might occur." In keeping with this "if-then" attitude several *considerations* which are "hypothesized" as essential for the development of art learning situations are introduced. These considerations serve as an organizational device for all of the art learning situations that appear in Chapters Four through Eighteen. The reader is invited to test and reappraise these considerations.

Also, a fourfold evaluative approach, based upon what one can infer from observations will be discussed. These organizational considerations and evaluative approaches are offered as useful information to be made more effective by personal investigation and possible modification.

Organizational Considerations

The following considerations are offered as a means for developing art learning situations: the group, the objective, the situation, materials, stimulation, and procedure. The sequence of each consideration in relation to another is designated for purposes of convenience. With the exception of the first consideration, the group, each will reappear in the same sequence throughout all of the forthcoming situations.

The Group

The very first consideration will be that of the group. Most likely there will be some information available regarding general social and ethnic background. Also, a teacher usually has some assessment as to children's performance in certain areas of learning other than art. These assessments might be interpreted from either national or local norms or both. (There are no norms for performance in the visual arts.) Further, it would be helpful to have some information about the educational and occupational backgrounds of the parents.

As the teacher presents the situations, he will learn more about art aptitudes, abilities, and interests of each child within the group. The children's current art abilities and interests can be extended. Each art learning situation will elicit many levels of response within a group. Observations of these responses (by means of some forthcoming evaluation suggestions) will also emerge as considerations to be made in reference to the group as further situations are presented and developed.

The Objective

Art, like other subjects, needs a background of expectations to become understandable and effective. The sixteen objectives discussed in Chapter One will reappear as primary considerations to be made in relation to all of the art learning situations that follow.

The Situation

The situation consists in bringing together a set of circumstances whereby art learning is likely to occur. In one sense each situation is a specific subobjective reduced to a lower level of abstraction from the major objective. In another sense, each situation is a statement of a problem that relates to the major objective.

Most of these situations involve open-ended problem solving. Each is intended to be provocative as well as informative. Each can have the situations that compose the last portion of each set usually have more intellectual appeal than those in the first portion. In Areas One and Two most of the situations from the third through the tenth are of this kind. Less academically inclined groups might use more situations in Area Three, but they should not exclude Areas One and Two. Most of the situations in all three areas are intended for a one-period presentation and development. Splits and follow-up situations are occasionally recommended.

Figure 2 is a device for assessing coverage, scope, and sequence. A teacher may use an

GROUP: _____   YEAR: _____

DATE	AREA	OBJECTIVE	SITUATION	MATERIALS	EFFECTIVENESS		
					−	±	+
					−	±	+
					−	±	+
						±	+
						±	+
						±	+

Figure 2. Presentation and Coverage Plan and/or Record

as many different and acceptable solutions as there are individuals. A means of estimating the validity of these solutions will be discussed under "Evaluation."

These situations differ from so-called projects. The latter usually consist of step-by-step procedures which, when completed, yield fairly safe, known outcomes with few differences among them.

The several situations in each set are presented in an assumed order of complexity, the first being the easiest, the last the most complex. This assumed order, however, will have to be tested in reference to a particular group and individuals within that group. For example, extension of it as a long-range plan (depending on his familiarity with the children, art, and the contents of this book), as a record, or as both. When completed, it will indicate which areas of emphasis (second column) and which objectives (third column) have been attended to or omitted. If most of the objectives have been met by way of appropriate art learning situations (fourth column) it is conceivable that some scope has also been secured.

The completed chart will also reveal a kind of sequence. It is difficult to specify an order of presentation among the sixteen objectives and related sets of situations. Actually, each situation contains ingredients that can transfer to another. Teachers and children can generalize from one situation to another. They can identify relationships en route. By means of this generalizing approach, sequence, as a neat continuity, gives way to cumulative relationships. Also, the climate communicated by responses within a group could reveal the need for presenting another situation that closely resembles the one preceding. Or, conversely, a group might be ready for a situation that greatly contrasts the one just experienced. It seems that sequence is fickle to the extent that what follows might even account for what went on before.

Materials

A brief list of necessary materials accompanies each art learning situation. None of the situations requires expensive or unusual materials. Very often children will share the responsibility of obtaining the materials. For teachers who prefer to plan ahead, the fifth column of Figure 2 is reserved for the listing and ordering of these essentials.

"Materials," as an organizational consideration, is broadened to include any aids that would be useful in a total situation. These aids include recordings, films, and books. A teacher might find it helpful to start and maintain a visual file that is organized according to the sixteen art learning objectives.

The materials listed are considered to be appropriate for each situation, but the teacher must ascertain their appropriateness in terms of individual responses within a class; some children will prefer a small brush to a large one, large paper to small, and chalk to crayons. After they have become acquainted with the properties of certain materials they are more qualified to have choices.

Stimulation

Not every child will be ready for a situation at a given time. Consequently, each situation contains suggestions that are intended to attract and sustain attention. Quite often the teacher can stimulate the children by what he says. At times the nature of the problem and the properties of the medium are in themselves stimulating. Here much of the success is dependent on a child's curiosity. Curiosity is partially dependent upon the values and attitudes he shares with others in school and at home. A teacher's attitude affects the total situation.

It would be desirable if this external stimulation might eventually be replaced by intrinsic motivation. At the outset, however, stimulation remains as a major consideration.

Procedure

After the teacher introduces the art learning situation, he may wish to demonstrate the use of art media. At the perceptual level of learning, he may want to help the group focus upon a variety of visual stimuli ranging from paintings to objects in the natural and cultural environment.

It is in this procedural phase of the situation that content knowledge, or at least information about the visual arts, will be introduced. Newly introduced information will, when appropriate, be related to prior experiences. Throughout all of these situations there will be an emphasis on concept formation. When possible some historical precedent for the current activity will be incorporated.

The function of an organized procedure is to enable a teacher to present and develop the situation concisely, without undue repetition, to a diversity of comprehension levels within a group. In art, as in other areas of the curriculum, the teacher must shift approaches and give individual advice to those children who accelerate or lag. On the basis of a clear presentation and effective stimulation most children should be capable of *approaching* a problem independently. However, frequent reinforcement accompanied by cogent generalizations on both an individual and class basis will usually be helpful.

Chapters Four through Eighteen end with outlines based upon these preceding considerations. The teacher is invited to develop thereon a problem-solving art learning situation that relates to the objective of concern in that chapter in further reference to the needs of a particular group. This feature may be referred to as the "in-service thinking" page.

Evaluation

All aspects of the art learning situation, the information offered in subsequent chapters, the teacher's manner of presentation, and the varying responses of children, must be evaluated. Evaluation involves complexities too numerous to reiterate at the end of each situation. Consequently, suggestions for a fourfold evaluation are included in this chapter with the intention that they be considered in reference to each art learning situation described. Evaluation should determine (1) whether or not the situation has fulfilled the specific learning objective (including an estimate of a teacher's effectiveness in presenting the problem), (2) the general group response to the situation, (3) the responses of each child based upon both his and the teacher's assessment, and (4) fulfillment of the sixteen objectives in terms of learning over a period of one semester.

known to a teacher, however, so he can be as aware as possible of precisely what he is trying to instill. As a checkpoint he might ascertain the effectiveness of the problem and the presentation by devising questions that could reveal objective-related answers. However, if the children are always aware of the objective some might merely reveal what a teacher would like to hear! Yet, with older children, their awareness of the specific objective can provide credence for the art learning situation. Their products and their behavior en route should provide some evidence for evaluation. At this

	Displeased	In between	Pleased
Our discussion—(what we saw and did)	−	±	+
Our problem—(what we were to learn)	−	±	+
What we did—(the experience itself)	−	±	+
*The art material—(what I used........)	−	±	+
*The art object—(what I made........)	−	±	+

Our problem was:

too difficult	difficult	interesting	easy	too easy

*Most applicable to situations in Area Three (Visual Organizational Learning)

Figure 3. Child's Rating of the Art Learning Situation

Fulfillment of the Objective by the Art Learning Situation

By intent, each art learning situation contains problems that relate mainly to a specific objective. It will be up to the teacher to determine whether or not the objective is kept in mind. Sometimes during the development of a presentation he can become sidetracked. There are certain advantages to this in that chance discoveries that relate to the original objective might occur. One of the disadvantages would be that of misinterpreting the objective-related problem to the extent that it was no longer related. This is not to say that improvisation cannot occur; it should be encouraged. The teacher is also encouraged to use the preceding outline of organization considerations and the detailed suggestions in each of the forthcoming situations as a means of evaluating a presentation.

The teacher need not always spell out the objective to the group. Its presence should be

point the teacher's chief question is, "Did the art learning situation, as it was developed in relation to my group, fulfill the stated objective?"

General Group Response to the Art Learning Situation

By observing the group's behavior, the teacher can determine whether or not a problem is too difficult or too easy. Observations of their behavior en route, although based only on inferences, can provide some evidence for this assessment. Lack of familiarity with a problem-solving approach as well as with certain media could temporarily induce some slowness in response. With this in mind the teacher can repeat a problem with certain modification rather than automatically abandon it. Some of the situations which might be appraised on the basis of a general group response as "too easy" might be deceptively simple. Moreover, in

15

response to nearly all of the forthcoming situations, there will be some children who excel and others who do not.

Occasionally, a brief questionnaire can be distributed to the group in order to determine their responses to an art learning situation. Figure 3 is an example. In using this, the teacher should adjust the vocabulary to the level of the group. Findings may be averaged and recorded in the extreme right column of the chart in Figure 2. At the end of a semester a profile of responses can be revealed accordingly.

With this information the teacher can chart a general group level of response. As noted, each learning situation follows another in an *assumed* ascendancy of complexity and possible difficulty. Since there are no *exact* sequences in art, the teacher can introduce a group to some situations that are one or two positions ahead of one to which they have favorably responded. With improvisation and time, older groups might run the entire gamut of situations in relation to one objective.

Assessment of Individual Responses

The ultimate here need not be a letter grade in art. Most important are the criteria employed in determining whether a child is learning what is intended. The content as well as the method of communicating it to the children should be evaluated. To say that there should be no evaluation in art is to evade the problem. And evaluation is a problem.

The suggestions in this chapter are made in an effort to cope with the problem; they are by no means offered as a solution. There is something other than subjective experience in art learning. And, most certainly, art is not entirely objective. The subjective-objective split has long been a center of philosophical and psychological debate. A synthesis might be in order.

A well-qualified adult can guide children through situations that are conducive to learning something about and in the visual arts. It is important that a child have opportunity for evaluating his own behavior and objects. The criteria listed in Figure 4, with vocabulary modification, compose what is intended to be a dual evaluation form. It may be used as a self-reporting device by a child and as a frame of reference for a teacher's evaluation of his responses. These observations can be made by and for each child twice a semester, while he

is working on a specific problem, or on the basis of responses to several art learning situations. The latter requires an averaging which, depending on a teacher's perception, could be less accurate. If a child is evaluated on two separate occasions in direct response to specific situations, the teacher should choose two diverse situations. One child might excel in one and do poorly in another. Another might be a consistent performer in both, unless other variables, such as a bad breakfast, have intervened.

Figure 4 is a general performance inventory which includes criteria for observing in all three areas of emphasis but in relation to *one* objective-related art learning situation. It is meant to be applied in a flexible manner. To be valid each criterion should become real in terms of observable behavior. The least desirable responses appear on the left (−), the most desirable on the right (+). There is an implied middleground (±) of response. It would be erroneous to assume that this scale is representative of equal intervals and easily discernible differences of poor and good performance. The teacher will have to decide what "−" and "+" mean in relation to each individual. It is also important to take account of a child's abilities and attitudes as they relate to possible achievement in each area of art learning. These are not easy to ascertain. Figure 4 is intended to be of some help with regard to this task.

Semester Coverage and the Sixteen Art Learning Objectives

Figure 1 in Chapter One outlines sixteen objectives in art learning. The teacher may use the chart as an inventory to evaluate the *scope* of art learning situations introduced to a group. Further, he may use it to assess general group behavior as far as these objectives are observable. A general improvement in vocabulary (first objective in Area One) within a group should be easy to observe. An appraisal of objects brought to school can indicate something of the children's visual perceptual growth. Increased sensitivity in relation to their visual organizations, though often more subtle, is subject to observation. One might not be correct in assuming that all of these changes occur as a result of *learning*. However, if an art program is organized to effect specific changes according to objectives in art learning, a teacher will be in a position to conduct a

VISUAL PERCEPTUAL LEARNING

	−	±	+	
seldom sees visual relationships between present and past activities	−	±	+	sees visual relationships between present and past activities
is unable visually to relate current activity to outside events	−	±	+	cites visual relationships between current activity and outside events
barely notices visual differences among objects and events	−	±	+	discriminates, notices visual qualities among many objects and events

DEVELOPING ART-RELATED BEHAVIOR

	−	±	+	
is unable to analyze and relate to the problem	−	±	+	is able to analyze and continually relate to the problem
is overly dependent on instruction	−	±	+	is capable of self-direction
is hesitant and apprehensive	−	±	+	shows genuine confidence
has few opinions	−	±	+	modifies opinions frequently
gives up easily	−	±	+	shows reasonable persistence
lacks ideas, imagination	−	±	+	has many imaginative ideas
relies on familiar and habitual ways	−	±	+	experiments and attempts different approaches
disregards constructive criticism	−	±	+	incorporates constructive criticism

VISUAL ORGANIZATIONAL LEARNING

	−	±	+	
has difficulty in carrying out ideas visually	−	±	+	can readily amplify ideas visually
uses same subject matter in same way	−	±	+	often varies subject matter
depends on repetitive symbols	−	±	+	introduces variation and modifies symbols
repeats similar arrangements symmetrically	−	±	+	develops unique arrangements asymmetrically
produces disorganized and chaotic visual work	−	±	+	produces work that has visual unity
is careless in selecting and using art materials	−	±	+	selects and handles art materials effectively

Figure 4. General Art Learning Evaluation Inventory

ORGANIZING AND EVALUATING ART LEARNING

more adequate evaluation. Otherwise it is even more difficult to determine if a change is, instead, a result of maturation, of other experience exclusive of the school, or of an innate ability coming forth.

Evaluation, it follows, is just as important to a well-organized art program as are objectives. The two affect each other. The reader is invited to utilize and improvise upon the remainder of this book with the considerations described in this chapter in mind. The forthcoming art learning situations are guidelines and points of departure for both the teacher and the children. It is the act of learning, not the structure embodied in the three areas of emphasis, which is of *utmost* importance.

Area One
Visual Perceptual Learning

A perceiver is confronted by the visible world, part of which is art. Art can be an interpretation of some other part of the visual world, a representation of it, or the development of new realities in terms of the work of art itself.

Since a perceiver is not passive, he seeks perceptual experiences that correspond to present values and concepts. Visual learning occurs when percepts and concepts reinforce each other. This circularity, rather than a polarity of percept and concept, when extended can be instrumental in refining one's perception of the visible world.

Accordingly, an important area of emphasis in art education is that of refining visual perception and gaining valid concepts in order to achieve visual literacy. The objectives and related art learning situations in Area One are directed toward this possibility.

A Vocabulary for the Visual Arts

3

Words are often symbols for other realities.

Words as symbols sometimes become realities in themselves.

The visual meanings of art are not entirely reducible to words.

Words about art can add meaning to art.

The verbal often supports and makes known the visual,
and the visual can add meaning to the verbal.

Though devoid of any specific art learning *situations*, this chapter is in a position of primacy because of its importance to art learning. Words can offer a familiar point of departure for both teacher and children as they encounter what is often less familiar in the visual arts. That the visual arts are often less familiar than words to much of civilized society is in itself ironic; the visual, historically, held a position of primacy. Now, for the most part, the world is verbally oriented.

One of the main functions of education is to make young people literate. Yet, in the early years, children are frequently held down in the development of a vocabulary that could help them attain literacy. In reference to art education teachers are often encouraged to speak to children about art "in words that are understandable" to them. But when "simple" words are inaccurate, children are deprived of literacy at the outset of their learning. Moreover, possible knowledge about art is distorted.

Quite early in the elementary grades children are capable of learning correct terminology. The following list of words has been selected and presented as a nucleus that can be helpful to young people in learning something about art. The teacher will recognize which words are most likely to be assimilated in the primary and in the intermediate grades. Many of these words will reappear in *italics* in the remainder of the book which, though employing the verbal, is mainly devoted to the beginning of a visual literacy.

ABSTRACT ART

Visual art that does not treat subject matter in a normative representational manner. Shape and colors derived from actuality are intentionally distorted and rearranged for expressive and artistic purposes. In a sense, all representational painting is abstract in that the "objects" have been flattened.

ABSTRACT EXPRESSIONISM

A kinetic approach to painting based upon the spontaneous interaction of the artist's arm movements and his medium often with few preconceived ideas or little reference to objects.

20

ALLA PRIMA

The completion of a painting in one sitting with a direct application and no retouching.

ANALOGOUS COLORS

In art, those colors that are grouped next to each other on the color wheel. For example: yellow-orange, orange, and red-orange.

ARCHITECTURE

The initial designing and the ultimate construction of a building in consideration of its use and visual quality.

ASSEMBLAGE

A three-dimensional arrangement of heretofore unrelated mass-produced objects. The actual objects remain unaltered but acquire special *visual meaning* when placed in this new context.

ASYMMETRY

An irregular arrangement wherein visual elements are unevenly distributed on each side of a central axis in such a way as to attain a visual order.

BACKGROUND

In pictorial art, that which represents the section most distant from the viewer.

BALANCE

One of the principles of visual order; a means of reconciling tensions in an artistic composition. The attainment of equilibrium among diverse elements of art.

BAROQUE

A style of art which was prevalent in Europe in the seventeenth and eighteenth centuries. It consisted of dramatic, swirling compositions in painting and of fantastically curved and ornate decoration in architecture.

BAS-RELIEF

The projection of shapes from a background, usually found on coins and wall sculpture.

BAUHAUS

A school in Germany in the 1920s, dedicated to the amalgamation rather than the division of the visual arts, architecture, technology, crafts, and industrial design; emphasis on the appearance as well as the utility of a designed object.

BRAYER

A hard rubber or soft gelatin roller, attached to a handle, used mainly for the application of ink.

CALLIGRAPHY

The use of free flowing line in lettering, drawing, and painting, evident in the rhythmical brushwork of Oriental handwriting.

CARICATURE

A drawing of a person with exaggeration of salient facial and bodily features.

CARTOON

Currently, a humorous drawing. Originally, a full-scale, detailed, preliminary sketch for a large work of art.

CERAMICS

A craft process involving the conversion of moist clay to decorative and useful products by firing and glazing in a kiln.

CERAMIC-MOIST CLAY

Actual clay, suitable for kiln firing, which has been packaged in 25-pound allotments. Must be stored moist.

CHIAROSCURO

The dramatic use of light and shade, as it flows over objects in a defined space, to produce an illusion of volume in a painting.

CITY PLANNING

The development of a design to control artistically the physical growth of a large urban area.

COLLAGE

A twentieth-century art form, pictorial or nonobjective, which is composed of castoff materials from everyday life.

COLOR

One of the four elements of art; the play of light on surfaces, which are seen by the eye in varying values (lightness and darkness) and intensities (brightness and dullness).

COMBINE

An art form made of three-dimensional objects harmoniously attached to a *format*, with additional shapes, colors, and textures derived from the application of paint.

COMPLEMENTARY COLORS

Those colors opposite one another on the conventional color wheel. If placed side by side they dazzle; if mixed, they neutralize each other.

COMPOSITION

Combining and organizing the elements of a work of art to effect a satisfactory whole.

CONTEMPORARY ART

Art forms that are produced at the present time.

CONTENT

The artist's way of expressing the subject matter; also, the ideological and emotional significance of any work of art whether or not it has subject matter.

CONTRAST

A means of opposing dissimilar visual elements in order to intensify a composition.

CRAFTS

The art of manually producing useful and decorative objects that are original in design.

CUBISM

An early-twentieth-century art movement that expressed concern for the basic structure of forms by simultaneously showing and combining several sides of objects in such a manner that the painting acquired a flat quality rather than one with the illusion of a third dimension.

DADAISM

An art movement which was, as an outgrowth of World War I, so negativistic toward the social and artistic traditions then prevalent that non-art objects and materials were combined, often in a random way, to create new forms that gave visual meaning to a deliberate anti-rational protest.

DECORATION

The surface embellishment of architecture and useful objects. Decoration is successful when it enhances a form, less so when it overpowers it.

DESIGN

The organizational properties of a work of art; also, a preliminary plan for objects of intended utility; to make such a plan.

DIMENSIONS

Measures. Two dimensions are the height and width of a plane; the third dimension is the depth or thickness of an area.

DISTORTION

The intentional and unintentional departure from the norms of reality in an effort to instill the necessary visual and expressive qualities in a work of art.

DOMINANCE

A principle of visual organization whereby certain elements are combined in such a way as to acquire more importance than any of the others in the same composition.

DRY BRUSH

The art process of loading a brush with tempera, wiping it partially dry, and dragging it lightly over a surface of contrasting color value to induce texture or the illusion of volume in accord with diminishing pressure.

EMPHASIS

See *dominance*.

ENGRAVING

The process of incising lines on various wood or metal surfaces.

ETCHING

The art process of incising lines through a wax or varnished covering (ground) which has been applied over a metal surface (plate). Subsequent exposures to acid etch the lines deeper. Eventually the plate is inked and made ready for printing on moist papers.

EXPRESSIONISM

Art works that are products of an intensified personal emotionalism as evidenced by distortion of shapes and colors.

EYE LEVEL

As used in perspective, the horizon as seen from the relative position of the viewer. Eye level persists even in interiors. All perspective lines converge from the viewer toward the eye level.

FAÇADE

The front of a building which is, as a consequence of this principal position, the most heavily ornamented part.

FANTASY

An extension of the imagination which leads to the formation of unprecedented conceptions ranging from the bizarre to the whimsical.

FAUVES

Literally, wild beasts. A name given by the French press at the beginning of this century to a group of expressionist painters whose brightly colored works departed from the more traditional concepts of painting.

FIXATIVE

A transparent colorless spray used as a protective coating for pastels and pencil drawings.

FOREGROUND

In pictorial art, the part that usually comprises the lower area of the composition or gives the illusion of being closest to the viewer.

FORESHORTENING

The representation of an object, such as an arm, as a shorter length, when the object is raised and pointed toward the viewer.

FORM

In art, the ultimate structure which fulfills and embodies, by means of appropriate materials, the expression of an artist. Often used interchangeably (perhaps incorrectly) with *shape* to signify an element of art.

FORMAT

The physical area occupied by a work of art. In painting, the two-dimensional boundaries are precisely defined; in sculpture, the air around and within the object serves as a less precise area in which to organize.

FUTURISM

An Italian art movement of the early twentieth century that tried to depict, by means of many echoing edges of objects, the mechanistic dynamism of an industrial-urban era.

GENRE

Originally, a Dutch approach to painting during the seventeenth century; portrayed in an unidealized and rather literal manner the ordinary events of daily life.

GOTHIC

The architectural style that dominated England and France from the twelfth century through the sixteenth century, often seen in buttress-supported, thin-walled, pointed-arched buildings.

ILLUSTRATION

Most often, a form of commercial art wherein the visual is employed in a narrative manner, primarily as a descriptive aid in books and magazines.

IMPASTO

Thick paint that retains the textural marks of the implements used to apply it.

IMPRESSIONISM

A French art movement of the 1860s that altered the traditional approach to landscape painting. The proponents were chiefly concerned about impressions induced by the play of natural light on objects outdoors. In an effort to record their observations of this phenomenon they used colors of paint in unusual combinations.

INDUSTRIAL DESIGN

The design of machine-produced utilitarian objects with concern for visual qualities.

LINE

One of the four elements of art. Line appears tangible as an independent entity or as an edge of a shape, and intangible as in the way of suggested directions that the eye may follow.

23

MEDIUM

The material the artist uses as a vehicle for his expression; also the fluid in which pigments are suspended.

MIDDLEGROUND

The area in a picture that resides between foreground and background.

MOBILE

A twentieth-century sculpture form made of lightweight, delicately attached moving shapes, usually suspended from the ceiling.

MONOCHROMATIC

Having one color with different values and intensities.

MOSAIC

A picture or design composed of bits of glass, tile, or other material adhering to a rigid surface; prevalent in Roman and early Christian art.

MURAL

A large wall painting that may tell a story or serve as architectural embellishment. Most contemporary murals appear flat in recognition of the two-dimensional quality of the wall.

NATURALISM

A style of pictorial expression that forces an art medium into an illusionary objective portrayal of the visible world.

NEGATIVE SPACE

The space that appears between the positively defined shapes (which are usually first perceived). For example, the sky appears as negative space between the positive shapes denoted by the branches of a tree. Often confused with *background*.

NEUTRAL COLOR

Various shades of gray that have been obtained by mixing any set of complements, the three primaries, or black and white, thus reducing the presence of any particular hue.

NONOBJECTIVITY

In art forms, the lack of any subject matter or reference to the objective, visible world; sometimes referred to as "pure" art.

OPAQUE

Impervious to light; the opposite of transparent. An opaque paint, such as tempera, completely hides the surface beneath it.

PAINTING

An art form produced by means of any one of a variety of painting media. Not all paintings are pictures in that many exemplify the quality of the paint rather than symbolize subject matter.

PALETTE

The surface upon which paint is distributed and mixed; also the range of colors a painter uses.

PASTICHE

A work that often is indiscriminately imitative of a style of another work or a combination of styles from many works.

PATINA

The encrusted, weathered quality that enhances a surface after a period of time.

PATTERN

In decorative design, well-articulated repetitive shapes that appear on a much larger scale than ordinary textural gradations.

PERSPECTIVE

A system of converging lines and edges of planes that give the illusion of spatial recession on a flat surface.

PIGMENT

Color substance, usually in powder form, that is ground and introduced to a variety of oil- or water-soluble bases.

PORTRAIT

An artist's interpretation of a person's visible features and character, usually painted with direct reference to the subject.

ART LEARNING SITUATIONS

POSITIVE SHAPES

Areas that are superimposed on a surface or first perceived in a view, such as words on a page, trees against a sky, or objects in a painting.

PRINT

An impression made from another object, for example, a lithograph, a photograph, or a woodcut.

PROPORTION

A principle of visual organization that describes the relationships of elements to one another and to the whole composition (for example, a space of red as related to a space of gray); often used in reference to size relations as they exist in nature and human anatomy.

REALISM

An approach in painting which is devoted to interpretations, not imitative renderings, of the significant aspects of the world in further consideration of the medium and of visual organization.

RENAISSANCE

Rebirth; most commonly, a revived interest in Classicism accompanied by a humanistic and inquisitive spirit that began in fourteenth-century Italy, affected the arts there, and spread to northern Europe.

RHYTHM

One of the principles of visual order; repetition of one or more of the visual elements in a composition, for example, the repetition of similar colors or lines.

ROMANTICISM

In painting, a style that is based upon the imagination rather than upon reference to tangibles; often involves an emotional, nostalgic response to bygone eras or vestiges thereof.

SCULPTURE

Three-dimensional art work made from one of three approaches: (1) subtractive, in which material is removed from a prescribed block; (2) additive, in which the form is enlarged by being built up with a plastic substance such as clay; or (3) constructive, in which separate segments of metal or other materials are joined together.

SERIFS

Lines that are perpendicular to the terminal points of letters.

SHAPE

One of the four elements of art; an area enclosed by a continuous edge or an area that emerges between other areas, for example, the hole in a doughnut.

SPACE

The area in which visual expression and organization occurs.

STEREOTYPE

In art, an overused uncritical symbol for an object, place, or event. A visual "average" of poorly perceived experiences as exemplified by tritely selected and handled subject matter (often sunsets) or *nonobjective* shapes (often in the appearance of kidney beans).

STILL LIFE

An arrangement of objects that shows the same scale of interaction between art elements and principles that could be found in nature; often referred to as a microcosm.

STYLE

The characteristics of an art movement or, more specifically, of the mode of expression attributed to an artist during a certain phase of his development.

SUBJECT MATTER

The topic of intended expression by visual means.

SURREALISM

An art movement which denied the validity of the rational in preference to obeying the uninhibited impulses of the so-called subconscious as a basis for subject matter and expression. The resulting paintings were precisely executed and possessed a rather dream-like quality; literally, super realism.

25

SYMBOL

In art, a construction that stands for something, material or immaterial, apart from itself.

TACHISME

A contemporary form of action painting whereby the artist relies on the properties of his medium by dripping, blotting, throwing, and splashing it to create accidental patterns that will be of possible visual and expressive merit. Nontraditional tools, such as human bodies and guns, are often employed.

TASTE

One's sense of what is personally gratifying; often confused with art judgment.

TEMPERA

A binder, usually water soluble, that holds powdered pigments together. When used in a moderately thick consistency, tempera dries opaque.

TESSERA

A small square of brightly colored glass or tile used in the construction of a mosaic.

TEXTURE

One of the four elements of art; the tactile qualities of a surface, which, when touched, range from slick to coarse. Small patterns may connote texture.

TRANSITION

One of the principles of visual order, used by artists to avert chaos or unintended abruptness. It is the gradual change of visual phenomena as exemplified by the diminishing size relationships in a tree (ranging from the thick trunk to thin branches to thinner twigs), by gradual color variation as observed in a spectrum, and by textural gradation from coarse to fine.

TRANSPARENT

The opposite of opaque. A transparent paint, such as thin water color, does not hide the surface beneath it.

UNITY

A completeness that is achieved when all of the visible elements in a work of art are in harmony with the interacting principles of visual organization.

VALUE

In color, the degree of lightness and darkness.

VANISHING POINT

In linear perspective, the point or points on the eye level (horizon) to which the edges of planes converge. Edges above eye level (the top edge of a façade) converge downward, while those below eye level (the edge of sidewalk) converge upward to the vanishing point.

VARIETY

One of the principles of visual order; the use of diversity as a means of attaining visual interest.

VISUAL MEANING

An expression which is embodied effectively in a visual rather than a verbal statement.

WASH

A thin application of any paint, used as a preliminary organizational device in oil painting and as a final product in watercolor.

WATERCOLOR

Pigment that comes in moist or cake form; the direct, fluid, transparent application of paint on paper.

WET ON WET

Primarily a method of applying watercolor on a premoistened surface to attain soft, atmospheric effects.

WOODCUT

One of the graphic arts; a process of relief printing in that the patterns are printed from the remaining original surface rather than from those lines or areas that have been cut away.

As noted, many of these terms will appear in italicized form throughout the following art learning situations. This first art learning objective, *the development of a vocabulary for the visual arts*, accordingly, will be met implicitly in several situations. The teacher is encouraged to add terms as the need arises.

26

Additional Terms

27

VOCABULARY FOR VISUAL ARTS

The Visual as Nonverbal Communication

In addition to verbal symbology, there is visual symbology.

4

In this context visual "symbols" are symbols that are encountered in our everyday environment exclusive of painting and sculpture.

They include such diversities as private and public places (all of which communicate a degree of care or neglect), people's gestures, and the symbols of traffic control.

Not all communicate in an intended manner. For that matter, not all of them will communicate. However, much of this world of possible visual communication becomes the raw material for art and the stimulus for a more sensitive perception.

The Objective
Recognition of the visual as nonverbal communication.

The Situation (No. 1)
A silent language. Discover how it is possible to "say something" with the hands and face rather than with spoken or written words.

Materials
Collect large photographs of faces and hands. Mount some of these in their entirety on neutral-colored sheets of construction paper. From other photographs, cut out expressive portions, such as eyes and mouths, and mount these on smaller sheets for class distribution. The children themselves constitute the main ingredient.

Stimulation
At an appropriate time, attract the attention of the group with a series of familiar hand gestures without using any words, oral or written. Then discuss the unique attributes of such a language. (Many of the Plains Indians relied on a sign language.) Focus on some of the larger photographs of faces. Elicit from the group possible meanings of the facial expressions (happy, sad, cross, surprised, sorry, puzzled, furious, thoughtful).

Procedure
At random, or to children who you know will benefit from such an experience, distribute the smaller mounted photographs of eyes, mouths, and other expressive features. Encourage the children to emulate the expressions they see on

28

the cards. These children may pass the cards on to others, who could, by contrast, try to show an expression *opposite* to that on the card. At this point you might review related observations the children have made from everyday experiences. It is important to indicate that facial expressions, like words, do not always mean what people think they mean.

At another time or in continuation of the present situation, encourage the group to think of something to say nonverbally, which includes at least three facial expressions and three hand gestures. Each child's problem is to communicate to the group; the group's problem is to "read" what each individual has to communicate.

If any of the children's drawings or paintings which include the human figure are present it would be worthwhile to direct their attention to the expressive properties therein. In further discussion, encourage the class to observe collective expressions and gestures that appear in crowds.

Notice which class members took these forms of nonverbal communication as something for granted and which ones could go beyond habit and find something about which to be enthusiastic. Notice which phases of the situation certain individuals responded to best. Follow this situation with one that involves depicting the human figure under different emotional circumstances.

The Objective

Recognition of the visual as nonverbal communication.

The Situation (No. 2)

Speed reading. Analyze some of the *symbols* that have been developed as means for traffic control. Recognize the necessity of a symbol as a means of rapid communication in keeping with the tempo of our times.

Materials

From appropriately colored construction paper cut some large shapes that denote common traffic signs, e.g., the octagon for a stop sign. Do not letter the words on the shapes. Have available four plain rectangular shapes of orange, brown, green, and blue, which symbolize the directions north, east, south, and west on many U.S. highway signs. Collect pictures, from safety posters and magazines, of other symbols for traffic control of all kinds.

Stimulation

Convert each desk or table into an "automobile." Make sure each one has a "driver." Indicate to the group that they are going on an imaginary drive and that they will have to "read," rather quickly, some shapes and colors that will enable them to cope with the traffic and find their way.

Procedure

For such a journey create any imaginary setting you and they would enjoy. From your traffic symbol collection flash some of the more familiar symbols, perhaps a yellow, red, or green circle to denote an ordinary traffic light.

Continue with several, repeating some until correct responses are obtained. Flash some of the more subtle symbols such as a solid line to the right of a broken line, comparable to lines that are painted on the highways to denote "no passing." Enlarge your visual collection to include a variety of highway symbols. The length of the "journey" will be partly dependent on the extent of the collection.

At the conclusion review the essentials of such "reading." Determine how many children had a "safe trip" or experienced "mishaps." Discuss briefly how man has always *designed* symbols to help him find his way. The first of these was probably a crude arrow, pointing, whereas now we have colors to denote the various directions (as indicated by the previously cited U.S. highway rectangles). Discuss some of the international traffic signs that are prevalent in Latin America and Europe. These include a picture of an auto horn on a red-rimmed circle with a red diagonal slash over the horn to indicate "quiet zone." Also, there are arrows bent at right angles, pointing left or right, on similar red-rimmed circles with red slashes across them; these mean "no left turn" or "no right turn." Try drawing some on the board. Discuss the importance of symbols as a possible international language (which the traffic symbols actually are).

As a follow-up activity, with cut paper, the children could design a new symbol, without words, which would indicate "School Crossing —Slow." At other times encourage them to think of new traffic symbols or possible changes in existing ones. They could also collect traffic symbols (in picture form, not off the streets) and make a visual design on a bulletin area which would designate a vicarious journey, complete with stops, turns, one-way streets, directions, and even the possibility of getting lost.

The Objective
Recognition of the visual as nonverbal communication.

The Situation (No. 3)
Colors, their many shades of meaning. Become more familiar with the intended and unintended symbology of colors.

Materials
Cut some eighteen-inch squares from large sheets of red, yellow, blue, orange, green, and purple construction paper. Reserve some chalkboard space equal in area to these sheets of color.

Stimulation
Replace whatever is usually located above the chalkboard space with the large squares of colored paper. Leave the space beneath the squares blank. Enable the group to focus on this simple arrangement by having one or more children write the word for each color directly under each square.

Procedure
Indicate that not all cultures have the same words for colors and that some have words for only a few. Indicate further that hereafter the usual procedure of naming a color will be different; they are going to look at the color and discover other meanings that might be present. From the preceding experience and their own daily encounters nearly all will equate red with "stop." Fewer will associate it with danger, fewer still with a political affiliation. Rather than to read from left to right, select any one of the color squares at random. Elicit verbal re-

sponses from the group that are in turn recorded under each color square. Continue until you reach a more subtle (for them) level of response as suggested with the range attributed to red. The following associations are likely to come forth: *red* (other than those cited), anger, excitement, fire equipment, war, intense heat; *yellow*, caution, illness, cowardice, sacredness (in parts of the Orient); *blue*, first prize, sad, cold, lonely, a kind of music, a kind of law; *orange*, autumn, warmth, Halloween; *green*, go, ignorance, envy, growth, freshness, immaturity, wealth, sickness; *purple,* mystery, mourning, range, royalty, Easter. Although black and white are not "colors" (black absorbing all and white reflecting all light waves), they nonetheless have meanings. Some of these seem to persist: *black,* secretive, mysterious, evil, unfortunate, outcast, bleak; *white,* sanitary, clinical, surrender, purity, goodness.

Ask the children how they think they arrived at the meanings they listed. Find out if any of them have preferences or aversions as a result of the meanings or attitudes they have learned and assigned to colors. Try assigning a meaning such as danger, from one color to another. Encourage the children to look at other colors by means of this approach. Is such a change in meaning possible? Why not? Remind them that if they lived in another culture these meanings might be very different. In reference to some of their previous or future painting, discuss how colors might affect *content*.

Keep a record of the varying levels of response to the meanings of color.

The Objective
Recognition of the visual as nonverbal communication.

The Situation (No. 4)
Visual object lessons. Become aware of the possible symbolic significance of *singular*, inanimate objects.

Materials
Go on a "detecting walk" in search of unintended symbolic objects. You might have on hand a contrived object or two for purposes of

30

stimulation, for example, a board with one cleanly driven nail and one bent nail. A well-worn pencil might be included. Each child should have a tablet and a pencil.

Stimulation

Explain the nature of the problem to the group. A walk through a nearby area is in itself somewhat of a stimulus by contrast to the ordinary routine. Through the visual example indicate how one nail seems to communicate success while the other echoes clumsiness. Invite them as "object sleuths" to become aware of similar messages that await them on the forthcoming walk. Keep a list of the discoveries.

Procedure

This is somewhat of an inductive approach for the group; en route they will discover objects that communicate. However, you might do well to have a route planned in advance that will ensure the availability of objects. Not all areas are as fertile as others in that regard. Organize the group in any way you and they prefer; some might enjoy operating in teams, others by themselves. Equip each one with a tablet and pencil so he can make a "symbol" (quick sketch) of each object he discovers. Each sketch should be accompanied by a brief sentence which describes the meaning of the object to the child. Each object may have different meanings to different children.

If you prefer, depending on the writing skills of the group in general, suspend the addition of descriptive sentences to the sketches and, upon return, give the children opportunity to talk about their discoveries. Some discoveries which could be amplified upon verbally might include a feather on the ground, a twisted television antenna, a tire mark on the pavement, different conditions of trees, a solitary weed in a sidewalk crack, a chipped curb, a candy bar wrapper, a flaking rubber ball, a shiny but very old automobile, a rusty illegible sign on a wall, a freshly dug hole in the schoolyard, or a wire fence enclosure around some playground equipment.

Discuss the discoveries in terms of the unintended symbology each possesses. Inquire as to whether or not these objects would have different meanings if they were seen somewhere

else. Actually, as partly demonstrated by the experience, the meanings reside in the "detective" or discoverer as much as in the objects. Here again, children might learn why they assigned certain meanings to objects.

Notice who picked out the subtleties. Conversely, what objects were most frequently detected and reported? What objects elicited consistent meanings?

The Objective

Recognition of the visual as nonverbal communication.

The Situation (No. 5)

The significance of shapes as meaning. Determine the function and at times the design quality of objects more from visible shape than from verbal description.

Materials

Allow the children to develop some responsibility by bringing with them a tool (hammer, pliers, wrench), a kitchen utensil (beater, peeler, masher), or a piece of sporting equipment (baseball glove, bat, golf club, fishing reel). Develop a well-lighted, elevated viewing table on which these utilitarian objects can be displayed one at a time. If possible, have on hand a tool or utensil that will be unfamiliar to them.

Stimulation

Discuss the concept of *shape*. Show that even though an object has volume it appears as a shape when viewed from any one side. Query the class as to how a particular shape, perhaps that of a claw hammer, might have evolved. Was it accidental? The shapes of eating utensils in Western cultures, knives, forks, and spoons, have been virtually unchanged since their inception. Why? Demonstrate the difficulty of eating with a hammer.

Procedure

Ask for volunteers to place their objects on the viewing stand. Encourage the class to look at each object as if it were something just dug

31

THE VISUAL AS NONVERBAL COMMUNICATION

up from another civilization. Encourage them to look at it as if they had never before seen it.

Orally, determine the most significant features of each shape. If there were no previous knowledge about each object, would one be able to figure out its use solely on the basis of its shape? Would one swing it, squeeze it, or push it? In other words, the shape, as a design, has some integrity in that it is not disguised. If the decoration smothers the object it tends to destroy rather than enhance this integrity. If a metal tray imitates a leaf, its function is disguised.

If an object has evolved honestly and has not been destroyed by overdecoration or imitative disguise, its utility should communicate. After the class has identified the unique visual quality of each object, the severity of a hammer claw, the taut resilience of the net of a tennis racket, see if they can execute some "drawings" or traceries in the air (with their fingers) that depict the essence of each form. Since many of the objects require manipulation (an egg beater) the idea of a "motion drawing" of this kind is feasible. Emulate both the shape as a stationary form and as a form requiring manipulation. Enlist the viewpoints of those who have had sufficient experience with the object they brought to determine if it functions as well as its shape indicates it might. The variable here, of course, is the agility of the user.

Near the conclusion, or when you feel the moment is right, reveal the unfamiliar object to them. See whether they can guess its function on the basis of its shape. Exclude objects that have been put to inappropriate uses, such as coffee grinders made into plant containers.

The Objective
Recognition of the visual as nonverbal communication.

The Situation (No. 6)
Animals: shape, texture, gesture. Study the visual qualities of animals in relation to the requirements of their habitats.

Materials
Ideally, have a small, live animal available. A small turtle might suffice. Photographs, films, and mounted animals are numerous. Have on hand a tool or utensil from a previous perceptual experience. Have some photographs of different habitats.

Stimulation
You might review one aspect of the perceptual problem related to the shapes of tools and utensils. Indicate how the shape of an object, if it is well designed, reveals its intended use. With a live or substitute animal example, point out similar communications revealed by its shape. In addition describe the kind of movements it makes. Also focus on the unique textural qualities. Since the animal is not inanimate, as was the tool, it occurs in special habitats. Show several photographs of different habitats and ask the group which one is likely to correspond to the animal presently being viewed. Why?

Procedure
In consideration of your group, go through a variety of examples or dwell on one or two animals. From the shape of the animal determine how it might walk, or possibly crawl or run. Would it be swift or lethargic? What are the textural properties of the animal? Is it equipped to withstand moisture, pressure of earth, and intense heat or cold? If an actual animal is present, invite the children to touch its surface. What would happen to it if it had fur instead of a shell or scales? Longer or shorter legs? No tail or the absence of certain teeth? Enable the children to discover how the gestures and movements of the animal communicate the kinds of growth that are likely to occur in certain environments. The webbed foot suggests swamp, a muscular tail suggests vines that permit grasping and swinging.

Many in the group will be familiar with the problem of extinction; the habitats of certain animals changed to the extent that the creatures could no longer survive. Ask the class to think of a composite animal and then construct an imaginary habitat that would be suitable for its well-being. The reverse of this could also occur. Ask the group to describe a habitat and then design an animal that would or would not thrive in it.

This particular situation, as are most in Area

One, is mainly perceptual and verbal. As an adjunct of this experience, however, the children might want to visualize some of the discussion by means of an appropriate art *medium*.

Evaluate their responses to the visual properties of an unfamiliar animal by asking them what kind of zoo enclosure they would construct to make it happy.

The Objective
Recognition of the visual as nonverbal communication.

The Situation (No. 7)
Plant shapes and textures. Understand visual properties as they relate to climate and terrain.

Materials
The perception is directed toward phenomena that occur in nature. Cacti or other small plants might serve as visual referents to large plants. In your visual file and in appropriate books vicarious examples abound. Films and photographs that depict differences in climate and terrain will be useful.

Stimulation
Encourage the children as much as possible to assume the role of a plant in response to verbal and visual descriptions of different terrains and climates. What kind of plant would grow in the hot moist climate of a flat land with deep pools of water at a low elevation near the equator? How would you, as a plant, adapt in order to survive and thrive?

Procedure
Reverse the above approach as you proceed. Introduce an actual plant specimen or a large color photograph of a plant. If a small cactus comparable to the barrelhead or saguaro variety is available, direct attention to it. First examine its over-all shape. What does the shape alone, without words, suggest? (You might explain in this instance that the plant does not change much in appearance during the entire year.) At first glance the cactus appears to be at the mercy of the sun. A closer examination

will reveal indentations and fluting that, instead, provide constant shade over most of the plant's surface. Notice the spikes that protrude at the outermost edges of the fluting. What might they communicate? Show pictures of the environment of this plant (or any other you might use). Notice the space between the plants. Perhaps it tells us that the roots of such plants radiate far from each of them, often close to the surface of the earth. Compare this environment and spacing of plants to one much different in character.

Depending on your locale and the experiences of your group, introduce them to a plant form that is likely to be unfamiliar. On the basis of visual cues, ask them to identify a possible environment in which it would thrive. While doing so, encourage them to talk about the appearance of the plant. Too often concepts advanced in this area of study relate to the nonvisual aspects of learning (the *use* of the plant) to the degree that the entity is ignored.

Encourage them to conjure images that place plants peculiar to the desert and jungle, as they have experienced them indirectly, in their immediate surroundings. How would they look? What might happen to them? This situation could be related to an art activity in which the children construct a scene in either two or three *dimensions*.

The Objective
Recognition of the visual as nonverbal communication.

The Situation (No. 8)
A view of windows. Focus upon a detail that often depicts the entire character of a building. Learn to generalize from part to whole, as well as from whole to part.

Materials
Collect large photographs of windows and cut them from the remainder of the picture. Mount the windows on separate neutral-colored papers. In addition, have the children bring photographs that show the entire *façade* or side of one building. Do not cut windows from these pictures. There will be need for

33

scissors, rubber cement, crayons, and some 12″ × 18″ manila paper.

Stimulation

Invite the group to look outside an actual window. Comment briefly upon the view. Discuss the traditional function of windows. Ask the group to extend their vision outside the room and a considerable distance away and "look" at the same window from that position. Assume they cannot see into the room; only the window is visible. In what way does it differ from the windows at home? What does it tell us?

Show some of the large photographs of windows cut from their original surroundings. Ask the children to guess about the kinds of buildings they represent. What happened within these buildings? From what country are they?

Procedure

Distribute the photographs of façades and sides of buildings. Provide each child with a sheet of manila paper, scissors, rubber cement, and crayons. Have each child do the following: Trim the manila paper to correspond to the outer size of his photograph page. Choose one or two windows from the photograph, darken the back side of the photograph with a crayon, put the photo over the manila paper, trace the favorite windows with a pencil, and cut the corresponding shapes of the windows from the manila. Mount the manila paper over the photo by cementing only the top and left edges.

After the photo is successfully hidden and only one or two windows show through the manila, redistribute the mountings.

Ask each child to draw around the exposed window the kind of building he thinks belongs there. What kind of façade and door would relate to a store window with an elegant display of gowns as contrasted to the cluttered window of a pawn shop? What kind of wall might surround a window obscured by weathered wooden shutters as opposed to a window made of a large sheet of glass surrounded by aluminum trim? A window which contains a carefully arranged row of flowers in pots is likely to elicit a response quite different from one which discloses a battered cowboy hat and a coffee pot.

Let them draw with a minimum of talking. Upon completion of the drawing, have them

lift their pictures and compare what they drew to the original photograph underneath. The intent is not to match what is there but to imagine what kind of building the window communicates. Remind them.

The Objective

Recognition of the visual as nonverbal communication.

The Situation (No. 9)

Sight-seeing. Rely on visual knowledge in recognizing symbols of other nations.

Materials

From your own visual file and several visual aids from social studies amass some pictures that are typical of other nations. On small cards letter the name of each nation that is represented in your visual file. Have one card made out for each person in your group; duplicates for a country are acceptable. Include, of course, only those countries with which the group would be familiar.

Stimulation

Pass out the cards, in envelopes, which bear the names of countries that correspond to your visual examples. Explain to them that each card is a "free ticket" to the country so inscribed. However, they are all going on one unusual flight which will encompass much of the earth. Each time they see a picture (displayed by you to the entire group) it means the plane has landed and they in turn will have to know where to get off. No one is to see the other person's ticket.

Procedure

If you like, you may arrange the visual examples of each nation in a logical order to make the flight "sensible." The sequence will depend primarily on their knowledge of geography. To add interest to the situation, each picture could be placed behind a cardboard opening that resembles a window on a jet aircraft. Reserve discussion until the completion of the "journey." Ask the group to give

34

the individual tickets to you, without comment, when each thinks his destination has been sighted. For subsequent discussion you may keep the correct responses in a stack separate from the incorrect ones.

Show the group each picture for about thirty seconds. If you know individuals in your group well enough, some of the more obvious "symbols," such as the Eiffel Tower or the United States Capitol, could be given to those who would benefit from a positive response.

Upon completion of the journey, handle the results in any manner you think would be suitable. Do explain the meaning of a *symbol*. Discuss the convenience of symbols. Ask the group how they learned to associate a symbol with a nation. Examine the accuracy of the symbol. Discuss also the danger of forming stereotypes about people and places. Encourage them to seek, perhaps in a subsequent painting session, other visual symbols for nations. For the present verbal aspects of this situation ask them to think of other possible symbols that would stand for the country they just "visited" (assuming they deplaned at the proper place).

The Objective
Recognition of the visual as nonverbal communication.

The Situation (No. 10)
The visible community: an appraisal. Through the eyes of a stranger, determine what your community reveals about itself at a purely visual level.

Materials
The children may use any means available of reporting on their findings. Many older children have cameras. Others could sketch or try to render their visual observations in written terms. A 16mm Swedish film entitled "People of a City" (18 min., b. & w.) would be a definite asset for this situation. Several camera magazines publish photography annuals that have considerable visual merit. Obtain a variety of visual "slices" from communities similar in size to your own.

Stimulation
Ask each child to play the role of a stranger from another modern country who has been given the assignment of making a visual report on the local community. His job is that of summarizing its "flavor" by using a minimum of words and as few pictures as possible. "Community" may be defined as that area accessible to each of them for such a venture.

Provide the group with a visual stimulus related to their problem. Indicate to them what others have observed about certain communities. Artists, photographers, poets, and architects have been highly vocal (and visual) on such topics. Some have decried change as chaos, others have extolled it. Some have confused change with progress. If your group lives in a city it might be interesting to note that by day some have found cities to be overwhelming forces that impel people through life in a grinding, unnatural manner. How many in the class have found this to be so? By night the same cities take on qualities so different from the day that the former appears to have been replaced by an illusion. A city to one observer might seem "proud," to another it might seem "arrogant" or "aloof." Before making a specific assignment, ask some of the children what they think of their community. What building, street, park, bridge, or cluster of homes exemplifies the community?

Procedure
After the children have gathered and presented their findings, ask them what they would change if they could. Ask them to defend any recent changes of the local scene. A suitable display or visual program with supporting tape-recorded findings might serve as a culmination to the situation.

If possible, compare a nearby community to your own. The activity could be a separate situation or an integral part of the present one. Very often nearby communities in similar natural environments take on contrasting visual qualities as a result of cultural and occupational differences. The problem is to determine what is visually most gratifying and unique to each community. More and more cities throughout the world take on a closer similarity. The intent of this art learning situation is to educate people who might someday become effective in stopping such a trend toward conformity.

35

The Objective
Recognition of the visual as nonverbal communication.

The Situation

Materials

Stimulation

Procedure

36

A Comparison of Art Forms

The word art refers to more than painting, drawing, and sculpture.

There are several forms of art; some require looking, some listening, some both looking and listening.

Many of the forms share some basic principles, among them rhythm.

Though the arts share some principles, their varying forms develop largely because they have many differences.

It follows that each form of art expresses by its own means and accounts for its own special structure.

By comparing the properties within the unique structure of one art form with those within another, a person can learn more about both.

The Objective
Ability to make comparisons of art forms.

The Situation (No. 1)
Sentences, stanzas, and illustrations. Listen to a stanza or a sentence and determine how it corresponds to an accompanying picture. Look at a picture and match it to a stanza or a sentence. What can each do best?

Materials
Select two books, one of stories and another of poems, that are profusely illustrated. Reserve some chalkboard space. If time permits, enlarge some key sentences or stanzas on the board or large story sheets. An opaque projector and screen would be helpful.

Stimulation
Ask the children to tell what they think art is. Many will associate it with painting and drawing. Ask them if they consider poetry, or at least rhymes, to be art. Explain that there are many kinds of art. Each helps us to express and understand feelings and ideas in a special way. Sometimes art comes forth in music, other times as a written story. Show the group some books that contain stories and poems accompanied by appropriate illustrations. Indicate that each could possibly be a kind of art.

Procedure
Read aloud one of the enlarged sentences, then another that is in close sequence. Show the illustration that accompanies that part of

the story. Which do the children prefer by it-self? Which describes the event most effectively for them? Read a different set of unfamiliar sentences, perhaps an entire descriptive paragraph. Ask the children to think of a picture that might describe the same situation. Check their images with the accompanying illustrations in the book. If possible, obtain an opaque projector to enlarge the illustrations. While the children are looking at the projected illustration, ask them what happened to the words (since they were read aloud, they have, of course, vanished into the past). The picture by contrast cannot be heard. It is there before them, confined to a space. It does not move in time and disappear as do words. Does the picture contain all of the objects and events that the words describe?

Reverse the procedure and project some illustrations from a book of poems. While viewing the illustrations ask the group to think of some words that might be in the poem. Read the stanza that relates to the illustration. Does the picture rhyme? No, because it has no sound.

Project another illustration. This time read stanzas from the related poem and two *different* poems. See if the children can match the stanza to the illustration. Why were they able (or unable) to match words to a picture? Read one stanza and project, or mount side by side, illustrations from that stanza and two *different* ones. Try matching again. Notice that very often the illustration can show only *one part* of the stanza; it must fit on a small page whereas the words can tell us about many things, far and near, past and present, on only one page.

The Objective
Ability to make comparisons of art forms.

The Situation (No. 2)
Sculpture and dance: still and moving figures. Focus upon the role of the human figure in relation to different forms of art. Identify sculpture as a visual art, dance as a performing art accompanied by music.

Materials
Invite a dancer from a physical education class or a group within the community. Perhaps a child in your group is enrolled in ballet or interpretive dance. Acquire the appropriate recorded music or sound for the performance. Obtain a sculpture (or a three-dimensional reproduction) that depicts the human figure. Several photographed views of one sculpture could serve as a substitute. Conceivably someone could assume, and hold, a pose comparable to that pictured in order to establish a three-dimensional context.

Stimulation
A dance performance is in itself a pleasure and a stimulation. Before the performance explain to the group that they are going to see two different kinds of art. Each, in this instance, uses the human figure. One uses no familiar art material, and it moves; the other is made of plaster (or whatever you have) and remains motionless. Both are "in the round," not flat like a painting. What kinds of art could these be? Their guesses may remain silent, to be verified by the actual event.

Procedure
If you prefer, let the dancer perform first without any further comment. Prior to a second performance, however, ask the group to observe through the following frame of reference: First, pretend that the dancer left a path or streak of light wherever he went within the area of the dance; what kind of design might this make? Second, during the pauses of the dance observe the human form as a shape, each shape being different as the body assumes a different attitude or position from where you the viewer might be seated. Notice also that the dancer becomes "a part" of the sound; both occur in a certain length of time. Each sound or movement is "frozen" only for an instant in time before it dissolves into another sound or movement. The movement and sound express and elicit different feelings at different times.

At the conclusion of the performance appraise their observations. Ask them which art material, two- or three-dimensional, they would use to show a part of the dance. Why could they show only one part of the dance? "Unveil" the other art form (or facsimile). Many should be able to identify it as *sculpture* (or at least as a statue). What would they as viewers have to do in order to see as many *shapes* in it as they saw in the dance. Obviously *they* would

38

have to move around it instead. What do they hear? If they traced lines with a light around the arms and legs of the sculpture how would this pattern differ from those imaginary traceries of the dancer? By the way, where is the "dance" now? Where is the sculpture? What does one do that the other cannot?

The Objective

Ability to make comparisons of art forms.

The Situation (No. 3)

Hearing color and seeing sound. Enjoy the opportunity of seeing and hearing a combination of art forms, namely, film, painting, and music. Extend the range of sensory experience.

Materials

Obtain a 16-mm sound projector and a screen. Order two or three of the following films: *Dots* (3 minutes), *Hen Hop* (2 minutes), *Fiddle De Dee* (4 minutes), *Hoppity Hop* (3 minutes), or *Begone Dull Care* (9 minutes). All are in color. Each film consists of a lively musical sound track interpreted in a *nonobjective* manner through lines, shapes, and colors. Only *Hen Hop* has subject matter. The others are nonpictorial visual interpretations of the music.

Stimulation

Many of the children have probably painted on a rectangular sheet of paper while listening to music. Discuss the difficulties of such a problem (those of reducing several rhythms to something visual from sounds and taking something that moves on in time and confining it to a prescribed space). Ask them if they could think of a better way whereby sounds could be "painted."

Procedure

Show one of the films. Since these films will be novel to many and are quite brief, a second showing of each will be worthwhile. To the uninitiated the intent is sometimes overlooked. Between showings explain that the artist, McLaren, in some instances painted directly

on the film to the beat of the music, which was ultimately recorded on the sound track. In what way does this differ from painting on a single sheet of paper?

In films like these it is sometimes difficult to determine whether the swirling colors or the music attracts our attention. Try to find out which (the visual or the aural), if either, impressed the class most. Regardless, the moving film seems to be an ideal way of bringing two diverse art forms together. Follow this discussion with the other film. From time to time ask the children to close their eyes and listen to the sound track. What colors might they "hear"? Tell them to glance at the film frequently to check the sound-inspired images. Turn off the sound and try "listening" to the film on the basis of cavorting colors and shapes.

Those who have experienced the color symbology situation (Chapter Four, Number 3) might try substituting colors of their own in keeping with what they feel is expressed by the sounds. Determine from them what colors they would paint on film to represent such familiar sounds as a school bell, police siren, the drone of traffic, or the overhead roar of a jet. For those who are interested, 16mm film leader, usually white, can be obtained for some direct painting and scratching on the surface to communicate the "visual" qualities of sounds.

The Objective

Ability to make comparisons of art forms.

The Situation (No. 4)

Rhythm in the arts. Focus on one principle of the arts, *rhythm,* and trace its occurrence in music, poetry, and painting.

Materials

Have the children select a favorite poem, a musical recording, and, if their experience is sufficient, a reproduction of a painting. A painting exemplary of rhythm would be Seurat's "La Grande Jatte," populated by myriads of people on a Sunday outing amidst recurring shapes and patterns. The original is extremely large. An

39

inexpensive reproduction is available on a 27" × 18" format. Have a record player available.

Stimulation

Before saying anything, attract the attention of the group, if you like, by playing their selected recording. Encourage them to let their bodies as well as their ears react to the sounds. The amount of physical involvement will depend on the kind of music they have selected —waltz, march, a current fad, or whatever. Ask them what made them move. Inquire as to whether they repeated similar movements regularly or at different intervals. In other words did they "keep some sort of time with the music"?

Procedure

Identify the concept of *rhythm*. Underline its importance as an ingredient in all *forms* of art. Each art form, such as music, has many ways of attaining rhythm, from the narrow range of a primitive drumbeat to the subtle recurrences in extended symphonic compositions. Ask the group how rhythm occurs in some of the poems with which they are familiar. Read one aloud. Rhythm is made not only by the words that rhyme at even intervals but by the pause of the voice. Look at the printed poem. Some poems have a visual rhythm—long lines, short lines, a stanza, a pause. (In some Oriental cultures poetry is meant to be seen rather than heard.) Poetry, unlike music, usually does not evoke foot tapping. Neither does a painting. Poetry sometimes creates images in the mind; painting makes them permanent on canvas.

Ask the group to find visual rhythm in the Seurat (or other) reproduction. (Explain that it is a reproduction and does not communicate all of the artist's original meaning.) First, they might look for repetitive colors. Notice if these occur at equal or unequal distances. Find some repetitive lines or edges (the women's skirts, the brims of men's hats, a monkey tail). Notice also the similarity of shapes among the umbrellas, parts of the land, and the trees. These visual rhythms are made up mainly of curves. Without the straight horizontal lines of the shore and water at the upper left these would not show up as well; they would be confusing. Rhythm in all forms of art also depends on *contrast*. Try

to find more evidence of rhythm, perhaps in the brushwork, in "La Grande Jatte." Look for unintended rhythms in your immediate visual environment. How would these be modified in a painting of the same place?

The Objective

Ability to make comparisons of art forms.

The Situation (No. 5)

Mobile sculpture and music. Compare musical form to a twentieth-century form of sculpture, the one being aural, the other visual, both blending in time.

Materials

Obtain or construct a *mobile*. An example from one of the group's visual organizational situations (Area Three) might suffice. Perhaps the group can make musical sounds as well. If not, use a record or the piano.

Stimulation

Review earlier experiences with traditional sculpture. Perhaps the children will recall that they as the viewers had to do the actual "moving" around the form. Introduce the concept of moving sculpture. Identify the mobile as an art form which in a way is in keeping with our own century; it possesses increased movement and speed. Music has changed also but in ways less obvious than this type of sculpture. Indicate further that the group will have an opportunity to listen to music and look at a mobile. The problem is to point out the similarities and differences in the two *forms*.

Procedure

The obvious and most consistent similarity between the two forms is that of movement in time. Stationary sculpture does not share this quality with music. The children might point out that, in responding to these art forms, the viewer or listener can remain in one position. From here on you will have to help them respond to the more subtle aspects of each form of art.

Enable them to notice that the mobile moves but stays while music also moves through time but fades away. Both the mobile and music are *compositions*. The parts of the mobile do not remain in the same place; they rearrange themselves, whereas the sounds of music, as audible parts, must remain in a specific order. Have the group look and listen from time to time during this discussion. Because the mobile is moving, it has a changing *balance*. Music must have a consistent harmony. Which form of art is more subject to "chance" as a result of this condition? The mobile, unless caught in a storm, turns slowly whereas most forms of music have a greater variety of movement. A mobile depends on gravity while music somehow, as sound, seems to float through the air in all directions.

It might be of interest to the group to know that Alexander Calder, an American sculptor who originated the mobile, did construct one that makes sounds. During the continual circuit of moving parts some strike one another and create sounds of varying pitch and intensity. Aside from this "blending" of the two forms many, many differences exist to make each a form of art in itself. Is a bell a form of mobile sculpture?

The Objective

Ability to make comparisons of art forms.

The Situation (No. 6)

Looking, listening, and listening and looking. Identify forms in art according to the way in which they elicit response through the various senses.

Materials

This situation involves the construction of a chart composed of concepts that emerge from the group. Rather than use the chalkboard, employ some materials that will be more lasting. A 24" × 36" sheet of manila oaktag and a felt-nib pen would be useful. Divide the sheet into three equal columns. Head the first column, "Looking," the second, "Listening," and the third, "Listening and Looking." Mount the potential chart where all can see it and in a position that enables you to do a superb job of lettering.

Stimulation

The alliteration among the L's on the chart is in itself a stimulation. Also, an empty chart implies that someone, in this instance each child, is going to have a chance to contribute something. The inductive approach can be stimulating. Let the empty chart be the initial focal point.

Procedure

Discuss with the children their own role in responding to different kinds of art. Perhaps if each child better understands his own way of responding, the concept of variation among *forms* of art will also be better understood.

You might ask them to list all of the kinds of art, or possible art, that they only "listen" to. By now most children will have listened to many *stories* and *poems*. An obvious candidate for this area would be *music*.

Those arts that consistently require both looking and listening, aside from the one example of mobile sculpture from a previous situation, usually are referred to as the "performing arts." What would they include? At times *television* might qualify. *Films* are art forms; movies are entertainment and sometimes qualify as art. Most of the children will have seen or participated in *plays*. *Operettas* and *dance* require looking and listening.

Elicit from the group a number of the "looking" arts. These of course include *drawing, painting,* and *sculpture*—terms usually held as synonymous with art. Children are less likely to (though they could) mention *prints, architecture, photography,* and *collage.* Try drawing comparisons between art forms in the same column and among forms in other columns. What can one form achieve that another cannot?

Use the chart as a review of previous experiences they have had concerning the interrelationship of art forms. Use it as a point of departure for subsequent situations in Areas One and Three. Meanwhile help the children to broaden their concept of "art," but be careful not to broaden it to the point where nonexpressive events that do not reflect human experience or involve the utilization of a *medium* are included. Encourage them in the future to test the

41

chart as a way of perceiving varying *forms* of art as they are encountered.

The Objective

Ability to make comparisons of art forms.

The Situation (No. 7)

The film as a combination of sight and sound. Realize how one subject is treated by two means of expression, pictures and sound, within one form of art: the film.

Materials

In addition to the usual projection equipment, order the film "Pacific 231." This brief film (10 min., b. & w.) pictures the journey of a locomotive. The visual document is synchronized with a musical composition by Arthur Honegger. The film does much to unite two forms of art into one new form.

Stimulation

Tell the class about the film. While doing so, regulate the projector to operate with only the sound, a contrived blunder. Such a faulty projection technique usually attracts attention. Encourage the group to merely listen to the music of the sound track while you slowly correct the situation.

Procedure

Continue with the presentation of the sound track without the picture. Encourage the children to imagine what the locomotive might be doing as suggested by the rhythm and tempo of the music. If possible try to imagine the terrain that is being crossed. After a few minutes supplement the images with the projected pictures on the screen. Run the film in normal fashion until its completion.

Upon completion of the film discuss some of the images. Ascertain the effectiveness of the music in revealing the journey of the train. Run the film, this time properly, once again. Let the children realize that films, like music, can be encountered over and over again. Also, pictures can be looked at more than once. Art can be pleasing without being new or novel.

After showing the film, inquire as to whether the sound or the sight of it was dominant. Determine whether for some children one form of art canceled out the other. It is possible that some could attend to only the music or only the pictures at one time. Some children might have felt a synthesis of sight and sound; essentially synthesis was the goal of the film maker. On the basis of the group's reactions, ask them if they think the film could function without any sound. Perhaps, time permitting, they would like to view the pictorial part of the film without the sound. You might remind them that movies began in just such a way.

During routine showings of subsequent films, note the comparisons that might be made from the preceding art learning situation. Is it possible for an "entertainment" type film to be artistic? How do the concepts of *form* and *content* (Chapter Seven) relate to film making?

The Objective

Ability to make comparisons of art forms.

The Situation (No. 8)

Single subjects as treated by different art forms. Select one subject common to many forms of art, the seascape, and examine the manner in which it has been handled by music and by painting.

Materials

Acquire the necessary equipment to play Debussy's *La Mer* or a comparable selection of your preference. Also obtain a reproduction of a seascape. Among the worthwhile examples are Winslow Homer's "Weather Beaten" and "Northeaster" and any number of the works by John Marin or William Turner.

Stimulation

Without revealing the *subject matter* of the recording or disclosing the presence of the painting play the second section of *La Mer*, "The Play of the Waves." Suspend discussion until later.

Procedure

Rather than dwell on visual properties or

...rceptual situations ...k about the kinds of ...ed. Ascertain if any ...o feel in the music ...ature. For example, ...vastness? Perhaps ...poser was trying to ...composers try to ...ures" with sounds. ...La Mer, "Dialogue ...Do not reveal the ...children have had ...nd, if they wish, ...icence on the part ...fter such an expe-...strued as a lack of ...ng (or painting). In ...are in the form of ...into words. The ...ildren are so skill-...escribe nonexist-..., will be able to ...ir responses with ...ask them if they shared what Debussy was trying to communicate. Reveal the title of the section after they have reported.

Contrast this audible experience with a visual one. Within the moist context now established let them view Homer's "Weather Beaten." From previous situations they should be somewhat aware of differences in the *forms* of art, e.g., music is sound and temporal (goes on in time), painting is visual and confined to one space. Invite the group now to discuss their feelings about the painting. In what way has Homer, through his art, been able to make them feel the forces of nature (if at all)? In what way do these feelings differ from those experienced in responding to *La Mer*? For the present which form of art is most effective in making them feel something apart from the routine of the day?

The Objective
Ability to make comparisons of art forms.

The Situation (No. 9)
The art of picturing people. Compare the handling of portraiture in literature, poetry, and painting.

Materials
Determine from the group which of the stories and poems they have read contain passages that best describe a person. Avoid going into a lengthy biography. Have a few reproductions of portrait paintings available for comparison. The following portraits have been inexpensively reproduced: Derain's "Harlequin," Modigliani's "Woman with Red Hair," Redon's "Girl with Flowers," Vermeer's "Seamstress," and Van Dyck's "Picture of a Warrior." Try to have one of each sex.

Stimulation
Read to the group an actual or fictitious police bulletin that describes a wanted person. Obtain their opinions as to why this bulletin is or is not a form of art. Discuss the concept of *portrait* as recurring subject matter in many of the arts. Ask them to identify portraits with which they are familiar.

Procedure
From the work of an author of good repute have one child read aloud a paragraph that "paints a portrait" with words. Invite the children to form an image of the person being characterized. Discuss with one another the images that occur within the group. Why are some different? Perhaps each child added something from his own experiences to the words of the author. In a way each person in the group was an artist in that his interpretation in part consisted of personal meanings. The author, too, interpreted his subject through his own feelings. In this one respect the excerpt just read differs from the police bulletin. Moreover, the author uses words, sentences, and paragraphs as an art *medium*, personally and with skill.

Read a "portrait" poem. Make suitable analogies to the development by the author of that particular form of art. The poem is likely to contain more metaphor. The poet might have to take greater liberties with words than the novelist to contain them within a more closely prescribed structure.

Introduce the class to two reproductions of painted portraits. Why do they differ from ordinary photographs of people? Here again, the painter interjects a part of himself in the work. Also, he tries to assess the character and background of the person he is interpreting; a well-painted portrait goes beyond the routine

43

duplication of a photograph. The portrait painter, like the photographer, has a limited format into which he must "fit" the person. The space around the head and body is an important part of the painting. It should not appear to be unrelated to the pictured person. A portrait is never a replica of a person (flesh and bone). Instead, it involves the use of an art *medium* in a particular *form* of art. Which form would the children elect for such a task?

The Objective
Ability to make comparisons of art forms.

The Situation (No. 10)
Films and plays. Compare the film, as a visual form of art, to the play, which is a performing art.

Materials
Rely mainly on the raw material of the children's memories of their own experiences. Many will have seen some form of drama on the school stage or in local theatre group performances. Nearly all will have seen "movies," which hereafter will be referred to as films. As a focal point for discussion have on display a movie screen and a large box with one side cut away. The latter will serve as a model for a stage. The children can project their images onto these as you compare the two forms of art.

Stimulation
Explain to the group that they are going to serve as human "projectors" and fill in images on the screen and stage that they see before them. (No need for them to seek an electrical outlet.)

Procedure
Determine how many have seen plays. If necessary take a survey of their film attendance. List some of the titles of plays and films they have seen. Ask them to have in mind a favorite play or film as you discuss with them some of the properties of these *forms* of art. Make a separate list of films that have been adapted from plays.

Ask the group to list the general structural properties of plays (acts and scenes) and how ideas are presented (through talking and sometimes scenery). They will probably realize that talking is the central means of communication in plays. Sometimes there is no scenery; the *visual* is usually *supporting* or secondary. Also, and they can look into the model stage, how does one change scenes quickly? How does one go back into time? By showing two things happening at the same time? By giving the audience more than one view of a scene or event? By showing distance and close-ups? It becomes apparent that the stage has visual limitations. It depends mainly on dialogue and intermissions to separate time and place circumstances. Yet some people are very critical of films that do not closely follow the script of a play or of a book.

A film is a very flexible art form. If it utilizes the visual properties just identified and uses sounds and words as means of support it is said to be *cinematic*. In seconds it shows a change from far to near or from past to present. In seconds it shows an object or person from the top, front, back, or side. The viewer might see through his own eyes or might seem to see through the eyes of another. These are but a few of the things that the film can do. Ask the children to look at the screen and make an imaginary movie about something of interest. How would they have to change these ideas to fit them on the stage?

44

The Objective

Ability to make comparisons of art forms.

The Situation

Materials

Stimulation

Procedure

Past and Present Roles of Artists

The role of the artist has changed over a period of many centuries.

6   The artist once represented his society as an artisan who shared their views and they his.

The personal feelings of the artist were often subordinate to accepted styles of art.

Eventually he asserted his individuality and began to focus upon the immediate world of his own interests.

He became a specialist, most often a painter, rather than a craftsman who would undertake many visual tasks.

In his specialization, and as a result of political, industrial, and economic revolutions, he became increasingly isolated from society.

Some artists have emerged as specialists in many kinds of art that are part of business and industry.

Many artists, through their vision and their medium, remain as interpreters and shapers of human experience.

The Objective
Understanding of the varying past and present roles of artists.

The Situation (No. 1)
Cowboys, community helpers, and artists. Inquire as to what an artist might be in contrast to more familiar roles.

Materials
Put on display reproductions of four paintings. Have a landscape, a portrait, a scene with figures, and a *nonobjective* painting by Miró or Kandinsky. You might develop a story chart with a heading such as "The artist—who is he?"

Stimulation
Review previous discussions that dealt with various occupational groups within the community. Assess the current list of hero types among both sexes. Encourage the children to try to describe the roles of the familiar community occupational groups and, perhaps, those of the more remote figures with whom some might have identified. Determine the level of accuracy of their descriptions (the role of a cowboy is likely to be grossly misconstrued, that of the mailman more correctly understood).

Procedure

Focus on the displayed reproductions. Indicate that the reproductions are not the actual paintings. From these "products" inquire as to who might have "made" them. Many will respond with the term *artist*. Ask them whether musicians, poets, and authors are not also artists. If they have not yet thought of these reproductions as "paintings," compare the physical process that these artists went through to their own when they paint at an easel. From this, substitute *painter* for artist.

Ask the children what they think a painter must know before he can do outstanding work. Indicate that he must study for years, by himself or with teachers. The serious painter never stops studying. What other people study throughout their careers?

Why does a painter paint? There are many possible answers to this question, perhaps as many answers as there are painters. Painting is a highly personal way of responding to their lives. Not all jobs allow people to express their personal thoughts. Maybe that is why many painters paint.

Most jobs are referred to as work. Is what painters do work? Is it fun? Children really cannot tell by comparing to their own attempts at the easel, because adult painters have had more education and different experiences. They are not children. Children are not painters. But since most painters like what they do it is at times, for many, both work and fun. They work because they want to and because they believe in what they are doing. In this sense painting is often satisfying.

What do painters do for us? Many painters, through their study and work, see things and think about things differently from most people. Their thoughts and visions often materialize in their paintings. If we bother to look we will see that painters have shown us things we have been too busy to realize. They give us fresh views, to both our pleasure and displeasure, of our lives and those of others.

The Objective

Understanding of the varying past and present roles of artists

The Situation (No. 2)

Pictures outside of frames. Identify the function of the commercial artist as one responsible for the visual material found in books, magazines, stories, and on television.

Materials

Gather some commercial art products other than school books. These could include sizable magazine pictures and advertisements, a well-lettered package, a colorful poster, and a record album cover.

Stimulation

Ask the children to open some of their favorite illustrated books. Most of them will realize the function of the illustrations. Establish the difference, by questioning, between a picture or design in the book and a painting. At the physical level the painting exists by itself. Though some paintings have been reproduced, none were painted with that intent. By contrast, thousands of books contain the same pictures. Of course they do not have frames. What do we call the person who makes these pictures?

Procedure

With the identity of this kind of artist not yet revealed show some other products of commercial art. Ask the children whether they think the lettering and arrangement of an advertisement might be art. Why? It does involve some visual organizing. Where else do they see advertisements? On billboards. Where else? On television. What do we call advertisements on television? These are referred to as commercials. They try to sell something. The artist who designs these tries to tell us something about the product. He is called a *commercial artist*. He very often illustrates books in an imaginative way to help tell the story, not necessarily to sell it. He designs record album covers to tell with attractive colors and shapes what the contents are like. A record album cover is a kind of package. Show the group another package. Indicate that the commercial artist often has to design the shape of a package to hold a special product before he adds colors and letters.

There are many kinds of commercial artists. In what way does the job of a commercial artist differ from that of a painter? For the most part he tries to relate his ideas to a specific job that someone hires him to do. Very often he has many people to please and a specific space, such as a package, in which to design. When he illustrates a story, his ideas have to match those of the author. The commercial artist usually works in relation to the products of other people. He works for and with them.

The painter is different because he works mainly for himself but in relation to his society. Although he sets his own goals and limitations, he usually has more choices to make than does the commercial artist. What are some other differences? Collect some products designed by commercial artists.

The Objective

Understanding of the varying past and present roles of artists.

The Situation (No. 3)

The three-dimensional man. Investigate the role of the sculptor as an artist.

Materials

Have available a sizable portion of moist ceramic clay, a large stone, a chunk of wood, and, if possible, some random scraps of metal. These materials will be employed only for purposes of visual reference.

Stimulation

Arrange the three-dimensional materials so that all the children can conveniently see them. Ask them what kind of *artist* might use any or all of these materials.

Procedure

After a few responses you might arrive at the terms *sculpture* and *sculptor*. The former term is often used erroneously to refer to the artist rather than to his product. After the words have been clarified, help the children form a concept of the sculptor's role in relation to society.

Like the painter, the sculptor works chiefly for himself. His work, however, may be seen more often because much of it is outdoors. Ask the children if they can recall any sculpture they have seen, perhaps within their own community. Remind them that many parks contain sculpture. Some statues are imitations in stone or bronze of soldiers with muskets and officers on horses. You might discuss statues that all the children have seen, adding that some statues show little imagination on the part of the men who made them. A sculptor is an artist who changes outward appearances to show his feelings about whatever he is sculpturing. He shapes his material in a way that is natural; he may follow the grain of the wood and he may leave his hand marks in the clay. He does not always try to hide the way in which his sculpture was made.

As mentioned, in many ways the sculptor's art is a public art. It is often used to commemorate a special event, for better or worse. The sculptor's product serves to remind us of certain aspects of our heritage. Moreover, if he is a worthy sculptor rather than an ordinary statue maker, he graces the landscape and makes the community more personal. For many centuries sculptors have added visual interest to the buildings and parks of cities. This was particularly so in ancient Hellas, now called Greece. In the Hellenic or Classical period, architecture was built to protect the sculpture. Soon, sculpture began to decorate the buildings. The sculptor as a consequence has for some time worked closely with the men who design our large buildings. Some painters called muralists have also worked with builders.

Not all pieces of sculpture are large or public. Like paintings, many are products of private feelings and thoughts. Some are never sold. Others are bought by people for their homes. Some may be seen in museums. The sculptor's art is so durable that he has served as a communicator of his culture for many centuries. He graced the cities while alive and left something behind that helps us understand the life of his times.

The Objective

Understanding of the varying past and present roles of artists.

The Situation (No. 4)

Ideas we live in. Discuss the architect as an artist who designs a variety of shelters for many uses.

Materials

Collect some materials that show *architecture* as art. For older groups, have one person act as a "guest artist." Obtain an actual blueprint that shows a floor plan and one or two elevations (side views) of an interesting home. Display photographs of some of the more publicized works of architects from Michelangelo to Frank Lloyd Wright.

Stimulation

Create a situation whereby the children will have to play the role of an architect. Describe what building materials are available, different kinds of brick, wood, and glass. Describe what kind of building is needed and in what type of climate and terrain it must be built. Indicate that there are men who know how to prepare and assemble these materials, carpenters and masons, but that in order to have a building that looks and functions well it is important to have a plan, or a *design*. What kind of artist makes such a design?

Procedure

Establish the term *architect*. Describe his role in more detail. Like the sculptor's, his work is often public, at least from the outside. Everyone sees what he does. We either live in buildings that reflect his work or visit them. List several kinds of buildings. Like the sculptor or commercial artist, the architect is often hired to design a building for people or organizations. Sometimes these people tell him what they want, other times they tell him to do as he pleases. In the latter instance he behaves more like a painter. He sets his own limitations, considering the use of the building. Not all buildings are well designed. Some are unimaginative, others are copies of other architects' ideas, still others are poorly suited to their purposes. Some buildings are erected with little planning.

A good architect, like a good sculptor, can do much to enhance the visual qualities of the area in which he lives. He is an artist who knows the principles of art. He is also a scientist who knows about strength, construction, terrain, and climate. His art differs from that of painters and sculptors in that, as noted, it has to function properly as well as to please the eye. An architect might be said to be an artist when he can meet both requirements effectively. He has to be somewhat of a psychologist in his dealings

with people. Like all artists he must have imagination superior to that of most people. He needs years of education before he is even qualified to plan and supervise the construction of a building. Ask the children who designed the building they are in. Which buildings near by appear to have been *designed* by an architect? Which appear rather ordinary as if they were built from a popular blueprint? Why can't all of the schools in a community be built from the same plan?

The Objective

Understanding of the varying past and present roles of artists.

The Situation (No. 5)

The unmechanical man. Cite the contributions of the present-day designer-craftsman.

Materials

There are a number of publications that feature the products of the present-day craftsman. Among these are *Crafts Horizons* and *Creative Crafts*. Amass some photographs from these and other sources that disclose *crafts* production ranging through weaving, jewelry, and ceramics. For purposes of clarity limit the examples to present-day products. Folk art constitutes another major area. If possible, have some actual contemporary products available.

Stimulation

Ask the children to imagine how they would manage to eat their food, clothe themselves, and decorate their surroundings if they were unable to buy the products that presently enable them to accomplish those tasks.

Procedure

Ask them further what kind of present-day artist might be able to help them fashion products to achieve the ends specified above. Show some of the visual examples. From their responses establish the term *craftsman*. A craftsman, in addition to being skillful with his hands and knowledgeable about his materials, must be more than an imitator; he is also a designer. He, like all artists, is influenced by the works of others but he refrains from copying them.

49

He *designs* by developing his own ideas in addition to what he has learned from others. He thus becomes a *designer-craftsman*. The objects he makes are products of the *hand* and *mind*. Not many useful objects are made in this way in our age of mass production and increased automation. Accordingly, most people might have difficulty if they were asked to weave their own fabrics or make their own utensils.

In a sense the craftsman is like a painter in that he ordinarily produces only one of each product—no two are exactly alike. They have a human rather than a machine touch. Like the painter he depends on people who appreciate handmade things to purchase his work.

Unlike the painter or sculptor, but more like an architect, his product must be useful. It has to do the job for which it was intended. Some craft objects are merely decorative; the woven cloth might serve as a wall hanging. But decoration is also a function. The craftsman is very much concerned about the appearance of interiors. The presence of his objects can do much to make a house more pleasant.

Unlike paintings and sculpture, craft objects are not *symbolic*; the craftsman is less concerned about expressing something apart from the object. Also, he is less likely to be concerned about visual perception and psychological introspection. He uses his materials for what they are; clay remains clay. He does not go beyond them as does the painter to express various conditions of man and nature. As a result his product is more frequently referred to as a *craft* than as an art form.

The Objective
Understanding of the varying past and present roles of artists.

The Situation (No. 6)
The man behind your chair. Identify the role of the industrial designer in relation to machine-made products.

Materials
Prepare nothing. Almost every manmade environment is replete with examples, good and poor, of industrial design. Actual reference to the *design* qualities of these products is made in Chapter Nine. For the present rely on the spontaneity of the group to perceive the role of the industrial designer through a few ordinary examples that appear in the room.

Stimulation
Review the concepts developed about the designer-craftsman. Emphasize his role as a producer of individually made objects. Ask the group what the present population of the United States is. Remind them that we have essentially an urban industrial economy. Could the craftsman produce enough to meet our needs? It is obvious that for the most part objects of daily use, from chairs to automobiles, are machine produced. But who is responsible for the *design* of these objects?

Procedure
Invite the group to focus on the chairs in the room. They will probably appear identical in shape. They are not handcrafted. Since machines do not have human sensitivity toward visual proportion the *industrial designer* now serves as a mediator between daily needs and the capacities of the machine to produce items to meet them.

The industrial designer is in a sense a "modern" artist. He has not been around as long as the painter or sculptor. He became prominent partly as a result of the *Bauhaus* school in the Germany of the 1920s. In this school no distinction was made between objects of use and objects of beauty. The present-day industrial designer studies the needs of people. Accordingly he determines what kind of chair is most suitable for lounging or for working at a desk. He must also consider where the chair will be used and by whom. Upon studying these needs the industrial designer then investigates the most appropriate materials available and relates these to what machines can economically produce. New ideas, even for chairs, often require new materials and new methods of manufacturing. The problem of the industrial designer is that of making changes that are better, not just different. In this regard good design goes beyond fashion. However, since these products are produced to be sold, he sometimes has to comply with the wishes of the manufacturer. Like the commercial artist, he often has less freedom than the painter. Like the painter, however, he is able to say something about the era

50

in which he designs. And, like the architect, he *plans* and seldom touches the materials that shape the final product.

He has to invent new shapes to contain things that did not exist several decades ago. Among these is the television set. Think of some other new industrial forms. How would you design an automobile that operated on a cushion of air rather than on four wheels? Here the answer is not obtained by copying an existent design.

The Objective

Understanding of the varying past and present roles of artists.

The Situation (No. 7)

The beginning of the artist. On the basis of inferences and ethnographic objects discuss the role of the *artist* in preliterate societies.

Materials

Some reproductions of cave paintings are needed. You might want to use one or both of the following films related to this situation. They have to do, respectively, with past and present preliterate societies. The first, "Lascaux, Cradle of Man's Art" (17 min., color), shows some of the early cave paintings discovered in southern France. The second, "The Living Stone" (22 min., b. & w.), depicts the story of a hunter who carved the image of his legendary wish from a piece of stone.

Stimulation

Either of the films will do much to gain attention and subsequent interest. With or without them, ask the children what they think art, and artists, must have been like before we had schools and all of the special needs of our present civilization. Many will think of the "caveman" artist. He, as a vague generality, might serve as a point of departure for what follows. Remind the group that there are a few isolated societies intact today that closely resemble those of the past.

Procedure

Emphasize the relative simplicity of a preliterate society. Each person had a well-defined role. Many of these roles were probably shared; several people might have served as artists. In some societies, the artist's role might be that of maker of religious artifacts.

At Lascaux someone left behind some remarkable paintings of animals. Archeologists have conjectured that these were created to insure fertility or success in a hunt. This kind of art could have been a basis for a ritual conducted by the artist. In a way each artist was a composite of his entire group; or at least he is now to us. The Lascaux art identifies the beliefs of the society. Out of the environment the artist *selected* subjects significant to all (the hunt, fertility) and *shaped* them through his own *medium* and *style*. Preliterate art was more socially oriented than present-day art in that it portrayed or fulfilled the daily needs of nearly everyone in the group. The artist served to strengthen social bonds. The artist was a practical man dealing with the immediate concerns of all.

Art seems to have become less practical in Neolithic societies. In looking at objects from that era one notices decorations that enhance surfaces of implements. It appears that the artist derived ideas from nature forms around him. Some closely resemble the outward appearances of such forms. Gradually he extended some of these nature shapes into symbolic designs of his own invention. Many of his scratchings were apparently appreciated more for their own sake than as "magic." Like his society the role of the artist was also changing and becoming more complex. Whoever he was, he was extremely close to his kinsmen and they to him.

The Objective

Understanding of the varying past and present roles of artists.

The Situation (No. 8)

The artist in ancient and medieval times. Develop concepts pertinent to the roles of the artists in these remote times.

Materials

In order to make the locale of this situation seem more palpable utilize a large world map.

51

To go back into time is difficult enough. Prior to this situation assign teams to look up information and pictures about the following eras: the Tang dynasty in China; the Hellenic period in Greece, and the medieval period in Western Europe. A chairman from each team should be prepared to give an oral report about the era of concern.

Stimulation

Rely on the three oral reports to serve as a background for the discussion. Indicate that each report will serve as "scenery" from which three characters will emerge. Each will be an artist, representative of his times. There have always been artists, even before they were named as such.

Procedure

You might begin with the Tang report. Supplement it (and those that follow) with a description of "the artist" of that culture. Indicate to the group that he often was a painter, a writer, and a poet all in one. His intent was to *blend* ideas rather than to separate them. Rather than develop a style of his own, the artist studied what his artist ancestors had done and tried to preserve their way. In this way the past blended with the present and offered a form of art for the future artist to continue. The individual did not assert himself because he believed (as many present-day Zen Buddhists believe) that man was at one with nature; he was of equal importance to all living things, not superior to them. The artist was in this context an obedient "unifier" of many arts, of past and present, and of man and nature.

In ancient Greece, at the time of Hellas, the artist was a servant to the state and to certain gods. His role was that of an artisan or craftsman. His work was also quite impersonal in that he created sculpture and pottery according to precepts of subject and beauty; he responded less to his own vision and the materials. In some Hellenic art pertaining to athletes, he did respond to the inherent possibilities of stone. In his society he was considered to be a rather lowly fellow because he used his hands. Actually, the term art was applied mainly to poetry and music, not to handmade products. His contributions far surpassed his status.

In medieval Europe the artist also created forms based upon the beliefs of the culture. As Christianity spread, great cathedrals were built. The artist decorated churches with *mosaic* pictures and sculpture depicting the Christian faith. A craftsman still, he busily illustrated and illuminated books. His place in society was increasingly well defined. His craft became more of a trade. In towns he joined guilds that offered years of apprenticeship for those who wanted to be artists. Towns became "craft universities." Although his way of doing things was becoming more personal in *style* his *subject matter* was largely limited to religion.

The Objective

Understanding of the varying past and present roles of artists.

The Situation (No. 9)

The artist as an individual. Examine the changing role of the artist from the time of the Italian Renaissance onward.

Materials

Utilize some of the visual materials and references from social studies to clarify the role of the Renaissance artist as he focused on the ancient world and his own world, with emphasis on the individual within it. Two films would be helpful in demonstrating the span of the artist's role from then until recent times. Because this topic might be extended to two situations the films could be viewed on separate occasions. The first, "Leonardo Da Vinci and His Art" (13 min., color), examines Leonardo's versatility and his importance as a Renaissance figure. The second, "Vincent van Gogh" (21 min., color), traces Van Gogh's career through views of his paintings and excerpts from his letters.

Stimulation

Either of these films would serve as a point of departure, forward from Leonardo or back toward the Renaissance from Van Gogh, in an effort to understand the role of the artist as an important member of society.

Procedure

Using appropriate social studies references, convey the following information. During the

52

Italian Renaissance the artist had a well-defined place in society as one who could take care of nearly any visual task. He catered more and more to nobility and businessmen. He decorated for their festivities, designed cabinets, and began to paint at the easel. He was not a specialist. When he did paint, he often depicted Greek legends and subjects of his own choosing. His work was often secular. His education was geared toward the development of many manual skills. Boys who wanted to be artists served as apprentices under master craftsmen. For the time being, the painter and the craftsman were not two distinct entities.

Those artists who were chiefly painters became more scientific in their appraisal of the visible world. They became concerned with visual perception through human anatomy and perspective in landscapes. Even religious paintings revealed a scientific interest in volumes and spatial relationships. Before the Renaissance the artist had been involved chiefly with architecture and sculpture. Near the end of the Renaissance he was becoming more concerned with painting, on walls in Italy and on small panels in Northern Europe. Wealthy people began to patronize him as a painter.

As the Renaissance spread to Holland the role of the artist changed. The Protestant religion did not foster art in the church and as a result the artist painted portraits, *genre* scenes, and detailed landscapes. Later on, toward the nineteenth century some French and English artists, on their own volitions, also painted genre subject matter.

The artist thus became more of a specialist; painting became his chief interest. His audience became smaller as his culture became increasingly specialized. Mainly his patrons were the aristocrats. He was regarded by them as an intelligent person, no longer a lowly craftsman. The artist, as a painter, persisted in this manner well until the time of the industrial, political, and economic revolutions of the nineteenth century.

In France, after the Renaissance and before the Revolution, the artist was almost entirely patronized by the aristocracy. The French government formed an academy that prescribed in a sense what was considered to be good art, generally heroic subjects that pleased the wealthy. Although the artist had become more of an individual as a result of the Renaissance, he was now becoming another kind of servant to another group. Fortunately many artists objected to such a restricted way of painting.

The French Revolution led to the formation of the middle class and the decline of the aristocracies. By now the artist had lost or had rejected his former patronage. The new middle classes, with less cultivated tastes, were not ready to consume his products. The craftsmen were being replaced by machinery. Some organized to counter the industrial trend, which until this day has put the artist out of the mainstream of society. As society at large became more interested in gadgets, the artist withdrew. He became an individual who could not accept the limited middle-class view of the world. In refusing to conform he often advocated *"L' art pour l'art,"* art for art's sake. The artist now became elite. Since then he has been accused of living in an "ivory tower." If this is so, his views from there have been remarkably clear.

The Objective

Understanding of the varying past and present roles of artists.

The Situation (No. 10)

The emergent divergent man. Appraise the possible role of the artist amidst the stereotypes held about him in an urban, secular, technological society.

Materials

Distribute to everyone a conte crayon and a large (18″ × 24″) sheet of manila paper or newsprint.

Stimulation

Invite the group to make a quick sketch of a present-day artist. Do not offer any details or description. In consideration of their drawing abilities assess each sketch as a reflection of a concept of an artist.

Procedure

Observe the completed drawings before beginning the discussion. Do not collect them. Ask the children to trace briefly the changing role of the artist from the time of the Renais-

53

sance to the present. Indicate that the artist is a part of a small group (subculture), voluntarily or not, within the total population (culture). Most of our population is located in cities. The cities contain a great variety of industries and businesses that occupy the lives and interests of most people. The products of the artist are in turn more likely to be found in galleries and museums than in most homes. More homes have television sets than have paintings.

After setting the scene ask the children to look at their sketches. If you like, take an inventory of the visible characteristics assigned to "the artist." Determine first how many artists are painters and if they are working or inactive. Check the type of attire, the facial appearance, the facial expression, and any object he (or she) might be holding. Probably most will be bearded males in equally stereotypic clothing.

It is true that some artists dress oddly. Their energies are often directed toward their art rather than outward appearance. Some appear as they do to perpetuate a romantic symbol of the artist as a rebel. Some just pretend to be artists. And many artists, more specifically painters, possess no outward differences. Most people tend to hold a generalized image of the artist.

The artist's role is not as well defined as that of many trades and professional men. His behavior is different from that of the salesman, the junior executive, and the laborer. His product reflects his different behavior—it has lasting qualities; it uplifts people from their daily cares. He values a countryside for its natural charm without thinking of turning it into a money-making venture. He appreciates experiences more than household appliances. He often works alone. He feels into events and sees deeply (empathy). Though often accused of being "unrealistic," he might be closer to a reality overlooked by most of our hurried population. He sees, thinks, and organizes in terms of an art medium. Thus, he offers us a reality other than our own if we pause to appreciate him.

54

The Objective
Understanding of the varying past and present roles of artists.

The Situation

Materials

Stimulation

Procedure

55

A Range of Art Expression

7

The intent of artists has long been that of expressing
aspects of human experience.

Among works of significant art there are as many
styles of expression as there are artists.

The styles range from the apparently understandable to the seemingly
incomprehensible; from *naturalism* to complete *nonobjectivity*.

Very often what appears to be simple is extremely complex.

Many viewers fail to respond to certain styles of art because
of a learned "inability" to see.

A viewer with a receptive attitude and an informed perception
can give, at the very least, an alert response.

The Objective
Recognition of a range of art expression from
pictorial to pure.

The Situation (No. 1)
Pictures that "show feelings." Acquaint the
children with something closely akin to their
own painting "styles," the visual communication of ideas and feelings as exemplified by
reproductions of various *expressionist* painters.

Materials
Start a visual file according to the ranges of
artistic style that you will encounter in this and
subsequent art learning situations in Chapter
Seven. Many magazines reproduce paintings.
Inexpensive reproductions of the following are
available commercially in junior, postcard, and
large sizes: Marin's "Region of Brooklyn
Bridge," Van Gogh's "Starry Night," Marc's
"Red Horses," Rouault's "Old King," Matisse's
"Interior, Flowers and Parrots," Soutine's
"Windy Day," Pechstein's "Yellow Irises," and
Kokoschka's "View of Dresden." Obtain all or
some of the above examples of work by these
painters. Have tempera paint or crayon and
large manila or white construction paper available. If tempera is used, have a supply of large
round and one-inch flat brushes. Dispense
tempera paint from plastic ketchup containers
into opened half-pint milk cartons. Have water
and paintcloths available for each of the children, who should also be well protected from
any of the forthcoming expressionistic endeavors that miss the target.

Stimulation
Do not show the reproductions to the chil-

dren at this moment. Have in mind some of the *subject matter* included in those you do have. Through discussion identify some of the feelings the children might have about similar subject matter, the noise of big cities, the wind, a bouquet of flowers. Encourage them to paint what they *feel* about something, yet keep it pictorial—show subject matter.

Procedure

Upon completion of their work, perhaps at another time, present or distribute the reproductions to them. Define *expressionism*. Discuss it in relation to their own experiences. Indicate that these artists are capable of drawing and painting in a way that would make the subject matter look "very real" (unlike the present abilities of the children), but instead they intentionally twist and change shapes of things to give them a special meaning. The colors and lines are also exaggerated to go along with the special meaning the artist wants the picture to have. The emotion of the artist might even be different from that in the picture. He wants the *picture* itself to express something special about a certain subject in *itself*.

Encourage the children to pick out color distortions. These works have minimal detail and will be within the range of perceptual ability of most young children. Indicate that these paintings were inventions that enabled the artist to rely on color for the sake of color to generate feelings. Yet the painters were very careful as to where they placed color. Look for color *contrast* and repetition. Also, look for lyrical or strong *lines*. Look at the arrangement and feel the total painting.

The Objective

Recognition of a range of art expression from pictorial to pure.

The Situation (No. 2)

Lasting impressions. Look at some examples of *impressionism*.

Materials

Utilize the natural surroundings visible from the room. Consult your visual file under impressionism and post several magazine reproductions. Reproductions of the following are available in postcard, junior, and larger sizes (the larger sizes would be more effective): Sisley's "The Tugboat," Renoir's "By the Seashore" or "The Skiff," Monet's "Coast of Etretat" or "Windmills in Holland," Pissarro's "Street in Rouen," and Whistler's "Battersea Bridge." Reproductions of nearly any of the works of these men would suffice.

Stimulation

On a sunny day invite the children to turn their chairs or desks to face outdoors. Ask them to squint at what they see. Have some of them describe the softer blurred forms and colors induced by this optical effort. With normal vision ask them to describe what happens to surfaces that are entirely exposed to the intensity of the sun. Allow them to comment on their perceptions. At one time have them close their eyes, open them for only an instant, and close them again, merely to glance at the exterior view. Some might be able to describe their impressions. Indicate that some painters tried to do just that with colors. Ask the group to imagine how the present view would appear on a rainy or foggy day. First, would they be able to see faraway objects clearly? Second, what effect would the atmosphere have on the colors?

Procedure

Introduce the children to Monet (through his reproduction). Tell them that as an impressionist painter he was so curious about the effects of light on objects outdoors that he painted the same haystack at different times of day. Although the subject was the same it appeared different each time. He also painted the same seashore during different times of the year to show the seasonal changes.

The impressionists all painted differently from one another even though they held similar ideas. They tried to do what the recently invented camera could not do. In a scientific way they wanted to show the outdoors and movements of people "at a glance." With paint and color they tried to "freeze" forever a general impression of the play of light as observed by anyone's eyes. They, unlike the expressionists who followed them, tried to keep their personal feelings out of the pictures. This, of course, really is not entirely possible.

57

Look at some of the examples. Notice how the painters used small brushstrokes of different bright colors side by side. Instead of painting a shape with one color, they broke up the shape with many colors. Moreover, the shadows are colored. What we see here are general impressions, in paint, of everchanging views. Ask the children to notice how things around them change. They might collect some examples of impressionist painting. They might try "breaking up colors" the next time they paint.

The Objective

Recognition of a range of art expression from pictorial to pure.

The Situation (No. 3)

Paintings without objects. Begin to understand the significance of paintings without *subject matter* by realizing the "object" behind *nonobjectivity.*

Materials

Refer to Situation No. 8, which pertains to *realism* in art expression, and utilize one of those recommended reproductions. Obtain reproductions of nonobjective paintings such as the following: Kandinsky's "Composition 711" or "Heavenly Bodies," Miró's "Comets," and Mondrian's "Broadway Boogie Woogie" or "Painting Number 1." You will often find reproductions of nonobjective works by such contemporary painters as Motherwell and Soulages.

Stimulation

Display one of the larger examples of realism upside down. Enable the children to focus their attention upon it. Invariably someone will be disquieted by the improper presentation of this style of painting.

Procedure

Ask the children what is bothersome about the position of the picture. Ask them to look at it in another way; view the objects as "shapes" that contain "colors" and "textures." Pretend that no subject matter exists; instead there is a composition without familiar objects. Show

them some of the nonobjective reproductions. Indicate that "objects" have been replaced by visual elements.

Tell them that many artists were dissatisfied with the limitations imposed by subject matter. Some thought that both the painter and the viewer could respond better to "pure" arrangements by doing away with remembrances provoked by subject matter. The musicians had been able to do this for many years; they arranged sounds made by the instruments in harmonies of tone—they did not depend on words or the sounds of nature to make up their symphonies. In fact, Kandinsky experimented with nameless lines and masses of color in an effort to get a musical or "pure" idea across in a painting. His painting, of course, is not like the music but the shapes and colors within it relate to no other "reality." Mondrian assigned a musical title to one of his works (Broadway Boogie Woogie). Again, his work is not music but is instead a thing all by itself; devoted to a harmony of opposing forces, composed of vertical and horizontal lines interspersed by a rhythmic arrangement of primary colors. Miró's shapes are almost lifelike but they too exist in the painting as shapes that must get along with one another, similar to sounds of music, in order to harmonize. These paintings are not as simple as they appear to be. The artist has to make every mark count; he wastes nothing. Also, many of the paintings express aspects of certain philosophical beliefs of the artists. Turn some upside down. Appreciate them as another kind of painting or design, one that sometimes appears pleasing from any direction. Some nonobjective paintings have numbers, but no titles.

The Objective

Recognition of a range of art expression from pictorial to pure.

The Situation (No. 4)

To take and change. Discuss the meaning of the term *abstract art* in reference to several paintings and an animation.

Materials

The *futurist* painters of Italy were among the first of this century to indulge in intentional

58

abstract painting. Many of their works have been reproduced in books and periodicals. Try to find examples of Carlo Carrà's and Gino Severini's work. Marcel Duchamp painted the widely reproduced "Nude Descending the Stairs." Mark Tobey's "Intersections," Nicolas de Staël's "Football Players," Stuart Davis's "Summer Landscape," and Lyonel Feininger's "Mariners at Dawn" are nonfuturist abstractions. Also, obtain the animated film "Le Merle" (5 min., b. & w.). In this film simple cutouts perform the action of a song about a blackbird that loses his beak, eyes, neck, etc., only to get them back in triplicate. The cutouts fall apart, dance, and reassemble according to the development of the story.

Stimulation

Ask the group if anyone knows the meaning of *abstraction*. Proceed with the film regardless of a possible lack of response.

Procedure

Though fragmented, the subject matter of the film is still recognizable. Ask the children to identify the "critter" from which the parts were taken (the bird). Inquire also as to the derivation of the idea for the pictorial part of the film (the story). Establish the concept of abstraction as meaning "to take from." Since this is general, relate the term to some of the abstract artists. The futurist painters, for example, took their ideas from modern cities and transportation. Before film cartoons were invented, they tried to show movement in a *still* painting. Ask the children how they might do this in their own work. If possible show some examples of futurism. The futurist painters realized that changes in the appearance of objects would have to be made in order to get their messages across. In the past most paintings resembled more closely the visible world. The abstractionists, however, believed that since the world was changing (technologically) art too must change. As a result they repeated edges of shapes, trains, autos, and the lights of a city at night, to give a feeling of excitement and movement. They tried to make the viewer feel that he was in the *midst* of all of this "modern" activity with things spinning and roaring past him. Consequently, cars, trains, and even people were fragmented into many shapes, lines, and colors. The shapes were simple but

the idea was complex. The shapes did not appear any more "real" than some of those in the film.

Tobey, De Staël, Feininger, and other abstractionists show things as if they were still. They try to distill what they paint and show only what is important. They take from the familiar and give us a whole new idea to view. Ask the children to look at things in such a way as to keep only "what counts" and then exaggerate that to make it even more important. Artists have to take liberties with, not merely "copy," what they see.

The Objective

Recognition of a range of art expression from pictorial to pure.

The Situation (No. 5)

Dada. Become acquainted with *Dadaism.*

Materials

Distribute some 12" × 18" newsprint and Blackie drawing pencils. Have the children cut some separate printed words and fill the bottom of a paper bag with them. Reserve some space on the chalkboard.

Stimulation

After the materials are ready, invite several children to take turns reaching into the bag and extracting one word at a time. Letter each word on the board. Develop a series of lines of five or six words each. If time permits, develop a few stanzas. Of what meaning is this? Some might identify it as nonsense, others as fun.

Procedure

In a way both of the preceding responses are correct in terms of the meaning of *Dada.* Several artists—writers, poets, musicians, and painters—were quite disgusted with civilization as it existed right after World War I. They decided that man as a thinker had merely blundered. The war was evidence of his foolishness. Also, they decided that most forms of art were equally worthless. In a sense they began to oppose rationality, society, and art as they then existed. The founders of the movement, being antirational, merely opened a Swiss

59

dictionary at random and extracted the word Dada, which, in keeping with the meaninglessness, means "rocking horse." (Also, explain to your group that Dadaists composed "poetry" by choosing words at random.)

These men were very bright. They were at times humorous as well as cynical. The painters among them included Marcel Duchamp, Kurt Schwitters, Man Ray, and Max Ernst. Since they were anti-art the things they did no longer resembled traditional *form* in art. Schwitters, for example, made *collages* by combining scraps of paper, old wrappers, tickets, and playing cards. Ernst made some magnificent collages. The artists invented titles that were in themselves works of art ("The Little Tear Gland That Says Tic Tac"). Ray combined photographs and made montages. Several made frottages by putting paper over surfaces and rubbing the front side, thus picking up impressions of whatever was underneath. They staged huge exhibitions in Cologne and Paris made up of *objets trouves*, everyday objects such as wash basins and hall trees that had been cast off but yet had a certain visual elegance apart from their former use. Sometimes the artists contrived things such as a fantastic room occupied by weirdly dressed manikins. Once they exhibited a fur-lined teacup.

Conjecture remains as to whether their work was "art." Aside from such conjecture they were an extremely imaginative group. They liberated artists from rigid thinking and habit. Their influence is seen today in such forms as *assemblage*. They invented a game called the "exquisite corpse": Fold a paper in half. On the upper half draw a "character" from the head to the waist, going slightly below the fold. Hide it and pass it, the lower half up, on to another person, who finishes by drawing from the waist down. Enjoy some exquisite corpses of your own invention.

The Objective

Recognition of a range of art expression from pictorial to pure.

The Situation (No. 6)

The super real. Become acquainted with some of the concepts underlying *surrealism*.

Materials

Ask the children to collect some large two-page color photographs from magazines. These may include both interior and exterior scenes. At a time prior to this situation have the children mount these on a manila backing. Have available several back issues of pictorial magazines, some scissors, and rubber cement. Obtain reproductions of Marc Chagall's "Violinist" or "Red House," Salvador Dali's "Persistence of Memory," Yves Tanguy's "Rapidity of Sleep," Peter Blume's "Parade," and Giorgio de Chirico's "Ears of Corn."

Stimulation

Distribute the mounted photographs. Inquire as to what compatible objects could be added to these scenes, e.g., a horse, another piece of furniture, etc. Distribute the other magazines and materials.

Procedure

Reverse the above question. Invite the children to "dream" in class. Ask them to find photographs of objects they ordinarily would *not* associate with the large scenes before them. Let the "dream" materialize with little hesitation or thought by quickly cutting and adhering the additions to the scene. Upon completion the children may make up appropriate titles for these paste-ups. At another time they might try "painting a dream."

Since the chief objective of this situation is that of developing a concept of surrealism, the activity is but a prelude for a perceptual experience. Review the nature of the activity. Enable the children to identify their dependency on "incongruity" as a means of developing a picture that went beyond what they would ordinarily expect in a certain context. Discuss the product as one which displays "fantasy" and "surprise."

Determine if any in the group can explain the premise of *Dadaism*. Indicate that many of the Dadaists eventually became surrealists. These artists were antirational and antiscientific. They did have some respect for psychoanalysis. Accordingly, they thought that artists could create a "reality" beyond that of the visible, waking world. Writers tried writing automatically, recording what happened to pop up into their minds. Painters began to paint via the same approach. Many of the paintings became "dreams" in paint—they possessed an enchanting, nostalgic, fantastic quality. Sometimes the painters became more concerned with this "super reality" than with the organization of the thing; the story of the dream often superseded the artistic merit.

Show the reproductions. Indicate that by depicting things in a way that was absurd these painters were actually pointing out that the so-called real world was to them even more ridiculous. To them a super reality was to be found in the "subconscious mind," in dreams, and in spontaneous thoughts that appear from nowhere. To the surrealists, thoughts were important. At times, however, the artists became excessively conscious of the "subconscious."

The Objective
Recognition of a range of art expression from pictorial to pure.

The Situation (No. 7)
Painting as action. Acquaint the children with some of the current events in painting. Introduce them to reproductions of *abstract expressionism* and *tachisme.*

Materials
In your visual file use reproductions from periodicals, which are numerous. The following recent works are reproduced commercially: Pollock's "Composition" and "Painting Number 12," Tapies' "Painting XXXXVIII," Dubuffet's "Figured Stone," and Rothko's "Painting Number 7." Collect examples of DeKooning, Kline, and Diebenkorn. Try to have a picture of an Indian sand painting. Reserve some chalkboard space.

Stimulation
On the board draw a tall thin line, a thicker diagonal, and a wispy horizontal line. Also, with the chalk on the side and with the group in rapt attention by now, make some energetic strokes.

Procedure
Focus on your artistry. These marks are obviously devoid of any subject matter. Some are mere "tracks" that register a certain mate-

rial by the stroke of an arm. Ask them if these marks possess any expressive qualities: Does the diagonal appear harsher than the vertical line? Does the horizontal line appear to be tranquil by contrast to the diagonal? Review some of the concepts related to nonobjective painting.

Focus on the sand painting. Do not ask what it signifies but, instead, how it was made. Indicate that the artist worked on the ground with his body *in* the painting. How are most paintings made? (On a wall or easel.) Introduce Pollock's work. It is nonobjective. It appears to be most dynamic. It also expresses a belief. Pollock enjoyed the physical contact of his *medium* and the format. He put the canvas on the floor and approached it from all sides. He applied the paint with sticks and at times poured it directly from a can. The result was a recording of his encounter with the paint and canvas. There was no preconceived plan. There was an attempt to use the paint in a "natural" way—to let it run. Everything happened spontaneously; he felt his way as the colors and lines merged into actuality.

Rothko, on the other hand, works more deliberately with large areas of color. He experiments with color interaction, how one area affects another, and in doing so tries to create surfaces that "present" themselves as experiences totally different from any encountered in daily life.

Tapies builds up textured surfaces by incorporating a variety of non-art materials in addition to paint. His work and Dubuffet's are often referred to as *tachisme.* Dubuffet often includes subject matter within a total textural emphasis. Artists are continually searching for different ways to express themselves.

The Objective
Recognition of a range of art expression from pictorial to pure.

The Situation (No. 8)
What is real in painting? As applied to art, *realism* is perhaps the most ambiguous term in use. It is the intent of this situation to at least modify some of that ambiguity and extend realism into workable concept.

61

Materials

Much of the painting and sculpture that remains from the time of the late Italian Renaissance until 1860 is in the style of realism. As an approach to painting, it still exists. Any list of realistic paintings is bound to leave out countless important contributions. Realism in this context is the perception and subsequent depiction of recognizable subject matter with evidence of a strong personal interpretive style. Examples of the following deserve consideration: portraits by Rembrandt, landscapes by Constable and Cézanne, people by Toulouse-Lautrec, and local scenes by Sloan and Hopper. Works by these men are widely reproduced. Acquire some. Also, collect some black and white photographs of similar subjects from magazines.

Stimulation

Ask the children to describe one of their favorite scenes or places. Ask them how they would record it in a way most "real" to them. Many would rely on a camera. Discuss some of the photographs you have collected. Ask the children whether they think these look "real." Why or why not? Many will treat them as realities. Have them look at the thin edge of the paper as a reminder that it is really quite flat. Moreover, what they identified as real is actually a gradation of grays. What would have happened if the photographer had used different shutter openings or treated the film differently during the developing? Several photographs of the same scene could portray different "realities." Yet, for many people "photographic realism" is the basis for judging the validity of a pictorial painting.

Realism in painting is more diverse. No one sees the same thing in the same way as another person. (Witnesses at jury trials do not always agree.) It is even less likely that they would paint it the same way! A "realist" painter, first of all, is one who draws and paints in *direct response* to what he sees. He uses his immediate perception. He carefully studies the *visual* significance of what he sees; he edits; he does not show everything. On canvas he moves things around to improve the *composition*. He tries to be objective, but since he was the selector of what he is painting he has already been subjective. Upon his careful observations he "stamps" his individual style. In other words

realism is at least fourfold: it involves (1) an actual *setting* or *place*, (2) the chosen *medium*, (3) the artist's *perception*, and (4) his *style*.

Invite the class to look at paintings by competent realists. What might have been moved or eliminated to improve the composition? In what way has the medium affected the painting? How would the subject appear in chalk? in pencil? Do the children think they could recognize a different subject painted by one of these artists? What is *content*? What is *realism*?

The Objective

Recognition of a range of art expression from pictorial to pure.

The Situation (No. 9)

Naturalism. Examine a more detailed type of realism in painting.

Materials

Obtain reproductions of works by two painters from different eras: Vermeer's "Milkmaid" and "Artist's Studio," Andrew Wyeth's "Marshall Point Lighthouse" and "Christina's World." Other works by these men would also suffice. Have available in the room some interesting objects for still-life material.

Stimulation

Ask the group to choose from within the room three or four inanimate objects which they consider to be interesting in shape and texture. Distribute the objects and the children in a way that affords a good view of at least one of the objects. Invite the children to look at one object as intently as possible for at least two minutes. Ask them to divide the width of the object into the height. Pick out similarities in surface texture. Determine which side is lightest and which is darkest. Ask them why the object appears to be three-dimensional (explain if necessary). Look at one object that is close, another that is farther away. How is distance communicated?

Procedure

Ask the group to describe the most "natural"-looking painting they have ever seen. You

62

might tell them about some of the seventeenth century Dutch still-life painters who tried to fool people into believing that objects contained in a painting over the mantel were actually standing on the mantel. The objects were painted in actual size and became known as "fool the eye" pictures. Such works required a keen eye and a skillful hand, and, it should be remembered, they occurred before the invention of the camera. Ask the children whether they could depict as accurately the objects before them. If they could, would this ability make them artists? Actually not. There is more to art than factual reporting. Even so-called natural-looking pictures go beyond imitation.

Look at the Vermeer reproductions. Focus on the play of light (*chiaroscuro*) over the surfaces of walls and objects. Study the light as an organizing factor. Notice further that the light is not the same in different areas of the composition; the artist has made the colors brighter or darker in order to accentuate specific parts of the picture. The same light makes the objects appear round. Textures of surfaces are also defined by light. Look again at the objects in the classroom. Notice that they are also defined by light. Moreover, they and the surrounding space are not in a frame. This is another task of the artist, to see details and organize them with feeling on a *format*.

Wyeth is a master of texture. While Vermeer's paintings are painted in oils to allow for gradual changes in light, many of Wyeth's are painted in tempera. In a sense he forces the *medium* into another textural role. Action painters would prefer to let paint run in its natural way —to them Wyeth's painting would be "unnatural" in terms of the use of the medium. Notice also how Wyeth controls distance by reduction of size, detail, and brightness of color. Both he and Vermeer employ *perspective* and chiaroscuro to give an illusion of a third *dimension*. To some this illusion "looks natural." However, their works are not of the "fool the eye" kind; the objects are not even depicted in actual size.

The Objective
Recognition of a range of art expression from pictorial to pure.

The Situation (No. 10)
Poetic paintings. Discuss *romanticism* as an expressive style.

Materials
Display or mount for purposes of closer inspection reproductions of Delacroix's "Horseman," Kuniyoshi's "Objects on a Sofa," and Burchfield's "November Evening." Again, works other than these by the same painters would be satisfactory.

Stimulation
Ask the group to think of an object, person, place, or event that is of special significance to them—something toward which they hold fond "feelings." If they could write a poem to what would it be directed? Since many of these feelings are private, let them remain so. If time permits, let them attempt a stanza.

Procedure
Extend the discussion to another art form. Rather than write their feelings about something, would they prefer to paint them? What style of painting previously studied involved the portrayal of emotions? (*Expressionism,* usually in a very dynamic way.) What style of painting depicted the actual world of people and places in a personal way and in consideration of the medium? (*Realism.*) Identify an art expression that depicted a reality made up of recognizable shapes but in improbable situations. (*Surrealism.*)

Begin with Delacroix. His *subject matter* is recognizable yet not as "real" in appearance as in paintings by some other artists. The edges of objects are more rhythmic; they have been exaggerated and given a swirling quality. The brushstrokes echo these swirling rhythms. Yet, the distortion is not as great as that of expressionism. Nor are the colors, with their strong *contrasts*, as garish and intense. Delacroix's painting is not a poem; no painting can be. But it does convey his feelings and, perhaps, does something to our own.

Kuniyoshi's work is usually more nostalgic and wistful. Ordinary objects and events, a woman's slipper, a train, are placed in a special reality with a peculiar mood but still in context, not surrealistic. Usually his colors are more somber, in keeping with the moods they help evoke. By contrast to expressionism, his

63

colors are quiet, almost delicate. These are only descriptive adjectives; look at the painting for the visual meaning. Notice also that these works are carefully composed. The rhythmic edges of the shapes and the related colors give unity to the paintings.

Burchfield's work is based upon a nostalgia for nature, evenings, and places that one would like to re-encounter and enjoy. The distortions in shape are apparent, yet the objects appear "real." He often limits his palette; his colors tend to be *monochromatic*. Romantic paintings require great skill from the painter; he must reconcile his emotions with the demands of his medium and composition and, finally, convey what he has to say to whoever views his work. He must first have something to say.

The Objective

Recognition of a range of art expression from pictorial to pure.

The Situation (No. 11)

All sides showing. Examine the visual properties of *cubism*.

Materials

Acquire a plain "cubistic" box that is thin enough to cut. Reproductions of works from the cubistic period of Braque and Picasso are easily obtained; Braque's "Le Jour" and "Le Billard," Picasso's "Portrait de Femme" and "Citron et Orange" are exemplary.

Stimulation

Inquire as to whether anyone in the group has heard of cubism. In reference to art speculate as to what it might be. The chief intent of the cubists was that of showing different sides of an object at the same time. Objects were often shown "flattened out" on the painting. Why is this a logical approach? (Because the canvas is already flat.) Cut and fold the box until it becomes flat. Indicate, however, that cubism was not quite as simple as that.

Procedure

Invite one of the pupils to sit before the

group. Ask them how they would draw this person in order to show more than one "side" at a time. Not quite as simple as the cube. Actually, the cubists were eliminating what had taken artists centuries to learn—*perspective*. They argued that, since the painting was really flat, perspective served only to lead the viewer's eye into a fake distance that violated the natural *two-dimensional* surface. Moreover, objects shown in a position of distance by use of perspective became so small and insignificant that the viewer could barely detect them. So the cubists tried to put everything on the same plane, the same distance from the viewer regardless of the position held in the actual world. Focus on some of the reproductions.

Indicate further, while looking at the examples, that these painters traded the illusion of the third *dimension* (depth) for a fourth dimension (time). By trying to show more than one view of the same object simultaneously, they introduced an entirely new concept to painting. Notice also that they eliminated *chiaroscuro* to further reduce the illusion of depth. Objects seem to be twisted around to confront the viewer (parts of a face) or stacked on table tops tilted upward on the *format* in a way to appear vertical rather than horizontal. By the way, Picasso in his earlier days painted in a very *realistic* manner. He has painted in almost every known *style*.

Some of the cubistic paintings incorporate bits of newspaper and wallpaper with the paint. This method is referred to as *collage*. It was assumed that these materials added to the everyday reality of the composition. To the cubists their work was "more real" than those pictures that "lied" by trying to lead people into illusionary scenes depicted on flat surfaces.

Ask the group if they see any relationship between *futurism* and cubism. (Both depicted time; in futurism the viewer was in the center with one-sided objects going around him; in cubism the viewer at times went around the object.)

The Objective

Recognition of a range of art expression from pictorial to pure.

64

The Situation (No. 12)

A continuum of art expression. Identify eleven general styles of painting and relate them to a continuum of styles of expression ranging from pictorial (*naturalism*) to pure (*non-objectivism*).

Materials

On the chalkboard or a large sheet of paper, draw a diagram that identifies a *possible range* of art expression:

(More emphasis
on *content*)
PICTORIAL   1-2-3-4-5-6-7-8-9-10-11   PURE
(More emphasis
on form)

Have available a number of smaller reproductions of the eleven general *styles* of art expression studied in the previous situations. These would include postcard and junior size reproductions available from commercial sources and those extracted from a number of popular periodicals. Distribute five or six pictures of different expressive styles to each person.

Stimulation

Indicate to the group that they are going to have a visual examination but unlike most this one is based upon what they know in addition to how well they see. Describe the function of the continuum. The extreme left relates to those paintings which closely resemble natural reality; the chief concern here is a portrayal of *subject matter* with special *content* (expression of the subject matter). This kind of expression does not ignore *form* (*composition* and use of the *medium*) but emphasizes the subject instead. These compositions are made up of "people" and "objects" that look "real." As the continuum extends toward the right this emphasis on content gradually gives way to an emphasis on form—form over the use of and feeling evoked by subject matter. The extreme right would include paintings that are made up of geometric or nonfigurative shapes and masses of color that do not resemble the natural world.

The numbers on the chart are representative of the following styles of art expression that range, in order, across the entire continuum (This could serve as a key to accompany the diagram): 1. *Naturalism,* 2. *Realism,* 3. *Romanticism,* 4. *Surrealism,* 5. *Impressionism,* 6. *Dadaism,* 7. *Expressionism,* 8. *Abstraction,* 9. *Cubïsm,* 10. *Abstract Expressionism,* 11. *Nonobjectivism.*

Procedure

Ask the group to look at their reproductions. After a careful perusal, based upon all of the preceding art learning situations, they are to put on the backsides a number that corresponds to one of those in the diagram. Upon completion of this, review the responses. Indicate that the continuum diagram is merely a device to help them see that there are many avenues of expression in the visual arts. Its accuracy and completeness are limited. Even so-called realistic paintings are abstract (they are really *painted* people, not actualities). In a sense the nonobjective paintings "lie" less than the naturalistic ones; some purport to be only what they are, color and paint on canvas; they are new visual experiences in themselves. As a follow-up situation, make a visual display on a plan similar to that of the diagram.

The Objective
Recognition of a range of art expression from
pictorial to pure.

The Situation

Materials

Stimulation

Procedure

66

Relationships between Art and Nature

8

Nature itself is not art.

Art comes forth as a form of human expression.

Nature and art do, however, have many affinities.

The visual elements and principles of art have been derived from nature.

A frame of reference can be developed from these formal, abstract elements and principles.

This frame of reference enables one to perceive additional meanings in both art and nature.

It enables children to see a nature form as a kind of rhythm or a landscape as a painting.

Nature and art remain as independent but significantly related forms.

The Objective
Awareness of visual relationships between art and nature.

The Situation (No. 1)
Motion, actual and implied. Focus on motion as it occurs in nature and as it is "captured" in paintings.

Materials
Obtain projection equipment and the film, "Art and Motion" (17 min., color). After having previewed it yourself, run it without the sound. Essentially it portrays movement as an aspect of the visual arts in relation to movement in nature, space, and time. Have on hand some reproductions of paintings that have "captured"

motion. These might include Degas's "Dancers," Marc's "Red Horses," and Seurat's "Circus" plus a number of seascapes and stormy scenes by other painters, among them, Homer and Curry.

Stimulation
With or without the film, ask the children to help you make a list of things in nature that move, change, and sometimes disappear. The following phenomena would be included: clouds, sunset, rain, ripples on water, a cresting wave, trees in the wind, reptiles. Tell the children that they are going to see examples of art that handle motion in different ways. One is aptly called a motion picture; the others are paintings.

67

Procedure

Show the film, as suggested, without sound because the text might be too mature for a young group. The visual, however, is helpful in demonstrating how motion as it occurs in nature can possibly be interpreted through various forms of art. Supplement the group's list of observations through this vicarious contact.

Look at and discuss the paintings that are of related concern. Inquire as to the problem the painter has in showing motion in a painting which, of course, is very, very, still. Determine what qualities of movement the painter has noticed and subsequently used in his work. Ask them whether, while looking at a painting depicting motion, they can predict what is about to happen next, or what might have happened immediately prior to the "frozen" moment. How many feel the movement? What has the artist done to keep the implied movement in the format? Does your eye follow successive shapes that suggest motion throughout the painting? How have certain objects been placed and treated to give the feeling of motion?

It is obvious that motion occurred first in nature. But even cavemen (Paleolithic) tried to depict motion in what are thought to be man's earliest paintings. Many of their animals appear to be moving. Encourage the group to depict motion in their own drawings and paintings. See whether any of the examples now in the room show evidence of "motion." Find examples of painting that do *not* attempt to show motion. What objects in nature are motionless? How might an artist, in his painting, give the illusion that even stationary objects are capable of movement? Perhaps the children could try to create such an illusion.

The Objective

Awareness of visual relationships between art and nature.

The Situation (No. 2)

Varieties of contrasts. Establish the concept of *contrast* as opposition. Discover a variety of contrasts as they exist in nature. Relate some of these to the visual arts.

Materials

Obtain a checkerboard and a reproduction of any one of Mondrian's nonobjective paintings. Some of his earlier abstractions of trees would also suffice. If possible meet with the group in a pleasant outdoor setting.

Stimulation

Show the checkerboard to the children. Most will be familiar with it as a game but not as a "design." Ask them whether they can find in it any evidence of contrast (the red as opposed to the black). The contrast is apparent but does the checkerboard have *variety*? Virtually none.

Procedure

Discuss the meanings of contrast and variety. If you are unable to obtain reproductions of Mondrian's work, use some from your own group. Indicate that an artist tries to go beyond the checkerboard, introducing a variety of colors, areas, and shapes in his painting. In order to organize this variety effectively, he must make some parts more important than others (refer to the sameness of space division on the checkerboard once again). He employs different contrasts, those of color, of size, of shape, and of "movement" to guide the eye of the viewer on a controlled "journey" throughout the painting. Some children might think Mondrian's painting is similar to a checkerboard. However, the areas in his work are all slightly different in shape and size even though they are composed of straight lines and edges. The colors are often limited to three, but they appear in different positions and quantities. The vertical lines and sections oppose the horizontal lines and sections with unequal forces. Yet, the entire composition "balances" amidst these oppositions. Actually, Mondrian was visualizing an idea based upon opposing forces as they exist in nature and in our civilization, calm versus upheaval, war versus peace. Like many artists, he has gained insights by observing nature, even though his paintings do not show nature.

Ask the group to list several "varieties of contrast" that they have observed in their natural surroundings. Find some in the present situation. These might include examples similar to the following: a slick texture (water) next to a rough texture (tree bark), the fluttering movement of a moth over a firmly implanted rock, an intense orange flower amidst dull earth or sand, or the soft rounded shapes of tree foliage against the jagged profile of a rocky terrain. Make a list of contrasting shapes, sizes, textures, colors, and movements in the nearby environment.

Incorporate these observations in subsequent drawing and painting problems. Start by observing the two most significant contrasts in nature, the horizon or flat ground and the verticality of man and much of what grows. Perhaps that is why artists paint on rectangles, which echo these very oppositions.

The Objective

Awareness of visual relationships between art and nature.

The Situation (No. 3)

Animals as shape, color, and unity. Notice how the visual properties of animals unify with their surroundings.

Materials

Extract some examples of animal life, in photographic form, from your visual file. Cover each picture with a piece of opaque white paper that corresponds to the shape of the animal (thereby showing only the background coloration). Attach these shapes with a speck of rubber cement. "Life in the Desert" (11 min., color) or a similar film would be helpful. Once again, make the visual qualities more apparent by eliminating the sound.

Stimulation

Show some of the blocked-out photographs of animals. Encourage the children to look at the coloration in the background of the picture, observing the shapes of any visible plant life. Include some examples of marine life. The white cutout shapes in lieu of the visible animal might provoke some curiosity. Indicate that the children are to look at each animal, much as an artist would, as a *shape*. Ask them to guess what colors and patterns might be under the white paper. To what might the varying colors and patterns within each "shape" (animal) relate in the background? Introduce them to the term *unity*.

Procedure

Show two very different animals simultaneously. Focus mainly on the shape of the animal, as crisply defined by the white shape covering it, in relation to the surroundings. A dolphin assumes a sleek appearance. Its shape is in harmony with the habitat. Ask the children to imagine the dolphin in a rocky terrain on land, not as an animal but as a shape. Reverse this visual procedure with a land-based shape in the dolphin's watery environment.

Remove the white paper and expose the patterns and colors of each animal shape. Were their guesses correct? Discuss these observations in relation to the immediate surroundings visible in each photograph. Inquire as to why the colors in the animal shape do or do not "unify" with those around him. Look for similar colors in both. Are there any shapes *within* the animal that are repeated in the background?

As observers of nature both biologists and painters, for different reasons, have been acutely aware of the visual properties of animals in relation to their surroundings. Artists have derived principles of art from nature. The chief principle in art is that of *unity;* everything must be in harmony with everything else. Although nature is by no means perfect, unity occurs consistently enough to provide insights for an artist.

Project the film without sound. Look at the animals in terms of shapes and colors, as elements of art, in relation to the surrounding shapes and colors. Be aware of visual unity.

The Objective

Awareness of visual relationships between art and nature.

The Situation (No. 4)

Disrupted unity. Introduce "disunity" by modifying the appearance of organic nature forms and well-unified paintings.

Materials

So as not to destroy any actual nature forms or paintings find substitutes for both. Have the children collect some photographs that show at least one plant, a cactus or a tree (no animals), in large scale. Have a large-scale repro-

69

duction of a landscape painting by Cézanne, Constable, Wyeth, or another reputable artist. Have a variety of thin colored paper scraps, rubber cement, and scissors. Have the reproduction in full view while you work on it.

Stimulation

What happens to a tree when it dies? Ask the children to think of a nature form they have observed in two diverse states, as a healthy organic specimen and later as a destroyed form. Perhaps some have noticed a favorite tree that was trimmed rather abruptly to accommodate utility line installations. Ask the children whether they think nature is visually perfect. Discuss their responses in relation to the principle of unity. If necessary review the meaning of *unity.*

Procedure

Distribute the materials and photographs of plant forms. Ask the children to examine their individual plants in terms of structural unity. Focus on the balance of each plant (symmetrical or asymmetrical). Examine clumps of foliage (if any are present) in relation to the length and thickness of supporting branches. Do they appear graceful yet capable of sustaining the weight of the clump? Search for textural contrasts.

Continue to analyze the plant forms for their visual unity. Determine which parts of a particular form contribute to this unity. Select scraps of tonal paper that correspond to the surrounding colors in the photograph. Tear different sizes and block out some of the vital areas that contribute to the unity of the plant form. Eliminate the essentials that made it appear balanced. When the formerly elegant forms reach an imposed bedraggled visual state, ask the group to focus on the landscape reproduction.

Identify the problem of the landscape painter as one which requires selection from nature and a reordering of visual unity through his *medium* within an appropriately proportioned *format.* If he is successful, his painting will possess unity. There are several ways by which he can attain unity. Sometimes by making changes on a completed painting he can achieve another kind of unity. Most often, however, subsequent changes result in disunity. Demonstrate how you can affect the unity of

the painted landscape by blocking out vital areas. Have the group identify these vital areas and then eliminate them by temporarily placing the paper scraps over the surface. If you happen to improve the unity, take joy in the discovery of a latent talent!

The Objective

Awareness of visual relationships between art and nature.

The Situation (No. 5)

Transition rather than contrast. As opposed to the contrasts previously cited, observe the gradual changes that occur among and within the forms of nature.

Materials

Try to provide an outdoor, scenic setting—directly or vicariously through color slides projected on a large screen with a 500-watt instrument. Obtain some reproductions of Cézanne's landscape paintings. Examples from his *Mont Sainte-Victoire* series would be fine. Also have a color comic section.

Stimulation

Ask the group the meaning of the word "camouflage." List some examples of camouflage as it occurs in nature. Several children will recall the protective coloration of animals. Ask them further how camouflage differs from *contrast.* Review some example of contrast (opposition) that they have previously observed in nature. What word would best describe something in between contrast and camouflage? Lead them to the term *transition.*

Procedure

Define transition as a gradual change from one shape and color to another within the same area. The area could be that found in a natural setting or in a format established by an artist. Art and nature both have their sets of contradictory forces. It has been said that modern physics has identified thirty-two elementary particles of matter, each with its twin anti-particle. These opposites supposedly keep our universe in balance. Nature continually serves as a basis for insights in art and science.

70

Project some color slides of landscapes or gaze upon an actual scene. The contrasts are still there. Look within shapes. Help the children to notice that tree foliage consists of gradual changes in shades of green. Grass nudges lightly up and around a tree root. Some tree trunks slope gently into the ground. Branches grow gradually from the trunk, tapering as they extend outward. The edges of clouds are soft. Like the spaces between clumps of foliage they admit sections of blue sky. Though rocks are hard edged, the color in them is weathered enough to give it a relationship to other colors in the surroundings. Moreover, the colors within rocks vary and gradually relate because of continuous repetition. If any manmade forms (a tin can) are long exposed to nature they are gradually absorbed by it through impinging growth and weather. Look for transitions along edges of forms as they appear next to other forms. Most are gradual. Continue to look for more transitions *within* forms. Though contrast is evident, few changes are abrupt.

Examine the visual, not the literal, properties of a comic strip (hold it upside down). Notice the hard black lines and solid colors. No transition occurs. Untutored painters, such as the American primitives, paint in a similar manner —everything is in a separate "package" with no transition. Look at Cézanne's trees and rocks. Notice the gradual changes of color inside shapes and among shapes. Which of these visual examples demonstrate a better understanding of transition?

The Objective

Awareness of visual relationships between art and nature.

The Situation (No. 6)

A *contrived unified landscape.* Develop a two-dimensional landscape of compatible plant, animal, and mineral shapes.

Materials

Collect some color photographs that show rock formations and plant life. Be prepared to distribute 12″ × 18″ manila paper, scissors, and rubber cement. If possible, obtain reproductions of Rousseau's "Jungle" and "The Sleeping Gypsy." These paintings deal with contrasting terrains, the jungle and desert respectively.

Stimulation

With or without the assistance of Rousseau, discuss diversities of landscapes. Limit the discussion to landscapes that have plant, animal, and mineral forms (thereby excluding the completely barren regions). Distribute the manila paper. Instruct the group to draw a horizon line across the entire paper (which may be in either a vertical or horizontal position). Instruct them further to imagine this as a setting for either a potential desert or jungle or any landscape that would differ from the actual one nearby. If your region is that of the desert, let the imagination move to the Midwestern hills and prairies.

Procedure

Distribute the necessary art materials and color photographs of diverse rock formations and plant life. Discuss the inventiveness of Rousseau in constructing an imaginative environment in his paintings. Examine the distribution of shapes and the repetition of patterns, lines, and colors that provide his work with visual *unity.*

Ask the group to trade back and forth and search through the photographs for shapes of rocks and plants that would "look good" in the potential landscapes they are going to organize on the paper before them. Remind them that the plants do not have to be geographically correct; the problem is strictly visual, not conceptual. If a jungle flower harmonizes with a desert landscape, put it there regardless of botanical impossibility.

After the "rocks" and "plants" have been collected, ask the children to cut the pictures apart and reassemble them in a plant and rock formation of their own invention. Discuss the principle of unity—each shape must be compatible with the other shapes. Moreover, unlike a checkerboard, there should be a *variety* of shapes.

You might encourage the children to develop one plant form in such a way that it attains *dominance* in the contrived landscape. Look at Rousseau's jungle, not for purposes of emulation but to discover why the eye notices certain shapes rather than others. Develop a variety of sizes of similar forms. Arrange them in consideration of proportion to attain a feel-

71

ing of distance in the picture. Cut and paste a variety of plants that culminate in a unified whole. Examine a local landscape in terms of visual unity. What could be done to improve the contrived landscape around the school? The community?

The Objective

Awareness of visual relationships between art and nature.

The Situation (No. 7)

Shapes in nature as near twins and distant cousins. Develop a display of shapes collected from nature in accordance with their visual and tactile affinity.

Materials

Prior to this situation have the children collect and bring a variety of nature forms. These may range from dried insects to pine cones and sea shells. Have at least three nature forms for each person. Supply a paper bag for each person, plus one extra. Have someone pack three shapes in each bag. Clear a long, elevated shelf or counter top for a display of the objects.

Stimulation

Ask a volunteer to reach into one of the bags and without peeking describe the contents. Encourage this person to describe the contents in visual terms, based upon the sense of touch, not by the name alone. Ask for a comparison among the forms. Are there any similarities or distinct differences?

Procedure

Give the volunteer a new bag and distribute the remainder to the group. Ask them to pick out two objects, on the basis of touch alone, that seem to be related to each other. Give them sufficient time to explore and feel the objects. After everyone has had time to respond, ask them to extract the most *unrelated* objects from the bag.

A few might be surprised by the visual discovery. The sense of touch does not always correspond to visual proportions and textures. And, although some recent experiments suggest otherwise, it is unlikely that color can be per-

ceived by touch. Some children may have *assigned* colors to the objects on the basis of prior experiences, but these could be inaccurate. Some children see according to *sets,* or predetermined notions about what a color should be rather than closely observing its presence. Now that the objects are out of the bags, encourage the children to perceive the possible color relations and pattern distributions that await the eye. Do the objects seem to be *more* or *less* related on the basis of a visual appraisal?

Reintroduce the term *transition*. Indicate to the group that they will have opportunity to make a display that shows a gradual relationship among the forms now before them. Approach it any way you like; one person might hold up *one* of his nature forms in full view of everyone. From here on you may establish opposites or try to find another form that relates to that one in terms of shape, color, or texture. Allow each child to place one form from his original three along the display space. Leave sufficient room between forms to allow for changes in sequence. Turn each form in different positions to create silhouettes that vary accordingly. Those farthest apart should be the extreme opposites. Between them there should be a *transitional* flow. Try a similar approach with cut paper designs sometime.

The Objective

Awareness of visual relationships between art and nature.

The Situation (No. 8)

The painted view. Reassess an actual landscape from the viewpoints of several painters and their unique styles.

Materials

Order some color slides representative of a variety of styles in landscape painting. These slides are inexpensive and can be stored and shared indefinitely. Order slides and reproductions as you would any other supplementary educational aid. Landscapes of at least one Oriental and of the following painters would suffice for this situation: Constable, Cézanne, Monet, Gauguin, Marin, Wood, and Dieben-

72

korn. The approaches included among these range from *realism* to *abstract expressionism*. Have one photographic slide of a nearby landscape. Use a 500-watt slide projector and a quality screen for maximum effect.

Stimulation

Project the slide of an actual local landscape. Keep it on the screen for a very brief time. Elicit a description from those who can convert their perceptions into words. Record the variances among these descriptions: who noticed what and how. Make the group aware of the varying perceptions (as revealed verbally at least) among them. Discuss the role of visual perception among artists. Indicate that artists do not "see" exactly as they paint but that they do often see certain *qualities* in natural settings according to their style of painting. They emphasize certain features and exclude others. A summary of the stylistic tendencies of the painters previously specified follows:

Procedure

(Continue with the slides.) *Constable:* sparkling, twisted, heavy laden trees amidst contrasting highlights, shadows, and areas of intense bright grasses. A feeling of growth and paint. *Cézanne:* facet-like forms in a range of soft colors from light to middle value. A feeling for great expanse with things in the distance remaining distinct and solid in keeping with the objects in the *foreground. Monet:* objects dissolving into the areas surrounding them through countless small brushstrokes and softly contrasted colors placed side by side. Almost the opposite of Cézanne's more "solid," faceted statements. *Gauguin:* bright, almost "lush" colors filling in flat shapes further described by visible, dark lines that unite a landscape in a tapestry-like manner. *Marin:* angular brush strokes denoting in an energetic way suggestions of land masses and active skies that seem to be bound up in one another. *Wood:* the Midwest reduced to bulbous, bursting trees and hills that flow together in swollen, yet rhythmic patterns that seem fresh and lively. *Diebenkorn:* the parched vastness and intermittent dark greens of California appearing as wide brushmarks and areas of color that reflect the flatness of the surface and the fluidity of paint in keeping with the perception and will of the artist.

Look at the Oriental example. Why is it so different? Actually, Oriental painters have been known to paint scenes in foreign lands in a similar manner. Why? Try imagining what nearby landscapes would look like through the painting styles of the men just viewed. Describe some.

The Objective

Awareness of visual relationships between art and nature.

The Situation (No. 9)

Human nature. Relate an often overlooked "nature form," the human body, to various art expressions.

Materials

Have the group collect magazine advertisements that utilize the ideal human figure. To contrast these find a photograph of Hellenic sculpture, perhaps from a social studies source, a reproduction of a Renoir nude, and a more abstract figure by Henry Moore (sculpture) or Picasso (painting). On the board inscribe the words *shape* (an art element) and *proportion* (an art principle).

Stimulation

Ask the group if they have ever used the words on the board in reference to the human figure. The *shape* will probably be the most familiar. Indicate that these words are also art terms. Moreover, the human figure, which is actually another kind of nature form, has been a subject among artists from the beginning of art. Paleothic man carved female forms from stone (Willendorf Venus).

Procedure

Refer to photogenic figures in magazine advertisements. Inquire as to the significant visual features that appear most frequently. Are the figures slim or stout? Young or old? Smiling or frowning? Discuss the general shape that most frequently emerges among females and males pictured in the ads. Ask the group to think of the last public place they attended. How many people there corresponded to the shapes depicted in the ad photographs?

73

Show an example of Hellenic sculpture. Discuss *proportion*. Indicate that the Greeks had determined mathematically what the ideal proportions of a human form should be. In other words, they determined proportion by an external standard, not from the expression of the artist. A male, for example, was about "eight heads" high, his knees two heads from the heel; the width slightly below the shoulders about 2-1/3 heads. By current standards (the ads), the Hellenic females were somewhat hefty. How many people recently observed in a department store resemble the Greek proportions?

It seems that artists of all eras have had a shape-proportion concept of the human form. In more recent centuries artists have ignored outside standards of proportion and changed the human form to suit their personal expression—what they wanted to say with and about the figure. As a result radical "shapes" have emerged. Renoir's figures are essays of robust color and shape. His pinks are history's pinkest. The shapes are full yet soft and delicate. Henry Moore rounded off his figures. He also penetrated them with voids (openings) so the space around them could be incorporated within them. He designed his figures for outdoor settings. In a way their edges echo the contours of land and invite the air. Picasso applied his *cubistic* approach to the human form. Try drawing from two approaches. Draw in "natural" proportions from a model. Draw another form as an entry in a "Martian beauty contest." What standards might Martians have?

The Objective

Awareness of visual relationships between art and nature.

The Situation (No. 10)

A principled view of nature. Examine an actual landscape through a viewfinder and the traditional principles of art.

Materials

Have the children make viewfinders. From tablet backs or other medium-weight cardboard have them cut two L shapes, each about 1½ inches wide and 8½ inches long. Distribute paper clips and overlap the two L shapes to form a rectangular opening that can be adjusted to form different sizes and proportions. If you cannot meet where a natural view is available project some slides of landscapes on a large screen.

Stimulation

Letter the following principles of visual organization on the board: *balance, dominance, rhythm, proportion, transition, variety,* and *unity.* Instruct the group to letter these principles on one side of the viewfinder. Clip the L shapes in position. Demonstrate how they can be adjusted to form varying rectangular openings. Practice isolating segments of the room by looking through the viewfinders. Indicate that the group will be going outside (actually or vicariously) on a principle-treasure hunt. Ask them to take a note pad to record their discoveries with a notation or quick sketch.

Procedure

Refer to the principles recorded on one side of the viewfinder as a "frame of reference," which will enable them to make some important observations that relate art and nature. Instruct them to pick a principle, turn the viewfinder so the lettering is on the side away from them, and look for the principle in the surrounding landscape. Encourage them to think of landscape paintings with which they are familiar. Remind them that nature is not art nor is it perfect. Look through the opening in the viewfinder as if it were a *format.* Focus on the scene according to the following approaches (in any order that is feasible):

Balance: Compose a view that is symmetrical or asymmetrical. *Dominance:* Move the viewfinder around until an object within the opening appears to be more important than any other. Avoid placing it exactly in the center. *Rhythm:* Select shapes, lines, and colors that echo one another within the landscape. *Transition:* Compose a scene that emphasizes gradual changes from shape to shape, color to color. *Variety:* Search through the viewfinder to find an area filled with a variety of shapes, sizes, colors, values, textures, and lines. *Proportion:* Look at a scene through a variety of proportions in the format: square, long, and narrow. Look at the same view with a predominance of land and then a predominance of sky. How do the varying proportions effect the mood of the landscape? *Unity:* Select a view completely at random and analyze it for compatibility of the visual elements.

Select some more random views. Analyze them according to the effective presence or conspicuous absence of the principles. Ask the children what they as artists would keep, eliminate, add, or change in order to improve upon the composition. Compare findings.

The Objective
Awareness of visual relationships between art and nature.

The Situation

Materials

Stimulation

Procedure

76

Relationships between
Art and Manmade Objects

9

Most objects, exclusive of those in nature, had their origins
on drawing boards or underwent some kind of design process.

In all, a well-designed useful object must meet the
physical and emotional needs of the user.

Very often the visual qualities, which fulfill an emotional need,
are overlooked by both designers and users of objects.

It is in fulfillment of the emotional need that a relationship
exists between art and use in an object.

A recognition of this relationship might help people
make the environment more pleasant.

The Objective
Awareness of visual relationships between
art and manmade objects.

The Situation (No. 1)
What makes a house a home? After drawing
a home, discuss the visual qualities that houses
can share with art.

Materials
Distribute 18" × 24" white construction
paper. Use either tempera paints with medium-
size pointed brushes or large crayons.

Stimulation
Ask the children what a *"house"* is. It is first
of all a kind of shelter. Some might be able to
identify a variety of shelters that man has
developed. Discuss the function of a house as

a shelter in that it meets many *physical* needs
(warmth, dryness, privacy). After these needs
are met what else does a house become? What
makes it a home? It is at this point where more
personal needs must be accommodated. Discuss some of these. Discuss the visible things
(decorating, arranging) that make a house
homelike (thereby fulfilling *emotional* needs).

Procedure
Allow the children to draw pictures of
houses. Offer technical advice as to the use of
media. The main expectancy here is that of
developing a perceptual awareness from the
drawings and paintings in which their ideas are
embodied. Upon completion of the drawings,
discuss some of the following points from the
standpoint of visual *elements* and *principles*.

77

Focus first upon *shape*. (By the way, what kind of artist designs houses first on paper before they are built?) Assess the number of stereotypic squares with triangles parked on top of them. Talk about the *proportions* of these shapes. Is the house really intended to be higher than it is wide? Identify shape as an element of art that appears in houses as well as paintings. Discuss some of the shapes that occur on the sides of the house (windows, doors). In what way can they be placed to appear best? Also, what do windows do?

Look at the implied *textures* and *patterns* in the drawings. How do they appear side by side? Are all the textures the same without any contrast? Discuss the kinds of textures found in houses (brick, wood, glass, shingles, gravel) and how a personal arrangement of these makes a house more like a home. Discuss *color*. Find out how many of their drawings have similar shapes and colors. If they are identical, these houses might not be "homes" after all. Determine which and how many children mixed colors or developed unusual combinations. In what way was *balance* achieved? Is the home symmetrical or asymmetrical? If any plant life was added, discuss the arrangement of it as well. Lastly, determine which children thought of their present homes as they drew or painted. Indicate that they will have opportunity to be "architects" at another time and, accordingly, they will be able to test out some new ideas. As a future activity you might enable them to draw floor plans (white chalk lines on blue paper).

The Objective

Awareness of visual relationships between art and manmade objects.

The Situation (No. 2)

Shapes that function within the home. Identify utilitarian objects as *designs* rather than things.

Materials

Have scissors, white glue, and vast quantities of manila paper for mounting magazine photographs. With the aid of responsible children, collect dozens of photographs of objects of a utilitarian nature that would be found inside a home. Try to have three examples of each item (stoves, chairs, television sets, etc.). Meanwhile trim, mount, and sort the photographs according to the items represented. Have available an area where one set of three items can be displayed simultaneously.

Stimulation

Amass before you the categorized mounted material. Indicate to the group that they, with you as chairman, are going to play the part of a consumer research panel (explain this). They are to look at three different designs of one object, such as a stove, that would be found inside a home and determine which of the three would gain recommendation. The object will be discussed according to "how well it works" and "how nice it looks." The one object from each set of three that gains recommendation will be called "Brand X."

Procedure

Ask the group which household object they would first like to appraise. Identify its function. From this point on, discuss the shape of the object in relation to its function. In response to a stove, for example, make a list of the tasks it purports to do. Discuss its location, eye level, and the accessibility of its openings. Are the knobs and dials within reach of whoever is supposed to use the stove and out of reach of those who should not? Is there too much to read, or have colors been used to simplify the meanings of dials in relation to burners? Is there enough space between the burners to allow for protruding handles? Are the burners of different sizes? Is the stove easy to clean?

Now, in what way does the shape relate to all of these uses? Why is the stove rectangular? Why could it not be curved? Do the *proportions* appear graceful? How do the dials appear as proportioned shapes within the total shape? Are they too large or too small? Why does the stove have a smooth texture? Does it have color? Does the decoration add to or detract from the stove? Look at it as a painting. What part is seen first? Finally, which of the three stoves would be awarded the label "Brand X"?

Follow similar procedures with any number of household objects. Depending on your group appraise one set of three items at one time, or clump several. What kind of artist designs these objects of everyday use (Chapter 6)?

The Objective

Awareness of visual relationships between art and manmade objects.

The Situation (No. 3)

From tiny to tremendous. Become acquainted with the wide variety of visual qualities in objects of frequent and ordinary use.

Materials

Collect a supply of popular pictorial magazines. Have at least one for each child. Have scissors. Reserve some bulletin board space for a display that will eventuate from this situation.

Stimulation

Discuss one meaning of the word *design* (a working plan for the production of something). Indicate that objects share the same visual *elements* that are found in nature and art. Ask the children to identify some of these elements. Indicate that these elements are often used according to certain *principles*. Enumerate some of the principles that are most familiar to them. It will be their job to search through the magazines to find some examples of designed objects.

Procedure

Distribute the magazines and scissors. Call attention to the large empty bulletin area. Indicate that some of the objects that will be cut from the magazines will become a part of an exhibition. Ask the children first to find pictures of very small objects that were designed for ordinary use (such as a thimble). As the pictures are found, they may be cut out and delivered to you. (If you anticipate a stampede employ another approach.) When you think they have enough, switch to another task. Ask them to journey through the magazines in search of extremely *large* objects that have been carefully *designed* for everyday use. These objects could include skyscrapers, bridges, and highways. Once again, when you sense a sufficient response, introduce another category.

As the search continues, you and those in the group who would benefit from such an experience could assemble some of the findings on the bulletin area. Arrange them from tiny to tremendous. Start at the opposite ends and fill in the center area with the objects that are representative of middle sizes (in actuality, since an accurate scale will be impossible in such a situation).

When the display includes sufficient variety, focus on it rather than the remains of the magazine (which may be saved for subsequent searches). Discuss the range of design problems that exist. Focus on the extremes in size. Speculate as to what the specific demands of each object might entail. Look at them for their visual qualities. Discuss the absurdity of one looking like the other (a bridge shaped like a thimble). Discuss the notion of honesty in using materials in a design (selecting the proper material for the task involved).

Ask the children to bring, within a day or so, a list of ten objects seen in their everyday surroundings that appear to be well designed in terms of the job each has to do. Discuss the deployment of *colors* and *textures* within some of the objects listed.

The Objective

Awareness of visual relationships between art and manmade objects.

The Situation (No. 4)

To touch and see. By contrast to the immediately preceding situation, focus upon one seemingly insignificant unit of industrial design —various kinds of handles.

Materials

Obtain a twenty-five-pound block of ceramic moist clay. Divide it into units, each about the size of a potato, for each person in the group. Keep the clay moist until distribution. Cover the children and the working surfaces. Have everyone bring a water vessel and a medium-size paper bag. Order some tapered-pointed orange sticks for proper finishing of the clay.

Stimulation

Ask the children what they touch first when they enter an automobile. When they enter a room or a building? What do they touch first when they pick up a toy gun, a frying pan, a kitchen pot or a telephone? What do they touch first when they turn on a lamp or manipulate a pencil sharpener?

Procedure

Distribute the materials, cafeteria style or any

79

way that works. Be sure each child has a container partially filled with water to remoisten the ceramic clay and a bag large enough to accommodate both hands.

Discuss "handle" as a noun and as a verb. What does it have to do with art learning? Look about the room for a variety of handles. Their use is obvious. Less obvious, however, is their derivation from the designers' concept. Look upon them as a kind of practical sculpture. Are these forms pleasant to both touch and sight? Like so many objects they must function well, but unlike most they must also be touched. They must be comfortable to hold.

Invite the children to put the clay and both hands inside the paper bag and think of a handle for some useful object, whether it be a knife or a potato masher. Instruct them to squeeze the clay into the general form (shape) of a handle they have in mind. Under no circumstances are they to look at the object. Thus, the first stage of production will be a tactile experience. As they model the form question them as to its "feel." Have them place the handle in different positions and pick it up in a variety of ways. When the handle has qualified as something which is "tactually pleasant," extract it from the bag. Make some technical corrections. Eliminate open cracks by working a few drops of water into the clay.

Subject the handle (which will at this stage appear somewhat crude) to a visual scrutiny. Check the proportions. Does it look squat? Clumsy? Too fragile? Too lumpy? View it as miniature sculpture. Refine the contours with the thumb and an orange stick. Inscribe lines. Add any texture that might allow for a better grasp and appearance of the handle. Pinch away clay for any additional indentations, or squeeze more out for protrusions that would add to the functional and visual properties. Upon completion remoisten the clay and return the handles, in potato form, back to the airtight bag. Wash hands before touching any actual handles!

The Objective

Awareness of visual relationships between art and manmade objects.

The Situation (No. 5)

Designed objects: a two-way view. Assemble an exhibition of useful objects. Evaluate the visual qualities from a twofold frame of reference.

Materials

Utilize some open shelf space or an enclosed display area within the building. Develop an accompanying chart that will contain some of the forthcoming information. Ask the group to bring examples of machine-made useful objects *after* the following discussion. For the present, use two or three objects of your own.

Stimulation

Ask the group to pretend that they are in an isolated region without any tools or utensils. The climate is temperate. There is water nearby but no way to acquire it in any usable quantity. How would they make a vessel to acquire, transport, and store it? What human needs would they have to meet in developing such a container?

Procedure

Encourage the children to think of the most obvious need. Develop the concept of the *physical* need or *what* the utensil is intended to do. It would have to be watertight, easy to lift and carry, and easy to pour from. The proper materials have to be employed to make the utensil usable. The container must be well engineered. It must be structurally sound and durable. Invite the children to think of some suitable materials and ways of joining them together in order to meet this need. At this stage the container is "taking shape." But what of its *shape?* Let us assume that it functions "physically." What of its appearance?

This need might be called an *emotional* or an aesthetic need. As previously noted, it probably took man a long time to develop useful forms that met *all* of these needs. The first consideration in viewing a useful object from the standpoint of an emotional need might be that of its *shape.* Is there a clearness of shape that bespeaks its function in a forthright way? Are the proportions sufficiently varied to create visual interest or are they monotonously repetitious? Do shapes, spouts and handles, within the shape *unify* the whole? Does the *texture* within the shape tell something of the material and

80

tools which were employed in the production of the object? (Even machines echo their marks.) Is there need for identification and *decoration*? How much? Would decoration destroy the clarity of the shape itself or enhance its appearance? Would the decoration be applied (painted on) or organic (woven in or inscribed in the actual material)?

This discussion has centered upon a handmade form. Relate the same two needs, however, to present-day machine-made forms. The same needs exist. They must be reconciled with modern materials and modern machines. Too often objects are well engineered (physically successful) but devoid of emotional gratification. Discuss some of your examples. Collect and display objects according to these criteria.

The Objective

Awareness of visual relationships between art and manmade objects.

The Situation (No. 6)

Moving shapes, changing shapes. Discuss some gigantic manmade objects, transportation forms, and their evolution.

Materials

Ask the group to bring models or "authentic" toys that depict automobiles of various ages. If necessary, use photographs of older autos and carriages. Supply the group with some dark 12" × 18" construction paper and scissors.

Stimulation

Ask the children in what way an automobile is like a package.

Procedure

Discuss the responses and eventually, inductively or by astute pronouncement, arrive at the possible answer. Discuss the automobile according to its contents, mechanical and human. Compare the outer surface to a "skin" over a frame that holds everything in position. In this sense most transportation forms are actually elaborate package designs.

Focus on a model or a photograph of a carriage. Examine the basic shapes, the circular wheels, that allow for movement. In what way are these organized to facilitate movement? How are they connected? How do these circular shapes relate to the shape above them? In further reference to the upper shape, how was it possibly arrived at? What does it hold? What provides the energy to move the entire apparatus? In what way is the energy contained or attached?

Instruct the group to cut the construction paper into four smaller rectangles of equal size. From the first cut the general shape (a modified rectangle) of the carriage. What major change in production of energy occurred to further modify this vehicular shape? Focus upon one of the incipient automobiles. Notice the small hoods. Develop another shape on the basis of the early automobile. Avoid detail.

Reintroduce the term *transition*. What gradual changes can be observed from the carriage to the early auto? Select a model from the early 1930s. Examine the *proportions*, height and length. In what way do these vary from the earlier ones? What might account for the change in packaging? Develop another shape that roughly corresponds to that one. Move up to the present. Examine the profile in terms of transitions *within* the shape of the auto. Notice the covered wheels (no spokes). Do they appear different when they move? What happened to the windshield? Is it perpendicular to the hood? Look at the junctions of the windshield and the roof and the trunk at the back window. Do these areas meet abruptly or do they show a *transition* and a relationship of parts that fit nicely into the entirety? Look at the automobile as a composition as well as a package. Is the hood too long in relation to the body? Is the automobile too big as a package in terms of the contents it holds? Does it express movement? Ask the children to cut a shape that might be an improvement over the present shapes of cars. Analyze the visual properties of other transportation forms.

The Objective

Awareness of visual relationships between art and manmade objects.

81

The Situation (No. 7)

Homes, hills, and unity. Analyze the visual properties of home designs in relation to those of the surroundings.

Materials

Have the group collect and bring several magazines that feature house plans. Supply them with 18" × 24" manila paper, scissors, white glue, a variety of colored tonal paper, tempera paint, and some small round brushes.

Stimulation

Ask the group whether they have ever heard of a house that floats in the air. Distribute the magazines and ask each person to select a house design of particular appeal to him. Carefully cut the favorite from its surroundings and return the magazine. Mount the house near the center of the large manila paper. At this stage it should appear to be "floating."

Procedure

Ask the children what would be among their first considerations if they were architects employed to design the very house they had selected. Discuss the kind of climate that prevails where the house is to be built. Does the house itself suggest where it might be? Is there a lot of glass? If so, in what direction is it exposed? Observe the roof line. The next consideration could be that of terrain, nearby and surrounding. Is the area flat or hilly? Rocky or swampy?

Introduce the concept of *unity* in relation to *architectural* design. Review the principle in relation to painting. Focus on the mounted house. It is obviously the most dominant thing on the page by virtue of its singularity. Ask the children whether it reminds them of houses they have seen that appear almost as obtrusive in a neighborhood. Some might think of large developments where houses are the *only* obvious things in the landscape.

Ask the children to provide suitable terrain and surrounding scenery for the house. Granted, such a sequence is not feasible in nature though some builders have succeeded in flattening small hills and removing worthwhile vegetation. Ask them to analyze the shape of the house. Study the angles. You might tell them that Frank Lloyd Wright was an advocate of organic unity. He actually echoed some of the angles of mountains that were in the vicinity of homes he designed. He also incorporated native materials in the houses to help them appear to be a part of the landscape.

Disregard the original context from which the houses were cut. Very often split-level houses are built on flat lots and Cape Cod houses are erected in the desert. Go beyond these sentimental absurdities and relate the *shapes*, *colors*, and *textures* of the terrain and the natural growth to the house. Develop the composition as if it were a painting. The house may remain as the *dominant* object but it will *unify* with the total. If necessary, modify features of the house as the idea arises. Think in terms of oneness. At another time try a more orthodox approach. Develop a terrain and design a house for it. Look for examples of house-terrain unity in the community.

The Objective

Awareness of visual relationships between art and manmade objects.

The Situation (No. 8)

Develop a pastiche exhibit. With actual objects or photographs stage an exhibit of copies, fake styles, and novelty oriented objects of everyday use. See how "bad" you can make it.

Materials

Invite the children to bring from their homes at least one "white elephant" or object of intended use that is no longer or never was useful. It is important to specify that the object they bring is *not* one of affection. For that matter encourage them to bring a useful object that they dislike. Refer to catalogues and pictorial magazines for other examples of non-design. Reserve space to exhibit the findings. Have 12" × 18" manila paper and drawing pencils for everyone.

Stimulation

Review the "non-art" expression, *Dada*. Explain to the children that they are going to have a chance to stage a whimsical exhibition not of non-art but of non-design. Select one of the objects contributed to the group as a focal point for the installation of the exhibition. Take one of the more absurd objects, such as a pair

82

of bronze hands (copied from Dürer's original prints) which now serve as book ends. Introduce the group to the concept *pastiche* in reference to these phenomena. Clarify the meaning of the term as the following typical examples avail themselves to scrutiny.

Procedure

For example, in reference to the "lifelike" hands as book ends, point out the obvious intention of imitating not only hands but another art form. Book ends, appearing as horses' heads, ships' wheels, and saddles, as well as hands, provide a fascinating area of search for the absurd in so-called functional design. Other likely candidates might be lamps which appear not as lamps but as hula dancers or trees. Try to acquire a ceramic cookie jar that conforms to the shape of a bulging "money bag." You are also likely to encounter clocks that are composed of a radial arrangement of twelve playing cards each with the appropriate numerical-hour relationship. Or, you might find timepieces within various anatomical locations.

Explain to the group that these objects were not designed (if they were that at all) by Dadaists. Dadaists were men of wit and intellect. These novelties do seem, however, to have been made in a similar vein when compared to well-designed objects. Many without doubt though are highly imaginative and provide their owners with considerable gratification. It is remotely possible that some are made "tongue in cheek." If not, we can look at them from such an approach. Arrange the objects. Enjoy the spectacle.

Distribute paper and pencils and invite the group to "design" some "practical" yet "wild" object that performs a task similar to or entirely different from some of the objects on display. In addition to freeing a few inhibitions by trying *not* to excel, some children might recognize and enjoy novelty objects for what they are—novelty objects. Personal preference may continue to reign.

The Objective

Awareness of visual relationships between art and manmade objects.

The Situation (No. 9)

The outside as a shaper of the inside. Be aware of the influence of the natural and cultural environments as forces which modify and at times account for the "shape" of designed objects. Develop an imaginary situation upon this premise.

Materials

The raw material of the imagination will suffice.

Stimulation

Ask the group to think for a moment about the design of the clothing they are wearing. How did we arrive at this particular costume? Why do we wear the different weights, cuts, and colors of clothing? In what parts of the world do we find different kinds of clothing? Or no clothing at all? Why? Identify two environmental factors that would account for variances: the natural environment (the physical elements of land and climate) and the cultural environment (the beliefs and habits of the majority of the populace). In view of these environmental considerations the kind of or lack of clothing, as a manmade object, becomes more apparent. Since, in our culture, the design of clothing is compounded by the dictates of fashion, select another manmade object for the focal point of discussion.

Procedure

With your group develop an imaginary "natural environment." List some of the factors that constitute the natural setting. Consider the terrain(s), for example; the landscape might be composed of immovable, extremely hard jagged rocks which cluster at the surface like myriads of tumbled cubes about one foot in size. There is no soil. Perhaps the temperature on the surface is a constant two hundred degrees while three feet above a strong chilling wind blows perpetually from the south.

Develop a "cultural environment" for this setting. Always men must be separate, by at least four feet, from the remainder of their families. Moreover, it is considered unmannerly to look behind by turning one's head or body. Develop a series of cultural folkways that would differ from our own.

83

Ask the group to consider carefully the imaginary natural and cultural environment they have constructed as a "force." In what way would this force affect the appearance of a transportation form such as the equivalent of our automobile?

Invite some children to sketch their ideas for such a vehicle on the board. Consider the environment in comparison with our own. Determine what features, if any, of our familiar automobiles could be retained. Some children might prefer to start from the basis of the unfamiliar environment and develop a transportation form that is original.

Most of the demands met through this discussion will be of a practical nature. Let us assume that the imaginary people possess emotional needs—they like to have things that are well designed in terms of appearance as well as function. Ask the group if they think painters are also influenced by their natural and cultural environments. (All are.) In what ways? Give some examples.

The Objective

Awareness of visual relationships between art and manmade objects.

The Situation (No. 10)

Appraise the local scene. Develop a diary that records manmade "visual pleasure" and "visual blight" as perceived in one's own community.

Materials

Writing materials and a notebook or a sketchbook. Some children might have cameras.

Stimulation

Ask each person to think of at least one outdoor, manmade object in the community that he thinks is visually pleasing. It might be an arrangement, such as landscaping. Make a list of some of the objects. Repeat the process by listing unpleasant manmade objects in the community. Indicate that each person will have a chance to develop a diary of similar personal observations. Some children may develop a visual diary of such findings through photographs or drawings.

Procedure

In consideration of your group define "community." For some this might be extremely limited. Let each pupil determine the extent of his own community. Decide upon a suitable time period in which to make the observations to be recorded.

In a sense this situation meets the current objective and the one immediately preceding in that these observations relate to manmade objects that have appropriately utilized or blighted the natural surroundings. Thus the two main sections of the diary, visual pleasure and visual blight.

In reference to the latter, ask the children to search for manmade things that seem to have "erased" nature rather than to have become a part of it or to have enhanced it. Obvious manmade intrusion of this kind would include haphazard utility poles and wires interrupting sky or mountains and blatant billboards that blot out views. Smaller manmade artifacts such as beverage containers dot the landscape (as intrusions) in a more temporary manner. Encourage your group to be aware of such intrusions.

And, as an opposing force, people have provided spaces in cities and have built barns in the countryside that gratify the eye. Contemporary architecture has combined large areas of textural materials to complement details remaining from older structures. The effect of lights in windows and along thoroughfares reveals an organic pattern that changes the complexion of a city at night (sometimes erasing its daytime visual deficiencies). Encourage them to look for pleasing combinations of pattern, color, and texture where objects join, where objects overlap, and things move past. How might these visual qualities be effectively combined in a painting or collage?

Upon receipt of their observations develop a "planning" panel to discuss proposed improvements. Perhaps this panel could include those who would play the roles of artists and architects or civic leaders.

84

The Objective
Awareness of visual relationships between art and manmade objects.

The Situation

Materials

Stimulation

Procedure

85

Area Two
Developing
Art-Related Behavior

The art learning situations in Area Two are intended to reinforce art-related behavior assumed to have been acquired, in part, as a result of perceptual experiences in Area One (Visual Perceptual Learning) and visual organizational experiences with art media and problems in Area Three (Visual Organizational Learning).

With regard to this concept of mutual reinforcement all three areas are integral, just as several aspects of behavior modified as a result of these art learning situations are related to total behavior. In the Area Two situations the emphasis will be on these changes in behavior rather than on the few tangible products that will be made. Evaluation of performance should be conducted with this "behavioral" emphasis in mind.

Such desirable behaviors as "imagination," "sound judgment," "individuality," and a "capacity for aesthetic response" are shared by art education with all other school subjects. Art learning situations do, however, offer unique ways through which these kinds of behavior can be developed.

Aesthetic Response

10

A person who is concerned mainly about the use of things
limits his capacity for aesthetic response.

Aesthetic response demands a special kind of attitude, that
of enjoying things solely for their own existence.

In developing this attitude, a person must at times erase labels
that stand as symbols for objects, places, and events.

A receptive attitude, free of utility and labels, often enables
a person to discover visual qualities in things previously overlooked.

This attitude, in being receptive, though by necessity
uncritical, could lead to unbiased yet critical art judgment.

The Objective
Cultivation of a capacity for aesthetic response.

The Situation (No. 1)
Emptied pockets . . . things noticed. Investigate both practical and impractical perception among younger children.

Materials
Utilize the objects that many boys and girls collect. Observe children on their way to and from school. Let some of these observations become material for discussion.

Stimulation
Have a treasure hunt. Ask the children to empty their pockets if they want to. Ask others what of interest they have recently noticed.

Procedure
Indicate that you are trying to find out what is visually interesting to them. For your own information determine which children seem to exhibit a "practical perception" in that the things they collect or notice have a use or relate to a fact. By contrast, notice which children seem to have a more "impractical perception" as evidenced by acquisition of objects that exist solely for their own worth—they are just "fun to have."

Allow them to talk freely about whatever they have collected or noticed. Encourage those who seem to possess an impractical perception (appreciating things for no utilitarian reason). This concern for the visual qualities of objects or places is more conducive to an aesthetic *attitude* than a perception which is *continually* directed toward a useful application among discoveries. Some of the following examples of "impractical" perception are likely to be revealed.

Quite often both boys and girls find visual

and tactile pleasure in dried plants, weeds, or flowers too remote from the higher altitude and distracted attitude of adults. When viewed out of context these bits of color and texture are even further enhanced. Many adults accept such treasures willingly from children, others dismiss them as rubbish, and, in consequence, dismiss the inception of a receptive aesthetic outlook toward the world. Among the children's gleanings from nature are myriads of rocks. Many well-intentioned teachers and parents would like to help the children categorize them only according to geological concepts, overlooking the aesthetic properties that might have been of initial worth to the collector.

Emptied pockets among the boys might reveal vast amounts of apparently "useless" items. One might find knives hopelessly rusted shut or fragments of broken tile or toys. When assembled these items might actually reveal an impractical perception that surpasses a "learned inability" to see among many adults who have viewed the world in a way restricted by utility and fashion.

Encourage bulging pockets and the acquisition of assumedly "useless" objects and observations. It is unfortunate that many girls do not have pockets. The absence of such wonderful repositories for treasured objects amounts to a cultural bias which inhibits or precludes this impractical perception which could be a basis for an aesthetic attitude.

The Objective

Cultivation of a capacity for aesthetic response.

The Situation (No. 2)

An aesthetic "ambush." Introduce several unfamiliar objects into the room. Observe the range of reactions.

Materials

Investigate your visual file for photographic material of particular visual worth that will afford the children a fresh view. Display a variety of three-dimensional things ranging from obvious flower arrangements to some more nondescript items such as a cluster of thistles, a well weathered brick, and a piece of crumpled white paper. Introduce without comment a variety of objects in the "nondescript" category.

Stimulation

Record the children's spontaneous responses to the displayed items for a day or two. On the second or third day ask them if they realize they have been "ambushed."

Procedure

Upon clarification of the question encourage the children to reveal what visual additions they might have noticed within the room. As their findings are voiced, chart the range of responses. As much as possible determine which objects placed about the room proved to be the most obvious or most subtle. Any obvious-subtle range depends, of course, on one's own value system. A daughter of a flower grower might be unimpressed or, conversely, elated by the unprecedented appearance of a dandelion bouquet in the room. A bricklayer's son might notice the brick as the most obvious item introduced to the room. As much as possible though, through your own perception, determine which objects most likely would be noticed first and which would likely be passed undetected.

Since most of the objects displayed in the "aesthetic ambush" have no meaning in the sense of visual aids, some children might be concerned about the "why" of such display. Listen to their comments. By contrast, some children might possess a visual sensitivity that enables them to look upon the posted crumpled paper as shadow and pattern for its own sake. The crumpled paper is of little worth as "knowledge"; it does not support a recent lesson. Moreover it is of no further use as a writing surface.

Aside from these bipolar responses there probably will be some children who are apathetic. Others might not have noticed any of your efforts to induce a response. You might remind those who failed to notice the visual additives that they were most thoroughly ambushed.

As for the apathetic and those who could not respond to the objects lacking practical worth, they might be said to have constructed their own "ambush"; they managed to keep them-

89

selves ensnared by a limited outlook. Subsequent tries might free them from this self-imposed trap.

The Objective

Cultivation of a capacity for aesthetic response.

The Situation (No. 3)

Visual disorder. Respond to intentional disorder among familiar arrangements in the room.

Materials

Rearrange several movable items in the room. Do not introduce any new materials. Probably the room is generally in good visual order. Strive to attain disorder in the following ways: Consider proximity. Move two pictures so close together that they cause visual discomfort, or separate them so widely that they appear scattered or unrelated. Or tilt them. Determine how many objects in the room can be disturbed by a change in proximity.

Probably a comfortable balance usually exists among items in the room. Try to disrupt the balance, quickly, whenever possible. (If everything were symmetrically balanced you might achieve a better arrangement by accident.)

Switch positions of some visible objects. You might move a table off center and put your desk in a position almost opposite from the present one. Hang the map in a space formerly occupied by a picture. Avoid moving the desks or tables occupied by the children. Most rooms have furniture and items arranged at right angles to the walls. Introduce a few oblique angles that disturb the eye. All of the disorder can be achieved in about ten minutes prior to the arrival of your group.

Stimulation

The disorder is the stimulus. Listen for overt, spontaneous responses and use these as a point of departure.

Procedure

Try to sort the negative responses from the positive. For your own information try to notice which children seem to experience no reaction. (But remember that you are only making inferences.)

Such observations have a variety of possible ramifications. Essentially, and assumedly, on the basis of a contrived visual disorder you might determine which children are sensitive to order. This is a kind of *aesthetic* response, a sense of order upset by the presence of disorder. Some authorities argue that such responses are innate or Gestalt. Responses could also be learned as a result of exposure to good visual order. If innate capacities to perceive order or disorder do exist, it is likely that they can be further modified by negative and positive visual experience that occurs at both aware and unaware levels. This current situation is of an aware nature.

Some children might tolerate the imposed disorder. To them, depending on their outlook, it might not represent disorder. Also, some of the children, assumed visually sensitive, who were immediately bothered by your rearrangement of a familiar setting might be more "rigid" than visually aware. These possible reactions are representative of but a few that are likely to occur.

The Objective

Cultivation of a capacity for aesthetic response.

The Situation (No. 4)

I do not see people in rocks and clouds. Learn to see natural forms in terms of visual properties.

Materials

If possible take the group outdoors to observe some passing clouds. If any rock formations are visible, refer also to these. Whenever these natural conditions are not available provide, from your file of photographs and slides, vicarious examples. Also display some large pictures of people and animals.

Stimulation

Focus on the pictures of people and animals. Ask the group if they see any rocks within the

90

people. Any clouds? Why is it that they often "see" people or animals in well-known rock formations or ephemeral clouds?

Procedure

Before going outdoors discuss with them two ways of looking at something. One way involves looking at something for the sake of its visual properties, those elements that are readily available to normal vision. This way of looking at something might be referred to as a "pure" response, independent of any meanings apart from what is immediately seen. The possibility of an entirely pure response is subject to conjecture. It is likely that very few adults look at things with a pure vision. Most people tend to view clouds, rocks, and nearly everything through a "secondhand" frame of reference. Instead of reacting directly to the object, they assign a word to it. Words are symbols that stand for things. They are essential for *verbal* communication. They enable people to learn. Some people have learned the words so well, however, that they think the words are the *real* objects! Accordingly, when looking at a cloud, one might identify what *kind* of cloud it is. One might even "use" the cloud to predict weather. And, as intimated in the title for this situation, one might evade direct contact with the cloud by assigning another separate "meaning" to it in the form of Lincoln's profile or a crouching figure. Likewise a rock with exciting geologic formations, stacked daringly, replete with contrasting textures, opposing tensions, and subtle color might be reduced to the foreign and banal description of "Indian Head Rock."

For purposes of this situation encourage the children to respond via the first approach—direct visual pleasure free of any symbolic or foreign attachments. The animistic thinkers might find this difficult. There is no need to report the findings. Those who are verbally equipped may do so if you and they prefer. If the perception is communicated further by words, encourage the children to select words that relate to the visual qualities embodied in what they viewed. Clouds are whiteness, grayness, and at other times mere swaths of reflected color against soft dusty skies or intense blue areas. Such discussion might lead to a more critical, artistic perception rather than an entirely uncritical outlook. The perception is

related to the *object*—not to Lincoln's profile in a cloud.

The Objective

Cultivation of a capacity for aesthetic response.

The Situation (No. 5)

Hidden shapes. Discover other visual meanings by concentrating on the negative spaces between and around objects.

Materials

Obtain several pictorial magazines, scissors, tempera paints, small round brushes, a mixing tray, and a paintcloth. Each person should have a water container to expedite brush cleaning between colors. Provide rubber cement (in tubes) and manila paper for mounting.

Stimulation

Select a large size, fairly complex photograph from a magazine and hold it before the group. Ask them to focus on the spaces between the main figures or objects in the picture. Identify these areas as *negative space*. Within this negative space try to find shapes that are pleasing in their own right, free of any subject matter connotations. As you proceed turn the photo sideways and upside down to further divorce their vision from the subject matter. Encourage them to concentrate on the negative space until it becomes the most obvious thing in the photograph.

Procedure

Distribute the magazines and art materials. Invite the children to look through the magazines, holding them so the pictures appear upside down, with the intent of finding a photograph that contains a variety of negative shapes. Cut and mount these photographs on a sheet of manila paper. Instruct the children to forget that the surface of the magazine photo is a "picture." Have them turn the photos in any position but the intended one and paint in the negative spaces directly on the original surface. Some temperas tend to "slide" on the slick surfaces; continued brushing will overcome this resistance. Encourage the children

91

to strive for a variety of shapes, sizes, and value contrasts. Allow some of the original colors and textures of the photographs to show through for surface variety. If the photographs are black and white, work in a range of grays. If they are colored, mix colors that are related but in contrast to those present in the photo. Paint in the negative spaces first. Assign a color or value to these shapes that will assure a degree of dominance upon completion. Dissect the original *positive shapes* (subject matter) in order to destroy their identity. Large negative areas, such as "skies," could also be divided into smaller parcels and at times combined with some of the remaining positive shapes. If one were to paint the areas of the positive shapes in a solid tone without dividing them the result would be that of several obvious silhouettes.

From time to time pause and check the perceptual effect. Assign values or colors in a way to make the negative areas *dominant*. Modify the shapes as work progresses. The edges defined by the figures in the photo are points of departure; not outlines to be rigidly followed. If possible save untouched photos that are duplicates of those being painted upon. Exhibit some side by side to show the reverse perceptual emphasis. Go outdoors and find other examples of negative space. Looking beyond the obvious increases one's chances of finding pleasurable surprise.

The Objective

Cultivation of a capacity for aesthetic response.

The Situation (No. 6)

A fresh view. Look at familiar objects under different circumstances of location, lighting, position, and scale.

Materials

From your own resources and those of the group gather an array of familiar items which include both manmade and nature forms. These items may range from rocks to pencil sharpeners. Have each person make a viewfinder by cutting an opening one inch square in the center of a four-inch square of heavy white or gray paper.

Stimulation

Invite the group to move their viewfinders over the surface of their hands until they isolate a one-inch-square area. Ask them to look intently upon this small area. Gather some of their observations. It is likely that through such isolation and prolonged attention they will discover lines and colors heretofore overlooked. Challenge them to seek out additional new views by looking at the items assembled about the room.

Procedure

Encourage the children to move about and discover "compositions" through the small openings in the viewfinders. Sometimes the most ordinary surfaces, when viewed as microcosms, reveal colors, scratches (lines), and textures that are visually pleasing and surprising in themselves. Emphasize the importance of isolating views from contexts that prevent us from responding aesthetically. Cite parallel experiences that are likely to occur on a larger scale in the actual environment. For example, few people would think it possible to discover something aesthetically gratifying in a barnyard or in an alley. A careful perusal, by the process of isolation from a known context, can, however, do much to cultivate the ability to find visual pleasure in supposedly unlikely places.

Focus on some of the items in their entirety. Hold some of them in different positions, a pencil sharpener on its side, with the light coming from behind. This reduction to a semi-silhouette might produce visual qualities previously undiscovered. Try this approach with several items that form interesting silhouettes.

Reverse the context-isolation approach. Place some items against different colors or combine them with different shapes in such a way that they become more highly visible. Contrast can also enhance. Butchers realize this when they display red meat amid green paper. Meat displayed against purple might appear repugnant. View objects in and out of context.

If possible, view objects through different transparencies. A frosted glass surface forces the viewer to see familiar objects in different ways. Obscurity sometimes enhances. Willingness on the part of the viewer is essential. Encourage the children to experiment with their vision. You might remind them that few people see the same item in identical ways—veridical perception is a questionable phenomenon. Encourage the children to break visual habits and find new views, just for the sake of new views, within their daily surroundings.

The Objective
Cultivation of a capacity for aesthetic response.

The Situation (No. 7)
Doors that are not doors. React to doors in terms of their visual properties.

Materials
Ask the group to bring in a variety of discarded pictorial, home, builders, and architectural trade magazines. Provide scissors and pins. Reserve a large area of the bulletin board. Cover it with neutral, semi-rough-textured oatmeal paper.

Stimulation
Indicate to the group that they are about to go on a door-to-door campaign. Without leaving their desks, they are to find doors in photographs contained in the magazines they collected. The doors they choose must be spontaneously pleasing. They need not be in working order. Invite the children to react to the doors as if they were not doors but compositions of color and texture. The children may cut out the doors they like best. Do not suggest any minimum or maximum number.

Procedure
Let the snipping and searching become the stimulation. After the children have covered enough territory, ask them to present their discoveries to the group. Each person may select a favorite door and pin it to the oatmeal paper. After a few doors have been posted, survey some of the evident visual properties. Invite the children, as discussion evolves from the few posted examples, to look at their chosen doors, examining them first for color (if present) and areas of light and dark, then for implied textural qualities. Weather sometimes modifies both wood and paint to the extent that a *patina* is acquired. Very often the weathered doors are more interesting than those in better condition.

On the bulletin area develop a texture-color arrangement of the doors. Allow each person to place his door next to one that would be visually compatible. Encourage the children to place the doors in different positions. Treat the doors as combinations of texture and color. Observe textural gradation among the examples. Try combining doors for textural contrast. Scale is not a factor—a small door cut from a large photograph may be thought of as a "smaller shape" and combined with larger ones. If some doors are not compatible, separate them from others by the amount of space necessary to relieve the eye yet relate them to the total composition. Discuss the over-all effect.

Save the doors that were not utilized in the collective composition. At another time (Chapter Twelve, Number 5) they may be used as a point of departure for an imaginative painting. In the meantime, find some actual doors that are of visual interest within the community. Bring them back for display—verbally. Enjoy them uncritically.

The Objective
Cultivation of a capacity for aesthetic response.

The Situation (No. 8)
A reading lesson. Organize letters and words into compositions of line, shape, and pattern.

Materials
In addition to an old magazine, each person should have a copy of a current events publication or a facsimile. There will also be need for manila paper, scissors, and rubber cement.

Stimulation
Conceivably this situation could be a contrived outgrowth of a session involving the perusal of a current events publication. Near the conclusion of such a session ask the group to turn the publications sideways. Invite them to squint at the mass of printed words before them. In doing so inquire as to what parts of the page "stand out" from the rest of it. Indicate that someone was responsible for the

93

layout or visual arrangement of the page. Instruct them to look through the remaining pages from such a frame of reference. Look at each page as a "visual surprise," exclusive of the news content. Look at the intervals of white that occur between the printed matter on each page.

Procedure

Distribute the art materials and the older magazines. Instruct the children to focus upon specific kinds of *printing* within the text and advertisements. Cut out entire words or single letters from a variety of styles. Some of these styles are examples of type faces, others of hand lettering. Regardless of origin encourage the children to look at individual letters as line and shape. These may be torn from the page and trimmed according to the contours established by each "shape." Invite the children to look at words as *designs* composed of different lines and shapes, not in terms of literal meanings.

Upon amassing several examples of letters and words that are interesting on the basis of visual properties alone, ask the children to separate a few and place them on the manila format. Do any of the shapes express a "feeling" beyond their literal meanings? Do some letters seem bold and others whimsical? Are some just enjoyable in themselves? The commercial artists who were responsible for the original layout were aware, of course, of these properties.

For the time being, however, focus mainly on the visual quality of each shape and line in the letters and words. Instruct the children to pick three or more different examples and paste them in positions of unequal distance from one another. Using these few letters (or words) as a core, add others to fill most of the remaining paper. Try to create recurring patterns of heavy and light print yet avoid a monotonous checkerboard arrangement (thus the initial unequal distances).

Notice which children find it difficult to turn letters and words in illegible positions. Encourage them to forget momentarily the meanings of the words, and, instead, "read" the entire format (page) at one glance. After all, this layout is no longer practical!

The Objective

Cultivation of a capacity for aesthetic response.

The Situation (No. 9)

Perceptual patterns. Develop shape and color configuration designs on the basis of the perception of configurations in the immediate surroundings.

Materials

Provide each person with two 12" × 18" sheets of manila or white paper, a set of crayons, and a portable surface on which to draw.

Stimulation

Discuss visual organization, how people see things in clusters, as one aspect of visual perception. Ask for some examples of "patterned perception" (various constellations in the night sky). Draw four dots on the board, about nine inches apart, as if each were in one of four corners of a square. Ask the group what they see. Most will refer to the drawing as a "square" though in reality there are but four separate dots. Refer to the example as a "configuration." Indicate that they will have a chance to make two different kinds of configuration designs outdoors.

Procedure

Distribute the art materials and lay any necessary ground rules for outdoor sketching. Explain the following two approaches to configuration composition:

Shape configuration: Select a scene with a variety of shapes in it. Include both manmade shapes (buildings) and nature shapes. Equate these with geometric shapes. Reduce the actual shapes in the landscape to *squares, circles,* and *triangles.* Alter the 12" × 18" paper into a *format* of pleasing *proportions* while keeping it in the *shape* of a rectangle. Start with any one of the three shapes and try to find its correspondent in the environment. Ignore scale. For example, in looking for square-like shapes treat them as similar sizes when they are recorded on the format. Do, however, pay attention to interval. Try to observe the scene by focusing only on the squares. Eliminate, as much as possible, everything else from the vision. In a way this approach resembles scanning a page with the intention of finding a few key words that relate to a topic of interest. Draw the shapes in grays. After completing all of the squares study the format for awhile, then look up suddenly at the

94

landscape in order to check the plausibility of the composition. Repeat the approach with circles and triangles, making separate sets of observations for each and reorganizing the perceptions on the format. When the composition is complete, study it in terms of similarity among three *sets* of shapes. Determine if these similar sets of shapes help organize the composition.

Color configuration: Repeat the above process, using three colors in lieu of the shapes. Yellow, red, and green might suffice. Record the colors on the format, one at a time, in rather neutral oval shapes. One might see a sign, raincoat, tree foliage, and automobile, all yellow, all to be reduced to yellow ovals in the design. Assess each set of colors as a rhythmic pattern that contributes to the whole of the design. Again, do not be concerned about actual proportions or perspective. Use color as a means of organizing the perception and the design. Repeat these approaches in different environments.

The Objective

Cultivation of a capacity for aesthetic response.

The Situation (No. 10)

What next? "Complete" a painting that has been partially obscured.

Materials

Obtain two large reproductions of work by Gauguin and Kandinsky or Miró that are "new" to the group. Cover them with white paper. From the white paper cut two or three openings that expose small but significant areas of the composition. Provide each person with crayons and white drawing paper trimmed to correspond to the size of the reproduction.

Stimulation

Display the masked-off Gauguin (or other expressionistic painting that contains "simplified" subject matter). Ask some children to describe what they see in the exposed area. It is likely that many descriptions will pertain to *subject matter*, e.g., "There are plants and a woman against a white background." Gather several observations. Then, ask them how they would complete the picture. Again, several will probably respond in terms of subject matter proposals; a dog and a tree might add something to the scene. Upon receipt of the observations and proposals for completion invite them to look at the *colors* present within the exposed subject matter. In what way and where could they be used again? Notice the *shapes*. What characteristics do they have (dark outlines in Gauguin) that would have to be repeated to insure *unity* in the *composition?* Focus more and more on the visual *elements* of the picture as a composition. Renew the discussion on the basis of this visually oriented approach.

Procedure

Introduce a *nonobjective* composition, appropriately masked off with a few vital areas exposed. The lack of subject matter may enable many of the children to focus upon the visible shapes, textures, and colors solely as shapes, textures, and colors. Suggest this possibility. Suspend any further discussion, however, of the possible ways in which the composition could be completed.

Distribute the art materials. Ask the children to reproduce, as closely as possible, the two or three exposed shapes and colors of the nonobjective painting. Using these as a nucleus, they should proceed with the remainder of the composition until much of the format is covered. Upon completion, unveil the masked-off masterpiece.

Indicate first of all that the intent is not that of matching the master (a remote possibility). Instead, study the different arrangements that evolved within the group as visual possibilities triggered by the initial stimulus. Reiterate the rationale behind nonobjective painting (Chapter Seven). Compare differences between their work and that of the mature painter. What did they do that seems to them to be more successful than his work or, in many instances, less successful? Discuss the subtleties of *transition* and *rhythm* that occur in the reproduction. In what way did they handle the *negative space?* In what way did the artist handle visual organizational problems? Try looking at both endeavors from different directions. Display some drawings. Respond to them aesthetically as "things in themselves."

95

The Objective
**Cultivation of a capacity for aesthetic
response.**

The Situation

Materials

Stimulation

Procedure

ART LEARNING SITUATIONS

A Basis for Art Judgment

Responses to art are often dismissed as a "matter of taste."

Opportunities to state *opinions* about *art* are limited. Consequently, opportunities to *examine* opinions, which are often limited by what is valued, are even rarer.

An examination of opinions and of values, however, could lead to a perception of art which can be sensitized by education.

In perceiving art, one is influenced by several "realities" (ways of noticing different things), some of which exist apart from the art forms themselves.

When children are afforded the opportunity to state opinions and examine values by viewing art through a variety of these realities they are better able to form a basis from which judgment can be developed in accordance with future learning and maturation.

11

The Objective
Examination of opinions and values as a basis for art judgment.

The Situation (No. 1)
An "ugly" contest. Collect objects and make discernments as to what is ugly and what is beautiful.

Materials
Reserve some bulletin board and shelf space. Ask the children to bring two objects, one that they consider "beautiful," the other "ugly." Their collections may consist of three-dimensional manmade or nature forms or magazine photographs of any subject of interest. For those who do not find anything, have some sheets of colored construction paper available so they may select a color for each of the above distinctions.

Stimulation
Early in the grades most children employ the adjectives "ugly" and "beautiful" or, perhaps, "pretty." Many of these younger children are also given credit for possessing an "innocent" eye toward nearly everything they view. The early presence of these opposing adjectives in their speech, however, very often indicates that many of their discernments are based upon biases. The innocence of vision is very difficult to maintain as one becomes a part of his culture. Before they show their own examples ask them how many think a rose is "ugly." How many consider it to be "pretty"? In consideration of their ability to verbalize, discuss the

possible reasons for these distinctions. Hold a similar discussion in relation to some popular "uglies," perhaps snakes and spiders. The discussion might be enhanced if the actual specimens were present.

Procedure

Begin wherever feasible with examples brought by the group. Have each person write on the back of the object his opinion as to its visual worth. Have some of the children show their examples to the group without orally identifying their opinion. Ask the group to vote according to the two opposing categories. Be especially aware of split decisions. After the poll each person may assign his "ugly" object to the display area and keep his "beautiful" one. Continue the process. Keep a record of the responses which at times might culminate in a near consensus of either agreement or disagreement with the child's rating of his contribution.

When all of the "uglies" are adequately displayed ask the children to change their habitual vision. Ask them to inspect the display with the intent of awarding a *positive* rating to one of the supposed ugly items. It might be helpful to assign numbers to the items on display. For the present discourage any discussion. Use "secret" ballots. Each person may vote for his choice upon return to the seating area. Meanwhile quickly tabulate the results.

Discuss the results. Examine the visual properties of the "most beautiful" ugly object. Discuss with the children the meanings of these words in relation to their attempt to view these objects with a fresher vision. Inquire as to how many were able to look at the objects in this way. Introduce the word "opinion." Discuss hurried and studied opinion as two different approaches to responding to something. Remind them also that people in different parts of the world hold varying opinions as to what is "beautiful."

The Objective

Examination of opinions and values as a basis for art judgment.

The Situation (No. 2)

Subject matter preferences as restriction or

departure. Discuss the effect of the subject matter of paintings on establishing preferences.

Materials

Borrow a doll house, or draw on the chalkboard a simple floor plan that shows the usual number and kinds of rooms (avoid being sumptuous). Have some small reproductions of a variety of pictures available. Use those you have cut from magazines or, if available, some of the commercially prepared postcard sizes. Have two available for each person.

Stimulation

Focus on the facsimile of a house. Identify each of the rooms. Ask the children to pretend that the model is a place in which they live. What, other than mirrors, calendars, and plaques, could they hang on the walls? After a few tangential responses they will probably identify "pictures" as possibilities. When they arrive at this stage, distribute the small reproductions among the group.

Procedure

Although the reproductions possess pictorial subject matter remind the children that they are also representative of *paintings*. In other words, pictures can be paintings though paintings are not necessarily pictures. Ask the children to study their reproductions. Some might prefer to trade.

Ask the children whether they would assign any of the paintings to particular rooms in the house. For example, on the basis of what frequently happens, one finds pictures of animals or clowns in children's rooms, fish in bathrooms, still lifes in eating areas, and landscapes in living rooms. Notice whether any of these trends occur within your group, either as a result of their experience with an actual environment or as a result of a momentary fancy. Try switching paintings into other rooms.

Ask the children to indicate further which paintings they would have in their house and which ones they would not hang under any circumstances. Ask them to explain, if possible, *why* they would select or reject certain paintings. Determine whether the preferences are made mainly on the basis of subject matter. Do the children think such a method determines the *artistic* worth of a painting?

Encourage them to find something other than subject matter in a reproduction which finds favor with them. For example, in what way has the artist given *content* to the *subject matter*? What parts of the picture have been subordinated in order to emphasize other parts? Ask the children to look at the color arrangement in terms of light and dark and bright and dull relationships within the painting. Invite them to look at the subject matter of the painting they like least and discover something about the way it was composed in order to become a *painting* rather than a story-telling picture. Suggest that a painting that is not wanted in a home could still be a good painting.

The Objective
Examination of opinions and values as a basis for art judgment.

The Situation (No. 3)
Quiet paintings, vocal respondents. Respond to an art exhibition made up of a variety of reproduced styles.

Materials
Refer to the various ranges of art expression described in Chapter Seven. From your file obtain reproductions that represent at least five or six styles of painting. Display these reproductions in an area where they will be easily noticed during the routine of the day.

Stimulation
Let the display be a form of subtle stimulation. Do not call attention to it until you have had a chance to observe and take notes on informal responses.

Procedure
As you observe the responses, try to determine which reproduction receives the most attention and which receives the least. Also, observe which reproduction receives the most praise and which, if any, receives derision.

Notice which children respond to certain reproductions and in what ways.

After two or three days check your own observations with some of their oral commentaries. Ask some of them to share their opinions about some of the paintings. Encourage discussion. It is unlikely that there will be consensus. Some children will not have stopped to observe the exhibition. You might ask them (in a curious, not vindictive way) why they did not look at it.

Introduce the word "value," not in terms of light or dark or a bargain in a store, but as a term defining the *worth* of something to a person. Ask the children why they value certain paintings more than others. Which paintings do they value not at all? Ask them to list a few things other than paintings, from water pistols to kittens, that they do value.

Label each of the reproductions with the name of the painter. Distribute sheets of paper. Ask the children to list the painter whose work they value the most and another whose work they value the least. Fold the papers. Collect them. About six months later present the same paintings in a different arrangement and give the children opportunity to reassess what they value without referring back to the first papers until the then current choices are stated. Upon completion of this assessment return the first papers and compare the "valued" choices.

The Objective
Examination of opinions and values as a basis for art judgment.

The Situation (No. 4)
Chimpanzees, donkey tails, and gimmicks. Recognize the limitations of nonexpressive "paintings" as compared to the nonobjective paintings.

Materials
Have reproductions of *nonobjective* paintings (Rothko, Pollock, Miró, and Kandinsky). Save news features about the "art abilities" of animals. For demonstration obtain a set of pan watercolors, water in a plastic container, a small brush, a paint cloth, 9" × 12" manila paper, and a sipping straw.

99

Ask the group whether they have heard of chimpanzees that can paint. Some children probably have. You might describe the achievements of some chimpanzees who have done quite well in distributing finger paint all over a surface. In fact, some of these "paintings" have been sold (a non-art criterion). Other children may have heard of donkey-tail paintings. These paintings contain a great amount of verve and, especially, swish. A renowned art critic was among the first to notice a resemblance between "modern art" and the possible trackings of a donkey tail dipped in paint. When someone actually dipped a donkey's tail in paint, he found that markings could be made in that manner.

Procedure

Begin a purposely spurious "easy art" demonstration of your own. Moisten each cake of watercolor by dropping a small amount of water on it. When the colors are moist and soft, load the brush with water, dip it into one color, and let a big drop fall on the paper. Blow against the drop with the sipping straw. Notice the uncontrolled striations. Repeat the process on several papers. In a sense this is fun. It is also a gimmick. It has about as much to do with art, as an expression of human experience, as do the products of the exploited quadrupeds. Ask the group to examine the "paintings." The repeated attempts will bear a monotonous similarity to one another, as do the chimpanzee swirls and the donkey-tail swishes.

Neither the animal paintings nor the sipping-straw blobs express ideas or feelings. Of course, not all artists have intent to express when they begin something. In the case of the animals, however, a human being did have some intent. Someone had to assemble the art materials, mix the colors, and, in the instance of the donkey, hold the format for him and move it about to insure adequate coverage. The donkey furnished the brush. The chimp, of course, had to be tied to the easel so as not to escape. The "art" of the chimp and the donkey is revealed as a human being's idea. The variety, however, is as limited as the sipping-straw approach. Art has to do with expressing something from a person's own experiences. By contrast, animal "art" and gimmicks, which by chance take on

quirks of attractiveness, remain at a superficial level.

The Objective

Examination of opinions and values as a basis for art judgment.

The Situation (No. 5)

What's on your walls? Take a survey of forms of decoration and visual art in homes.

Materials

Provide everyone with 12" × 18" manila paper, colored pencils, and one ordinary pencil.

Stimulation

Indicate to your group that they are about to go on an "art hunt." Where? In their own homes. How? By bringing, in the abstract, their homes to the desks or tables in front of them. Ask them to "remove the ceilings" from all of the rooms, go up high, and look down into all of the rooms on one floor. Draw a general floor plan on the chalkboard to get the concept across. Treat each room as a rectangular shape (unless someone is fortunate enough to live in a free-form shape) next to another rectangular shape. Wherever a door appears, "open up" the line at that place. For the present eliminate windows. If a home has more than one floor, use a separate sheet of paper for each. Spend a minimal amount of time on drawing the floor plan. Do not be concerned about scale.

Procedure

Draw the floor plan with ordinary pencils. Distribute colored pencils for the listing of "art objects" that are found during the room-to-room search. On the board list a color code. For example, red could represent original paintings, green could represent reproductions, and yellow could represent "number" paintings. Orange could identify original craft items, while blue could identify mass-produced craft items and ceramic ware. Purple could identify miscellaneous decor, plaques, and bric-a-brac.

Ask the children to letter the name of the item, in the coded color, in relation to its approximate location within a room. Encourage them to imagine carefully the contents of the

100

house, one room at a time, or, if they prefer, one item at a time.

Discuss the results of the art hunt. Ask those who possess original paintings to describe them. Many of these will include amateur efforts that depict standardized scenes, but do not judge them without having seen them. The very presence of an original painting usually means that art is valued. Reproductions vary in quality. Try to discover the names of artists so represented. Discuss the "number" paintings as something quite different by contrast to the preceding. Original craft items might be as rare as original paintings whereas highly glazed, mass-produced figurines and ash trays are likely to abound. Discuss the notion of buying original (not imitative) art and crafts. Tell the children that middle-class Japanese homes have niches with original art forms in them.

The Objective

Examination of opinions and values as a basis for art judgment.

The Situation (No. 6)

Ways of responding to art: experiential reality. Find out how the conditions under which we view paintings might affect our preferences and judgments.

Materials

Refer to your file of large-size reproductions. Select three or four, each with different *subject matter.* Include another which is *nonobjective.* Within the range include one that is somber in color and mood and another that is vivid. Introduce more variety in accord with your group.

Stimulation

Ask the group to identify "indoor places" that they visit. You are probably familiar with most of these, but a listing might be helpful (and perhaps surprising). Stop after you have listed about ten private and public indoor environments. If a church was listed, ask the children to close their eyes and pretend they are in the church when they open them again.

Procedure

Hold the vivid painting in a position where all will be able to see it when they open their eyes. Remind them that they are in a church, then have them look at the painting. In consideration of where the painting is viewed, how many like it? How many *strongly* like it? Does anyone dislike it? Accept their opinions and suspend discussion until later. Transport this same painting, via their imagination, to another place, perhaps the wall of the music room (or a room with a similar mood) in their school. Now, in consideration of this environment, how many feel the same way as before about the painting? How many have altered their preferences one way or another? Repeat similar operations with the other styles of paintings. Gather their opinions. Upon receipt of their preferences for the same paintings under a variety of imagined conditions, ask them why their responses did or did not change. Confront them with the actuality that the painting, the physical object before them had not changed, yet, depending on where it might be, their preference for it could be altered. Why? Is this a valid way to decide upon the worth of a painting? Why or why not? What kind of worth?

Next, alter the *actual* conditions under which the children are looking at three of the reproductions at the same time. Ask them to pick one they like. Turn off the lights, or turn them on. What happened to the values and colors? Does the change have any effect on preference? Also, tell the group the actual sizes of the paintings reproduced. If one of them in actual size were eleven feet wide and another only eleven inches would this affect their opinion?

Determine whether any of them have painted subject matter or have experienced visits to places similar to those depicted in these paintings. Does the association, whether pleasant or unpleasant, affect the preference? Are they able to respond in a "purer" sense to the nonobjective painting? Discuss this kind of associative thinking as an influence. Why are these kinds of "experiential reality" *not* a valid way of judging the artistic worth of a painting?

The Objective

Examination of opinions and values as a basis for art judgment.

The Situation (No. 7)

Ways of responding to art: social reality. Examine the ways in which social influences affect our art preferences and judgments.

Materials

Obtain five large-size reproductions of *non-objective* paintings. Refer to Chapter Seven for examples. Place the reproductions in different areas throughout the room.

Stimulation

Write a formula, such as $E = mc^2$, boldly on the chalkboard. Solicit reactions to this supposedly ambiguous statement. Because it has a scientific aura about it, some responses might border on the awesome and profoundly curious. Some children might be repelled. Human behavior is far too complex to allow for an accurate predictability. However, some rather general cultural traits are likely to emerge. Ask the children to respond to some of the "ambiguous" reproductions of paintings about the room. Because the paintings have no subject matter, the children will have to rely mainly on what they see before them, the paintings themselves, to form responses. Compare these reactions to those generated by the formula. What attitudinal differences are revealed? Which of the two stimuli elicited the most respect? The most derision? The most laughter? The greatest amount of curiosity? Would similar responses occur in a less technological culture? All of these questions, of course, are subject to experimentation.

Procedure

Focus on any one of the reproductions. Ask the children to identify its visual strengths, apart from any possible meaning. Invite them, as individuals, to select another reproduction that they like "equally" well. You might tell them that the original painting from which the first reproduction was taken might be valued at so many thousand dollars whereas none of the others is valued at more than a few hundred. Regardless, would the monetary value of the painting in any way alter their preference?

Focus on another painting by a reputable nonobjectivist. Discuss the artist's reputation as a painter. Indicate to the group the basis of his fame. Build up his importance. Focus on the painting as a painting, apart from the famous person who executed it. Now, what if it was suddenly learned that the signature on the painting was faked? Let us say that someone had copied the work of Kandinsky or Mondrian. In what way might this affect the viewer's response?

Look at another painting. Again invite preferential responses. Who likes it or dislikes it or is neutral and, if possible, why? For the moment you might intimate that this painting is well liked by a certain authority figure (a current idol) with whom they would find favor. The same painting, however, happens to be a favorite of ————(a current *un*popular figure). If these supposed authority opinions were so, what effect might this have on their own responses and possible judgments?

Authority figures (this book), cultural norms, morality, prestige, vogue and social class are forms of "social reality" that affect, often without the viewer's knowledge, *untutored* responses to art. Enable the children to identify this influence as a "reality" that often gets in the way of the "physical reality" of the painting itself.

The Objective

Examination of opinions and values as a basis for art judgment.

The Situation (No. 8)

Ways of responding to art: logical reality. Discover how art often serves as a historical or cultural document or reflects a statement of intent by the artist. Examine the strengths and weaknesses of these "logical" realities that exist apart from, yet largely account for, the actual work of art.

Materials

Use an upper-grade social studies textbook as one example of logical reality. Numerous paperbacks about art are also available. Try to acquire some exhibition catalogs from such institutions as the Whitney Museum and the University of Illinois, which contain statements by artists next to reproductions of their work. The latter institution has published catalogs from twelve exhibitions (1948–1965) of contemporary American painting and sculpture.

102

Art publications intended for teacher and classroom usually feature a painter and his work in their monthly issues. Utilize any worthwhile material that "describes" art.

Stimulation

From a social studies textbook read one of the typical paragraphs about a well-known artist and his work. Did the commentary try to relate the work to the era in which it was made? Did it attempt to teach something about that era from the work? What, specifically, was emphasized regarding the work itself? (Medium, composition.)

Procedure

Ask the group how they react to such presentations about art. Does the art become a document or a thing to be valued in and by itself? Does a historical account of the times in which it was made help to make a painting more understandable? If the painting or sculpture were an informative document, typical of its time, but poorly composed and executed—would it still be a good work of art? Or, the converse, perhaps a painter of today works in an "old-fashioned" style but turns out superbly executed compositions. Is his work "bad" because it is not typical of his era? Discuss these and related logical historical and cultural approaches to viewing art.

The artist himself often constructs logical realities to accompany the actual reality of his work. He may voice an intent or a set of intentions in reference to his art. A sculptor might intend to produce forms in welded metal that have a sinewy appearance in order to emulate what nature might do if it had the same means, intense heat and steel, at its disposal while nurturing plants and animals. Or a painter, by using unconnected fragments of paint, might intend to show the movements that exist in nature. (Review some of the rationales behind art expression identified in Chapter Seven). Very often a logical statement by the artist allows the viewer to enter into the work and investigate it in a more knowledgeable way. Without this logical reality many people might choose to walk by the painting. Yet, does an artist's statement enable us to judge the artistic worth of a painting? Perhaps the artist fulfilled his intent but the painting is clumsily composed. Or, again the converse: he failed in his intent but the work is artistically sound. Also, his intent might have changed en route or been multiple. Perhaps he had no conscious intentions. As with all of the words on these pages, logical reality goes just so far.

The Objective

Examination of opinions and values as a basis for art judgment.

The Situation (No. 9)

Ways of responding to art: physical reality. Discuss and test out the possibility of viewing art mainly in terms of its structural properties (*form*). Examine the *subject matter* and *content* in relation to the immediately visible *medium* and *composition*.

Materials

Original paintings viewed in a gallery are most desirable. If a gallery visit is not practicable, rely on slides, preferably projected to the actual size of the original, or the other modes of art reproduction. Make sure everyone has writing paper and a pencil.

Stimulation

Focus on a painting by way of any of the above means. Without discussion, ask the children to record what they noticed first when confronted by the painting. Ask them to study the painting for a few minutes and, if they can, list some secondary observations.

Procedure

Instruct them to go through their lists and check each comment that relates to something directly in the painting. Comments that describe *their* reactions, such as "it makes me feel cool," would not be applicable, in that they reveal more about the viewer (experiential reality) than the painting. List the painting-related responses as they are derived from the children's notes. Use these as a frame of reference for a collective viewing of a painting (on the assumption that many different valid observations were made).

Identify the painting-related observations as those that have to do with a "physical" reality,

103

the actual substance before their eyes. Sort these observations into categories for further perception and discussion of paintings.

Subject matter is an obvious physical reality. Yet, a closer scrutiny reveals that familiar objects are shown by *symbols*, there is no actual flesh, bone, or foliage on the canvas. These symbols convey *content*. Content, as generated by the medium and the subject matter, has to do with the general feeling that prevails. As a physical reality, a painting is difficult to "read," as everyone is bound to inject into a painting a part of his present and past experiences.

More clear-cut physical realities do exist. The medium, when effectively handled, contributes to the form. (The studio-oriented situations in Area Three help reinforce this concept.) These realities are highly visible if one can get past his own biases to view them. Focus on the manner in which the medium was employed. Look for brushmarks, transparent areas, and textures. Think of the medium first and the subject matter second. Switch the perception to the totality. Does each shape and color correspond to or "go with" the others? In contrast to making an aesthetic response, wherein you react solely to the visual properties, look at these arrangements of the art *elements* critically. Try adding, subtracting, and switching shapes and colors. In what way do such perceptual modifications affect the total *unity*? Such an approach to viewing is termed "formal." Though also limited, it enables one to learn more about the work of art as a thing in itself than do any of the other ways. Consequently, judgment is based mainly on what is seen, along with what is expressed.

The Objective

Examination of opinions and values as a basis for art judgment.

The Situation (No. 10)

Ways of responding to art: a multi-realistic approach. Organize four panels, each delegated to report responses to favorite paintings according to one of the previously discussed realities. Realize that responding to art is more than just "a matter of taste" (good, bad, or apathetic).

Materials

Reserve some chalkboard space, or develop a chart on a large posterboard that can be kept for future reference. Across the top, letter four headings: experiential reality, social reality, logical reality, and physical reality. Provide space under each heading for observations. Have available two or three of the children's favorite reproductions and, in addition, one with which they are unfamiliar.

Stimulation

Review the four ways of responding to art. Refer to the realities, in reference to art, listed on the chart. Divide the children into four voluntary groups, each of which will be responsible for detecting one of the realities that might occur in the responses to paintings they are about to see. Perhaps each group could have a chairman who could record observations in the appropriate space on the chart.

Procedure

If practicable, seat the participants according to the reality they represent. Present the unfamiliar painting first. Encourage all the children to comment informally in all four categories. Instruct the chairman of each group to record pertinent responses in his area. The following are likely to occur (each sample comment will be parenthetically identified by initials representative of the "reality" involved). "I wouldn't care to have it in my house; it makes me feel unhappy" (E.R.). "It must be good because it was painted by a very famous artist" (S.R.). "It looks confusing because that's the way we live nowadays" (L.R.). "The red and green seem to vibrate whenever they meet" (P.R.). "The house reminds me of a haunted house I saw in a movie" (E.R.). "Konrad Zilch (a current idol) says art like that doesn't make sense" (S.R.). "The artist was purposely trying to see what would happen if he flattened the perspective" (L.R.). "All of the colors and lines become dull and blurred near the edges" (P.R.).

Try relating these likely comments yourself: "This picture, like a Gothic cathedral I once saw, makes me feel reverent" ( ). "You can tell this is old fashioned because of the funny clothes the people are wearing" ( ). "The paint was applied so thickly that the brushmarks seem to tie it all together" ( ). "I think nudes are indecent" ( ).

After discussion of the unfamiliar painting is completed, elicit reality-oriented responses in relation to some of the other paintings. Encourage the children to look at these favorites from a fresh viewpoint. Discover heretofore overlooked realities. Invite the children to identify their opinions and to decide how valid those opinions are. In what way could the opinions be modified in the effort of learning more about art or about themselves? The aim of this discussion is art learning, not acceptance of any innovation that appears. Enable the children to begin to separate fashion from art.

A BASIS FOR ART JUDGMENT

The Objective
Examination of opinions and values as a
basis for art judgment.

The Situation

Materials

Stimulation

Procedure

106

Resourcefulness and Imagination

Responses to art problems demand considerable reliance on intuition.

Though these responses are likely to differ from individual
to individual within the group, each could be valid.

Solutions to problems in art tend to be open ended;
they are not limited to singular optimum answers.

Reliance on intuition, accompanied by a growing knowledge and a
receptive attitude that goes beyond habit, might enable a person
to develop a capacity for original rather than stereotypic thinking.

Stimulating explorations and diversities in approach help
children develop resourcefulness and imagination.

12

The Objective

Utilization of intuition in developing resourcefulness and imagination.

The Situation (No. 1)

Parental shapes. From three identical shapes,
cut three sets of identical shapes which are to
be rearranged to form three different kinds of
animals.

Materials

Everyone should have two 12″ × 18″ sheets
of manila paper, three 6″ × 12″ sheets of construction paper in varied colors, scissors, paper
clips, and rubber cement (in tubes).

Stimulation

Focus on the ordinary rectangular shape of a
sheet of colored construction paper. By way of
demonstration, with the scissors, modify the
shape by cutting away parts from the entire

circumference yet allowing one original edge
to remain if only for a half inch or so on each
of the four sides (thereby preventing the reduction of a large sheet into a minute one). Invite
each of them to transform a rectangular shape
(colored paper) into one which will be totally
different from that of anyone else. Distribute
the scissors and only *one* 6″ × 12″ sheet of
colored construction paper at this time.

Procedure

Remind them that for now the shapes are to
be just shapes, not representations of things.
Encourage differences. Upon completion of the
shapes, which include parts of all four edges of
the original area, distribute two additional
sheets of colored construction paper to each
child. Ask them to trace the cut shape onto
these two sheets, cut them, and have as a result
three shapes that are identical except for color.
Distribute paper clips. Instruct the children

to clip the three identical shapes together, hold them tightly, and from these cut at least ten small shapes in a variety of sizes. These shapes should range from large to small. Upon completion of this have them sort the shapes into three separate groups according to color. Distribute the large manila sheets and rubber cement.

Present the problem to what is by now, hopefully, a curious group. Instruct them to rearrange the shapes, from *one* of the original colored sheets, on manila paper to resemble a known animal. Encourage them to try turning the colored fragments into several positions. They are not to reassemble them into the original shape. Whenever the total configuration resembles an animal familiar *to them* they may cement the pieces to the page. Before cementing, however, the children should try several combinations of parts. Color in relation to the subject matter is irrelevant; yellow-green rhinos are acceptable.

With the two remaining sets of shapes ask them to develop two prehistoric or imaginary animals and paste both of them on another manila sheet. Encourage them to relate the two "animals" to one another in a *composition*. Some children might want to borrow a colored shape from one animal and integrate it with the other. For those who are sufficiently interested, it would be feasible to add, using additional colored paper and crayon, a habitat wherein such creatures are likely to thrive. If they do this, however, encourage them to keep the animals as the most *dominant* shapes in the composition.

The Objective

Utilization of intuition in developing resourcefulness and imagination.

The Situation (No. 2)

Fit the format. Obtain cues for subject matter from formats of varied proportions.

Materials

With the aid of a paper cutter reduce the standard size sheets of manila or white drawing paper to rectangles that vary in proportions from long and thin to almost square. Provide each child with at least three differently proportioned rectangles and a set of crayons.

Stimulation

Identify the surface of a sheet of paper as a *format*. Discuss the meaning of the term. Focus on the standard size formats, 9" × 12", 12" × 18", and 18" × 24". Indicate to them that an artist often alters a format to suit his expression. And sometimes the *proportions* of the format generate ideas as to what might appear on it. Show and distribute the prepared formats.

Procedure

In order to eliminate any preconceived notions as to what subject matter they will draw, ask the children to choose, quickly and at random, one of the three formats. Invite them to look at the format as a shape; all of the shapes are, of course, rectangular. Encourage them, while looking at the empty shape, to think of subject matter that would correspond to the *proportions* therein. Indicate that they can choose any subject matter that relates to the shape with the qualification that it must come close to all four edges of the format at least once. Those who have formats in shapes other than squares should look at them in different positions; a long narrow shape viewed vertically might elicit a response different from that obtained when it was viewed horizontally. Focus on only one of the three shapes. When the imagination is in force, distribute the crayons and let the drawing begin.

With regard for care and a sensible use of the medium, encourage the children to repeat the process (now or at another appropriate time) with the two remaining formats. Encourage them further to think of different subject matter in response to each format. Eliminate background treatment because the subject matter itself will, or should, occupy the majority of the space.

Upon completion some children might enjoy cutting the drawings from the original formats and arranging them, regardless of subject matter relationships, on a larger format. One drawing could overlap another or all three might remain separate. As the arrangement is being made, call attention to the shape and proportions of the new format on which they are placing the cut drawings. The drawings, when pasted, need not touch the edges of the new format but they should show *balance*. Encourage the children to notice how the *negative* space interacts with the shapes and how it can be used to create a feeling of distance and in turn affect the balance of the *composition*.

In subsequent drawing and painting experiences, encourage the children to depart at times from the standard size formats. Their ideas, you may remind them, need not be regulated by paper manufacturers.

The Objective
Utilization of intuition in developing resourcefulness and imagination.

The Situation (No. 3)
Facial fluency. Learn to modify and extend symbols for facial characteristics and expressions.

Materials
Each child should have three 6" × 12" sheets of white drawing or construction paper, an 18" × 24" sheet of the same, a Blackie pencil, scissors, and white glue. Have one or two hand mirrors available for optional reference.

Stimulation
Distribute the pencils and *small* sheets of drawing paper. In the middle of the first sheet ask the children to draw a full size front view of a nose. Upon completion of this repeat the process with a pair of eyes on the second sheet and a mouth on the third one. All are to be front views. Pause after each sheet contains one completed part.

Procedure
Select at random a few drawings of noses, eyes, and mouths. Look at them with the group. Discuss the various ways in which these facial features have been depicted. Noses, for example, will probably range from triangles, with the apex usually toward the top, to two closely placed dots. Some eyes will be circles with interior dots surrounded by concentric lines perpendicular to the circle. Mouths might resemble two filled-in cupid bows back to back. Praise the differences that have occurred.

Ask the children to try drawing the same features, in the same size, on the same sheets but in different ways. Ask them to see how many different ways they can draw a nose, a pair of eyes, and a mouth while maintaining a front view. Remind them to draw each feature life size. Encourage them to look at some of the "live" differences that exist among their friends. Others might prefer to examine their own features in a mirror. Encourage them to draw after, not while, looking at themselves in the mirror.

As they finish, at varying times, have them pick up the larger paper, scissors, and glue. Ask them to cut the various drawings of features from the small sheets. Instruct them to group the formerly separate drawings into facial arrangements. They are to use at least three or four noses, pairs of eyes, and mouths to make a corresponding number of faces. While they are arranging, encourage them to switch the features from one "face" to another. Notice the change in expressions as this occurs. (Keep the eyes in their original pairs.)

When three or four satisfactory combinations of features are completed, they may be secured in position. Crayons may be used to add the configuration of heads and additional textures. Remind the children to try different approaches while adding ears and the outlines of the heads. Or, if you prefer, say nothing and observe any possible transfer that might occur as a result of the previous emphasis on variety in depicting the facial features. Some children might rely on their habitual symbols for facial shapes and ears while others might vary them according to cues received from the interior features. Continue these observations in future work. Encourage the children to modify and extend their symbols for all subject matter, from horses to airplanes.

The Objective
Utilization of intuition in developing resourcefulness and imagination.

The Situation (No. 4)
From where to here, from here to where? Go through a "thinking away" process while drawing in response to visual stimuli.

Materials
Over a period of time collect pictures of

vehicles on roads that come on to and go off the page or terminate in an assumed distance. Petroleum and automobile companies have many advertisements of this kind. Similar pictorial material that implies an immediate "past" and an immediate "present" would also suffice. Have a picture for each child. If possible obtain (and preview) a film that has sequential transportation scenes. "Pacific 231" could be utilized again. Have available any drawing or painting medium the group prefers. Some might have need for two sheets of paper. Reserve display space.

Stimulation

Show the film. Stop it briefly, just before a change in scene regarding the presence of whatever vehicle is employed in the particular journey. Ask the group whether they can imagine a scene that is likely to occur next. Discuss the possibilities. Repeat this process as often as the film and the response of the group permit. Do not strive for "correct" predictions. Encourage divergent thinking.

Procedure

Distribute the art supplies. Give each child a picture. Duplicate examples, as long as they are not distributed immediately next to one another, are acceptable. Duplicate examples might be desirable as a means of ascertaining different responses that could occur from identical material within the group.

Ask each person, without any discussion, to imagine where the car (or other vehicle) in the picture came from a few minutes or hours before it arrived in its present position. The intervening amount of time may vary according to their own wishes and ability to conceptualize time and space. When they have an image in mind encourage them to give it substance on the *format*.

Some children might have time to continue the process. Others might prefer to follow up at another time. Regardless of when, encourage them to try drawing or painting the future tense of the vehicle in relation to its possible destination. In both illustrations encourage them to depict the vehicle in a manner that somewhat resembles the one in the photograph, not in terms of front or side view, but in color and general shape. It is conceivable, however, that some might want to alter the condi-

tion of the vehicle as a result of intervening episodes. Some might even prefer to make several episodic drawings, similar to a comic strip, that reveal the events en route. Encourage a variety of solutions to the problem.

Upon completion of the journeys develop an exhibit that includes the original photographs and the drawings. At another time use a similar time-space approach with different subject matter.

The Objective

Utilization of intuition in developing resourcefulness and imagination.

The Situation (No. 5)

Beyond the door. Extend the imagination beyond the opaque surface of an unusual door.

Materials

Utilize some of the photographs of doors previously used in Chapter Ten or collect new examples. Try to have a door for everyone. Provide each person with a 12" × 18" sheet of white construction paper and a choice of art media.

Stimulation

Mount a photograph of an unusual door. Walk around the group so everyone has opportunity to examine it closely. In addition to pointing out the visual attributes of the door, encourage them to speculate as to what lies beyond. List several of the conjectures. Responses will vary in accordance with the characteristics of the door, the children, and the time of year. If it is near Halloween, the imagery might revolve around more mysterious possibilities. Try to elicit a variety of responses. Indicate that all the children will soon receive their own secret doors. Upon receipt of the doors, they may speculate in private as to what might be on the other side.

Procedure

Distribute the doors at random (unless you know for certain which person is likely to respond more effectively to a specific kind of door). Encourage the children to study the characteristics of their doors before they "go inside." Just what does the type or condition

110

of the door communicate? What kind of activity, if any, might one find beyond the door? Encourage them to develop an indelible image of what lies beyond. As the image becomes more vivid ask them to think also in terms of an appropriate art *medium*. Allow them to choose a medium that would be most effective for the *content* they wish to connote.

As they work encourage them to treat their discoveries as secrets. Discuss with each of them, as privately as possible, what he wishes to show in his picture. Help him determine what is essential. Help him to "edit" his image in a way that makes its final visual message effective.

Those who finish sooner than others might enjoy reversing the approach. They might illustrate what they would see if they were opening the door to the outside. Upon what kind of scene would it open?

When everyone finishes the first phase, mount the work on the display area. Collect the photographs, shuffle them, and redistribute them. Ask the recipients of the shuffled doors to match the photographs to the paintings or drawings. It is not to be assumed that there is one correct drawing or painting for each door. Instead, each person has an opportunity to share and trade other possible images for the same stimulus. Eventually, mount each door adjacent to the picture that does actually correspond to it. In what way was the "thinking process" experienced in relation to this situation different from that employed in social studies? In arithmetic?

The Objective

Utilization of intuition in developing resourcefulness and imagination.

The Situation (No. 6)

The most from the least. Adapt to an "economy of means" by making a complex design from a limited number of materials.

Materials

Obtain some $9\frac{1}{2}'' \times 12\frac{1}{2}''$ manila envelopes, which can be used over again, to serve as packets. Place in each envelope a $9'' \times 12''$ sheet of white and a $6'' \times 9''$ sheet of gray construction paper accompanied by two plain sipping straws and a random length of black thread. Provide scissors and white glue for everyone.

Stimulation

Distribute the packets and ask the group to see what each contains. Ask them to pretend that the materials therein are the only ones available in the room. Because this limitation exists, the children will have to use *all* of the materials in an effort to make a design that is complex.

Procedure

In consideration of the age and background of the group, discuss some of the properties of the materials. Discuss, for example, some of the possible uses of paper. Since this is the last available paper, and the only tools to be employed are their hands and scissors, how can it be employed most effectively? With a sample (the last one!) indicate that it can be torn, shredded, rolled, folded, curled, looped, twisted, and joined in several ways. You might mention that the sheets of paper may be altered in size and shape and used in any way possible, as long as all of it is used. The straws and thread, likewise, should be exploited to the greatest extent. (Do not remind them at this time, however, that their designs may be either two or three *dimensional*.)

Distribute the glue and scissors. Encourage parsimony with material and flexibility of thought.

After the children have worked for some time, pause and offer a demonstration of simplicity as opposed to complexity in using the limited materials. Hold the small gray sheet in the center of the white format, flanked by two unaltered straws further circumscribed by the random length of black thread. Encourage them to proceed in the opposite direction. For the present relate complexity to *variety* in the use of materials. Out of variety, however, they should attain unity and avoid confusion.

Upon completion, notice which pupils departed from the conventional two-dimensional pictorial approach. Develop an exhibition which demonstrates the range of complexity achieved within these limited means. Discuss "adaptation" as a way of working like an artist. What, accordingly, is meant by a "limited palette"?

111

The Objective

Utilization of intuition in developing resourcefulness and imagination.

The Situation (No. 7)

Limited clay, unlimited ingenuity. With a limited amount of moist clay, build something as *tall* as possible while using the clay as *thin* as possible.

Materials

Order some ceramic-moist clay. This type of clay is packaged in airtight plastic bags, each containing 25 pounds, which keep the clay malleable enough for repeated use throughout the year. Have someone slice the large block of clay, with a wire, into cubes of about three fourths of a pound each, or the size of a potato. Keep the cubes in the plastic bag until distribution time. For this and subsequent work in clay, order 32 one-foot-square pieces of masonite (which can be sawed from an inexpensive 4' × 8' sheet) to serve as palettes for the moist clay. Ask the group to furnish newspapers for desk coverings and tin cans for water containers. Each person should have a paper towel. You will need a yardstick.

Stimulation

Distribute the clay cafeteria style. When everyone is ready, present the problem. Indicate that they will have about twenty minutes in which to use the apportioned clay to build something which is very *tall* and capable of standing without additional support while using the clay as *thin* as possible. Repeat the instructions because many will misconstrue the problem to mean "build something as tall and thin as possible." Actually, the structure can be very wide if the *clay* within it is very *thin*. Thinness might be thought of as corresponding to a heavy piece of cardboard. This cardboard could be employed as a gauge. The twenty-minute limit is important because the clay will remain moist during this period. If the clay is used over a longer period of time it gains strength through the drying process and, as a consequence, reduces the challenge of the problem!

Procedure

Encourage the children to join things together in any way that works. Remind them that

this approach is almost opposite to that ordinarily recommended for clay. The usual approach stresses solidity and compactness. In all fairness, for now, ask them to refrain from observing how others might be solving the problem. If cracks appear in the clay they should add small amounts of water by wetting the fingertips and working it in. Too much water will soften the clay to the extent that it will lack sufficient strength to stand in its extruded condition. Let the children know when the time limit is about to be reached; some might want to add extensions in order to increase the height for a few minutes until the inevitable collapse occurs. Indicate that the structures must stand, free of any support, until you have had time to measure them. Invite the children to walk among the tenuous forms and examine the ingenious approaches. After viewing and discussing the various ways of using the thin clay, roll each structure into a ball, add water, and return it to the airtight bag for future use.

The Objective

Utilization of intuition in developing resourcefulness and imagination.

The Situation (No. 8)

One thing, then another. Overcome rigidity by suddenly using an information blank in a way entirely different from its intended use.

Materials

If possible, have available some mimeographed information forms that require name, date of birth, etc. If these are not available you could manufacture some facsimiles or merely have the group letter their own on blank sheets in response to your directions. In addition to the information blank, each pupil should have access to scissors, white glue, paper clips, a stapler, and a ruler.

Stimulation

In a non-art context, distribute the vital information forms. Commence filling them out with the pertinent instructions. After a few minutes, pause, have them stop writing on the forms, and, instead, exchange their pencils for scissors, which can be rapidly distributed at this time.

Procedure

Indicate that the information blank is going to serve, rather abruptly, as a medium for paper sculpture. List the following as limitations to be considered in approaching this problem of paper sculpture. First, the original blank should remain in one piece; it may be cut but no part should be entirely *separated* and reassembled. Second, by cutting, folding, twisting, rolling, or any other process which maintains the singularity of the original sheet, they should develop a vertical free-standing structure that exceeds the length of the original information blank. Third, they should develop protrusions and indentations in an effort to create patterns and shadows that enhance the surface. Fourth, the area of the paper containing the name should be in a clearly visible, perhaps dominant position, within the completed structure. Do not, after all of these limitations, impose a time limit. Do, however, observe the varying levels of ease and difficulty encountered by those in your group.

To get them started, demonstrate a theory of structural strength. Hold a limp sheet of paper before them, focus on its flaccid state, then fold it and suddenly transform it into a self-supporting entity. Review some other three-dimensional methods of controlling paper. Let the children generalize from these suggestions and depart on divergent solutions to the problem.

Advise them to use paper clips for holding glued portions together until dry, thereby freeing the hands for other tasks. While working, they should continually rotate and view the form in different positions. In what way can the name be placed in a dominant position? Notice how, when viewed in different positions, form is altered by light and shadows. Think of the shadows as substitutes for color value. Remind the children of the engineering problems—the structures should be rigid, not flimsy. They, the pupils, however, should be anything but rigid. Determine which pupils were bothered by shifting the use of the information form. Discuss with them their reactions to the problem.

The Objective

Utilization of intuition in developing resourcefulness and imagination.

The Situation (No. 9)

Chair- or auto-synthesis. Design a chair or an automobile from one of its parts.

Materials

Have the children bring several unwanted pictorial magazines. Each person should have access to scissors, rubber cement, scraps of colored paper (magazine colors or tonal paper), and colored pencils, all of which are to be used on sheets of white drawing paper of appropriate size.

Stimulation

Distribute the magazines and art materials (exclusive of the colored pencils). Ask the children to search for and tear out pictures of automobiles and chairs. Instruct them to find fairly large photographs that show, as much as possible, straight side or front views of those objects. Avoid perspective photographs. When each person has one or two examples, ask them to carefully cut one complete part from the total and cement it to the plain sheet of paper in an appropriate position. For example, if someone takes a leg from a chair, he should adhere it in its intended position near the bottom of the paper; an arm would be placed midway on the page. Grilles, doors, or bumpers, as separate parts of an automobile, should also be placed in logical positions. Instruct everyone to mount two examples, one from a chair, another from an automobile.

Procedure

Collect the mounted parts. Shuffle and redistribute them in such a way that no one receives a part similar to one he mounted. Give only one to a person. Offer a choice of an auto part or a chair part. Distribute the colored pencils.

Review the role of an industrial designer (Chapter Six, Number 6). Indicate that quite often these artists redesign objects in consideration of the existing form. Yearly changes in automobile designs attest to this. The current problem, however, is somewhat different in

113

that each person is given only a slight clue as to how the remainder of the object might appear. The problem is that of designing the remainder in such a way that it *becomes* compatible with the clue provided by a separate part. Emphasize that they should not relate their ideas to any previous knowledge about the total object. Even if they know from what model automobile the bumper has been extracted they should go beyond and design another car that incorporates, in a visually pleasing way, that particular bumper.

Invite them to examine the linear quality of the part. In what way might the rhythms be repeated elsewhere? What textures would relate to or contrast with those inherent in the part? What colors would be maintained or introduced? Stress the principle of *unity*.

The main emphasis in this situation is, of course, a behavioral one in that the children have opportunity to relate new ideas to one previously established. This act in itself requires a fluid imagination and an approach beyond habit. Very often the best drawings are the products of those who are flexible and imaginative.

The Objective

Utilization of intuition in developing resourcefulness and imagination.

The Situation (No. 10)

The method of difference. Through drawing or painting imagine how the present locale might have appeared if the historical course of events had differed from what actually did occur.

Materials

On the basis of prior studio experiences (Area Three), allow each person to choose an appropriate illustrative medium. Encourage them to work on a large 18" × 24" format. Oatmeal paper would suffice for pastels; heavy white construction paper would be practical for crayons, pencil, or tempera. Rely in part on one of the social studies films that portrays community development to set the mood for this situation. "Belo Horizonte" (17 min., b. & w.)

shows the unique planned development of a community which at the time of filming was less than fifty years old. "Cities: Why They Grow" (12 min., b. & w.) could enable the children to examine and apply concepts to the development of their own community.

Stimulation

Lead the group into a discussion based upon the historian's method of difference. Ask what might have happened had the Spaniards, and no one else, colonized the eastern coast of the present-day United States. Speculate on some of the possibilities. Try, on the basis of current knowledge, to imagine what visual differences in housing and clothing might have occurred. Examine, if possible, one of the films which depict community development. Apply the method of difference to the content of the film.

Procedure

Bring the discussion around to the local community. Introduce a few variables such as what changes in appearance might have occurred if an industrial community had no factories and had become, instead, a resort area. Introduce whatever subtleties they can handle. Analyze the actual historical precedents for what did happen and think away in relation to those. When sufficient enthusiasm has been generated, distribute the art materials.

Encourage them to assess first the natural environment. Would it be as it is now or would the difference in historical precedent have altered it? In the case of dam constructions and large earth-moving programs such variations in landscape are likely to occur. What obvious changes in architectural style might have occurred? Would there be any streets or parks? In what kind of shelter would people now live? Question them as they work. Try to infuse in the drawings and paintings a general mood that connotes the possible differences.

Upon completion of the pictures, review orally some of the imaginative differences. Also look for some constants that might have defied change. Review the current status of the community. Perhaps a city planning panel could be formed within the group to direct future changes, if any, that would be beneficial to their community. At another time visualize these ideas with a painting of the community as it might appear in the future.

114

The Objective
Utilization of intuition in developing resourcefulness and imagination.

The Situation

Materials

Stimulation

Procedure

Individuality amid Conformity

13

Each person has behavioral attributes which are different from those of others.

Behavioral differences account, in part, for a variety of approaches and solutions to art problems.

Art problems have requirements and limitations that demand knowledge and discipline. Solutions that are merely individual, and even at best based upon a vaguely defined identity, are not in themselves sufficient.

A person conforms to the *limitations* of the problem and a medium by way of his individual knowledge, intuition, and self-discipline.

Many art problems require solutions to be made within groups, providing another opportunity to achieve and maintain an individual identity in relation to intelligently evaluated external demands.

The Objective

Individuality as well as intelligent conformity.

The Situation (No. 1)

See the forest for the trees. Design a unique *symbol* of a tree that will retain an individuality even when placed within a total cluster.

Materials

Provide everyone with a variety of colored construction paper (whole sheets and scraps), scissors, tempera, brushes, and white glue. Have available some actual trees, via a nearby walk, or some good visual examples that could be used for *initial* discussion and observation (and then put aside). Reserve some bulletin board space.

Stimulation

Indicate to the group that they will have a chance to "plant" their own "forest." In it they can grow any kind of tree they prefer. For that matter each person, from his knowledge and imagination, can invent his own special kind of tree. Discuss the concept of "tree." Couple the concept with visual references, outdoors or vicariously, in an effort to develop visual knowledge. Study general tree shapes and how they vary. Look for *transition* as evidenced by the gradual diminishing of thick to thin from trunk to twig or from crown to frond. Encourage the children to find a variety of greens (or other colors) rather than one average shade. Compare the textures of bark and foliage within one tree and among others. Discuss *proportion* within and among shapes.

116

Procedure

Upon return from the actual or imaginary trip, distribute the papers, glue, and scissors. Since paint will probably receive minimal use, a few jars and brushes may be located in a suitable work area for those who have intermittent need for it.

Who was Luther Burbank? You might tell the class that this man combined parts of some trees to develop different ones. In a sense they are "artistic Burbanks" in that they can combine ideas and visual knowledge about trees to develop a symbol for one that will differ from that of anyone else. For that matter, ask each person to try to make a "tree" that also differs from any that he has made before. In doing so he might try "looking" at trees from the viewpoint of other people. This might help him notice something previously overlooked. For children with sufficient background such variant roles as birds, tree surgeons, lumberjacks, or firefighters might be assumed.

Also remind the children of the possibilities of the *medium*. Paper need not remain flat. Shapes need not always be cut. For the present disregard climate and locale. Invite the children to make any kind of tree they like. This tree is capable of growing anywhere. Moreover, it will not be used as a means to something else— lumber or paper—it will remain as an individual tree. Allow the children sufficient time to elaborate upon their tree symbols.

Upon completion, at a convenient time, allow each person to "plant" his "tree" amidst the total "forest." Discuss the *variety* (hopefully) present. Ask individuals whether they can readily find their own. Why are they able to do so?

The Objective

Individuality as well as intelligent conformity.

The Situation (No. 2)

Ditto sheet innovation. Use a ditto sheet in a variant and personal way.

Materials

Most art educators agree that ditto sheets, containing poorly drawn purple outlines of stereotypic symbols, are detrimental to the ex-

pressive development of children. However, before throwing away any that might be present, amass enough of one kind for this one and final experiment. Everyone will need crayons.

Stimulation

Hold up an example of a ditto sheet. Inquire as to which children have colored on this type of surface. How many have colored in coloring books? Discuss with them the limitations of the process, namely, the fact that someone else has decided how something should appear and has, very often, done so by way of a very poor drawing. Sometimes one is even told what colors to insert—and these colors must stay inside the lines! Of course, anyone could draw his own lines about anything he wanted to and stay inside those if the purpose was that of a physical coordination drill. One might even learn to be "neat." However, neither of these abilities is very important as directly related to art. You might remind the group that if everyone had a diet of pictures made by someone else, all ready to color, some children might get visually lazy and see less and less in the world about them. If one looks at himself and his surroundings with the intention of better understanding and expressing both, through writing, poetry, painting, or song, the chances for developing an acute perception are enhanced.

Procedure

Distribute the crayons and the (final) edition of identical ditto sheets. Encourage the children to use the *format* and *some* of the shapes and lines as a take-off point for a drawing that will be quite different from the original purpose of the ditto sheet. Upon completion, every drawing should be different from every other drawing.

Those who prefer may depart from *subject matter* entirely. Encourage some to turn these usually restrictive sheets into different positions, upside down or sideways. Invite them to pick out spaces between the intended shapes (*negative space*) and emphasize those instead. Encourage them to divide, combine, ignore, conquer, go beyond, and generally transform the original purple monotony; use the latter only for visual cues as a means of generating other possibilities. Ordinarily ditto coloring involves the use of flat shapes filled with one

117

shade of one color devoid of any further pattern or implied texture. Reverse this limited habit.

Display these modified ditto sheets. Discuss with the group differences which have occurred by way of such an approach. Notice first that many of the rectangles are displayed in horizontal or vertical positions. What would a display of ordinarily executed ditto work reveal by contrast? Would individuals be able to pick out their own work?

The Objective
Individuality as well as intelligent conformity.

The Situation (No. 3)
Egocentric shape organization. Develop a design wherein shapes made by others are incorporated with a dominant shape of one's own in the total composition.

Materials
Each pupil will need a 12" × 18" sheet of heavy white paper (which he can alter in proportion), a 3" × 4" piece of oaktag or thin cardboard, scissors, a pencil, and a choice of media of individual interest at this time; some children might have need for a refreshing change.

Stimulation
Let the problem be the stimulant. Distribute the scissors and small oaktag pieces. From the oaktag ask each person to cut a shape that has some "ins" and "outs" but no subject matter. Remind him to touch at least three of the original edges as he cuts. Examine the shape for its visual appeal. If some children are dissatisfied, provide them with additional time and cardboard. When everyone has a satisfactory shape cut out, ask him to letter his name on what he considers to be the back side.

Procedure
Give each child a sheet of the heavy white paper and a pencil. Identify the paper as a *format.* Invite him to trim the paper if it appears too long and narrow. Discuss *design* in terms of arrangement and *composition.* Ask each child to place the cutout shape on the format in such

a way that it seems to "rest nicely." As much as possible discourage dead-center placements. Indicate that each format will soon contain other shapes that possess color and pattern. However, when the entire design has been finished, the first shape should be the dominant item on the page. Have each person check the position of his cutout shapes. He can try it in various positions. When the shape seems to be "at one" with the format, have him trace around it lightly with a pencil and trade that shape for one that was cut by someone else. Encourage each child to incorporate as many different shapes as he likes into the composition, without repeating any of them. Help him to realize different possibilities of overlapping and "underlapping." Not all shapes will remain in their entirety; some will partially cover others. As a consequence, some shapes might lose their original contours.

Whenever each pupil thinks the format is adequately populated by well-arranged shapes, have him proceed with the addition of color and pattern with a medium of personal choice. These media could be picked up at a well-arranged supply table. (Avoid watercolors.)

Remind the children that not all shapes have to be filled in with solid colors. Some shapes could possess pattern or a variance produced by the natural texture of the medium. As the children work, ask them how *dominance* can be preserved or attained. In what way will the original shape assert itself in the final composition? After they have finished, hold a "dominance test." Ask members of the group to pick out the dominant shapes in the work of others.

The Objective
Individuality as well as intelligent conformity.

The Situation (No. 4)
A group comic strip (or "movie"). Illustrate a story, each person contributing one drawing.

Materials
Each person will have to conform to a standard format held in a horizontal position. Medium-weight white drawing paper trimmed to 12" × 16", to be used with crayons, will suffice. Be prepared to suggest stories that are of sufficient

118

complexity to provide everyone with a different paragraph or key descriptive sentence which may serve as a basis for an illustration. If a "comic strip" approach is to be employed, reserve enough display area to accommodate one drawing from each person which in turn will be arranged in a total sequence. If the group prefers a sequential "movie" presentation, the drawings will have to be joined, one below the other, on a long strip of thin wrapping paper cut to a 16" width. This "film" could then be rolled through a cardboard box with a 12" × 16" opening cut into one side. Two broomstick halves, one inserted well above and the other below the back of the opening inside the box, will suffice as take-up "reels." The same device could also serve as a "television" set.

Stimulation

Ask the group in what way a story resembles a movie or a comic strip. Discuss the role of "time" in these forms of art. Mutually decide upon a story that would lend itself to such an adaptation. Underline the importance of adaptation. A movie cannot imitate a story because it is a different form, as is a comic strip. (The comic strip adaptation is a more legitimate translation since the children do not have movie equipment.) Through any suitable means distribute significant parts of a story so that each person has a different part (that is of personal interest), which he may adapt. In other words the story has to be "edited" in terms of what is significant. Try to gain as much consensus as possible on this issue. Also, some children will be drawing their versions of the same character in different situations. For sake of recognition and consistency try to reach some agreement as to the general appearance of this character.

An artistic problem of *unity* must also be met. Most comic strips have a unity of style because they are the products of one hand and mind. Films are under the control of one director. Among the contributions of thirty children some visual unity is bound to be sacrificed. A limited use of color, however, might promote some visual relationship. Also the children could be encouraged to apply the medium in a fairly consistent way. Stress the thick waxy application of crayon rather than the faint, light one. Remind them that the ultimate product

will be viewed from a slight distance. Emphasize *contrast* accordingly.

Upon completion develop a sequential arrangement of the individual drawings. Each person should be able to identify his own contribution. Some identification of the original story, in consideration of changes brought about by the *medium* and method of adaptation, should also be apparent.

The Objective

Individuality as well as intelligent conformity.

The Situation (No. 5)

Holiday symbol analysis. Conform to existing holiday beliefs but go beyond the usual stereotypic symbolism.

Materials

Because the chief emphasis of this situation is idea-oriented, nearly any of the ordinary two- or three-dimensional art media could be used. Discuss ideas for holiday symbol modification. Accordingly, select the medium that would serve best as a means for amplifying the idea. *Idea first, medium second.* Freedom of choice is feasible only after the group has had adequate experiences with several art media via situations recommended in Area Three. If their experiences with media are limited, you might prefer to limit the choice accordingly.

Stimulation

(Halloween will serve as an exemplary holiday. Generalizations can be made from this situation to those that possess similar problems regarding stereotypic symbolization.) Ask the children to list and describe the visual properties of the traditional Halloween symbols. This list could be supplemented by visual examples. Examine the historical development of this holiday. Why did it become a tradition? Why are traditions important to a culture? Should some traditional holidays be eliminated and new ones initiated? Account for the formation of the present symbols. Though it is unlikely that holidays will be changed, it might be possible to modify the symbols for those in existence. Indicate that the group will have an opportunity to do just that.

119

Procedure

The existing symbols for Halloween, as revealed in the usual decorations, are impoverished stereotoypes. They are maintained by unreflective acceptance and easy habit to the extent that children have a perceptual barrier that prevents further experimentation. Lead them through this barrier via an analysis of their own feelings about Halloween. What is to them of *emotional* significance? How could this be "pictured" (symbolized)? What *entities* or objects other than those usually thought of appear in relation to the holiday? What *events* occur that could be communicated visually? Invite them to analyze and interpret these emotions, entities, and events in relation to the direct and vicarious experiences they have had with them. Try to develop new (to them) and personal symbols rather than to habitually repeat those that are remote and trite.

Also, modify existing symbols. Perhaps a witch could be horrendous and still beautiful. Her cat need not be black. A modern home could be haunted. Colors other than orange and black could be used. Paper pumpkins could be dissected and reassembled in sculptural forms. Various media could be combined to inject the intended mood (*content*) into otherwise prosaic subject matter. Encourage the children to surpass, with a personal interpretation, the hackneyed commercial offerings that surround us (usually three weeks too soon) once each year.

The Objective

Individuality as well as intelligent conformity.

The Situation (No. 6)

Collective mobile sculpture. Develop a series of mobiles with individually made components.

Materials

For individual shapes within the mobiles use thin lightweight materials such as posterboard and sheet balsa wood. These can be modified further with the addition of colored construction and metallic papers. For the armatures (the rigid supports to which the shapes are attached, directly or with thread) use wood dowel rods, balsa strips, sturdy paper straws, or rigid lengths of precut wire. Refrain from using unbent coat hangers as they always look like unbent coat hangers. There will be need for thread, white glue, scissors, and a few Exacto knives.

Stimulation

Review the concept of mobile sculpture (Chapter Five, Number 5). Suspend some string or thin wire from an overhead fixture. Tie one of the armatures to the string. Slide the armature back and forth horizontally until it balances. If you like, cut two geometric shapes of different sizes (weights) from thin posterboard, punch a small hole in each, attach thread, and tie them to the opposite ends of the armature. Drop some glue over each knot and trim off the excess thread. Slide the armature back and forth until it once again assumes a horizontal status. Ask the group to speculate, using this demonstration as a basic principle, as to how a mobile could continue to "grow" and maintain balance.

Procedure

Discuss the possibility of a "thematic" mobile, wherein the components would be made of shapes that *relate* to an over-all subject matter. Form interest groups of from five to eight people. Each person, depending on the size of his group, could then make one or more shapes that would be assembled in the final sculpture. Remind the pupils that some shapes, though they relate to subject matter, should be simple and not pictorial. The essence of a mobile is the movement of related shapes, viewed as a totality, not as something made up of tiny unrelated imitations of whatever is being symbolized. Some groups might prefer to eliminate subject matter and work in a nonobjective manner. Either approach is fine.

Distribute the materials. For each group, hang from the ceiling a piece of string from which the sculpture may be suspended. Remind them to compare the individual shapes as they work in order to obtain a variety of sizes. Some shapes may dangle a few inches below the armature, others might be glued directly to the ends. The inclusion of both types adds visual interest. Before they begin the assembly, ask them to lay the shapes out before them. Try to repeat parts of some shapes in others. Echo an edge, line, material, or color from one into another in an attempt to attain a degree of *unity*. Determine which shapes should be close

120

together and which should be far apart. Assemble the mobile from the bottom up. Each time an armature is completed, detach it from the overhead string and replace it with an empty armature. Attach the first completed armature below the one above and add shapes to the one above to offset the balance of the former armature. Use armatures of varying lengths. When complete hoist them all up higher. Enjoy the view. Notice how each individual's contribution (shape) can be compatible with the whole.

The Objective
Individuality as well as intelligent conformity.

The Situation (No. 7)
Portraiture: individual interpretations of an individual. Exercise individual variations in response to a single theme.

Materials
Provide oil impregnated pastels and 18" × 24" oatmeal paper for everyone. Have three reproductions, in slides or printed form, of work by noted portrait painters. Reproductions of Picasso's "Woman in White," Modigliani's "Little Peasant," Rembrandt's "Golden Helmet," Renoir's "Lady Sewing," and Hals' "The Jester" are commercially available. Many other portraits by these painters are plentiful. Have a large photograph of a face.

Stimulation
Seat the pupils so that they will be able to see what you are about to show them. Indicate that they are going to have but a few seconds to look at a facsimile of a person (a photograph of a face) and from this brief exposure they will be asked to give a description of that person in terms of their immediate reactions. When ready, flash the picture (or use any means you wish, perhaps a live stranger, to elicit similar responses).

Procedure
Gather the visual descriptions—what were the children able to observe about the person? (Coloration, space between eyes, fullness of mouth, the line between the lips, general facial proportions, hair styling and texture, and other pertinent *physical* characteristics.) List the observations on the board. After compiling the list of physical characteristics, ask for expressive properties that might have been observed. Discuss the possible intent, occupation, status, disposition, and emotional characteristics of the person. Remind the group that this is sheer conjecture.

Look at the picture (or person) again in reference to the list of spontaneous observations. Where did the group gain consensus? Where did individuals "read" something as individual as themselves into what they saw? What went unnoticed the first time?

Put the photograph aside and focus upon the reproductions of painted portraits. Discuss the obvious role of the artist in reference to what he sees and paints. Why do the styles vary so? Indicate that the painter often paints "a part of himself" in every picture regardless of who is sitting for him in the portrait. He does, of course, try to give visual equivalents, in terms of his style and medium, for both the physical and emotional characteristics that he perceives in the person. Each portrait, though, is in a sense a "self-portrait" of the painter as well. Identify the dominant characteristics of each sitter.

Look again at the photograph (or person). Speculate as to how each artist, through his individual perception and style, might have interpreted *this* person. Emphasize the individual, human role of the painter. Many photographers also have personal styles that transcend the camera. However, greater variance in interpretation exists among painters. Ask them to decide upon a common subject for a portrait (you, or the school principal). Have them "execute" it, using the pastels, from memory. Encourage *differences* in response.

The Objective
Individuality as well as intelligent conformity.

The Situation (No. 8)
A personal communicable alphabet. Experiment with lettering styles that depart from manuscript "printing" but remain legible.

Materials
Some of the children will be able to use India

121

ink and various sizes of round and flat lettering nibs, which are interchangeable with the same penholder. Felt-nib pens also provide an effortless "flow" of line. Other children might prefer the more familiar fountain or ballpoint pens, and HB drawing pencils. Use hard-surfaced paper or thin posterboard for *formats*. The size may be personally determined. Use 12" × 18" newsprint for practice. Some children might have need for rulers as an aid in constructing guide lines, not for drawing the letters.

Stimulation

Ask how many in the group can read Japanese. If none can, ask why they cannot. How many are familiar with the style of "lettering" used by the Japanese? In what way does it vary from lettering used in Western languages? Introduce the word *calligraphy*. Further, identify lettering as a hand process different from writing whereas "printing" is something accomplished by pressing an inked design against paper. Indicate that the former can be very personal, and, as evidenced by some Oriental cultures, a kind of artistry in itself.

Procedure

The problem is to restyle some of the existing letter shapes. The pupils will have an opportunity to be inventive while conforming to a necessary system.

Instruct the children to letter with a pencil on newsprint the presently used upper case (capital) alphabet. Parallel guide lines, to be drawn faintly with pencil, are optional. Focus on this conventional alphabet that they have gradually learned to master. Study each letter as an entity, as a linear shape in itself. Examine the proportions within each shape. For example, compare the division of space in the upper and lower areas of the letters *A* and *R*. Examine the visual properties of "open" letters as compared to "closed" letters (*O, D, Q, B*). Encourage modification of existing letter shapes by manipulating these spaces and proportions.

Distribute more newsprint for practice. Perhaps the children could use only those letters that appear in their full names. Introduce further modification in terms of thick, thin, curved, and straight lines. Discuss the inclusion and omission of *serifs*. Experiment also with slanted and vertical positions of letters. Try some with double lines and split ends. Remind the chil-

dren to maintain legibility as well as design quality.

Follow this practice session with the distribution of hard-surfaced paper and various media. Treat this format as a design. Have each child letter his "personalized" name on the format in a way that will give it dominance. Distribute the remaining letters of the alphabet, in a lettering style consistent with that in the name, throughout the format. Use the letters as components of a total design. The letters may be varied in size and position. Each total design can be as individual as the person who organized it.

The Objective

Individuality as well as intelligent conformity.

The Situation (No. 9)

An autobiographical symbol book. Reflect on what makes a person what he is. Develop separate visual symbols for each factor identified.

Materials

Provide everyone with from six to ten 6" × 9" sheets of white construction paper, tempera, small brushes, partially filled water containers, and paintcloths. Have a stapler available.

Stimulation

What is a biography? What does it have in common with a portrait? What is an autobiography? What visual art form is comparable to the latter? (A self-portrait.) Discuss the conventional ways of writing autobiographies and painting self-portraits. Which method enables the artist (writer or painter) to portray a *variety* of events that are of importance to his life? Which form of art can best handle events that have occurred over a long period of time? What could be borrowed from these two art forms in order to develop a visual autobiography?

Procedure

Interweave some of these possible answers into the presentation of the problem, namely, that of a *symbolic visual* autobiography. For purposes of this problem define "symbol" as

122

a brief visual statement that represents something else. It might be compared to an emblem or insignia with which many are already familiar. A symbol in this instance is not a big picture that fills an entire space. There is no *background* or *foreground*. Each symbol is a self-contained, emblematic design based upon either an event or subject matter. A simplified drawing of an ornate crown might, for example, symbolize "royalty."

Invite the group to think about events in their lives and beliefs they hold that have exerted important influences. Ask them to examine their capabilities, interests, or any other possible factors that might account for their present concepts about themselves. Each person could make a list of those factors that he deems important to his present status as an individual.

After this period of introspection, discuss the possibility of making a *visual* symbol for each factor that has been identified. These symbols could range from *nonobjective* (streak of color to designate a sad or happy event) to simplified *subject matter* (sporting equipment as indicative of an athletic ability). Invite the children to make symbols that might communicate a particular factor.

Distribute the materials. Because tempera will be used, encourage the children to make preliminary drawings with a brush and tinted water rather than with a pencil which might establish details too small for completion by painting. Each factor should be symbolized on a separate page. It need not fill the entire page. On the back of each page, if the child wants to, he can write the verbal equivalent of the symbol. When the symbols are finished, have the child sort them, using the most important one as page one and so on. In another year he would probably arrange them differently. Staple them with a cover that could contain his personalized name from the previous situation.

The Objective
Individuality as well as intelligent conformity.

The Situation (No. 10)
Houses with similar shapes, but different interiors and exteriors. In one period, make varying floor plans within the limitation of a rectangular shape. In a second period, make varying exterior designs in consideration of a similar limitation.

Materials
Install a long strip of white butcher paper on a suitable wall area. On this a small group could design a street which will accommodate individually designed houses. Lots, about nine inches wide, could be designated along the streets. If you have a large group, have two parallel streets, one above the other. Do not be concerned about perspective. In addition to this common format each person will have need for a 2½" × 6" rectangle of heavy paper or oaktag for period one and a 1¼" × 6" rectangle of similar material for period two. There will be need for colored pencils, scissors, scraps of colored paper, rulers, and rubber cement.

Stimulation
Focus on the large format containing the streets. Have everyone choose a lot. As a property owner, each person will have opportunity to design his own home. However, only a minimal amount of money is available for mortgages. With this in mind, and in consideration of zoning restrictions, each house has to be designed with a restricted cost and square footage.

Procedure
Distribute the largest rectangles, which will be used as floor plans, rulers, scissors, and colored pencils. Examine the rectangle. Also examine the size, terrain, and location of the lot. Consider the scale to be that of about 1 inch equals 10 feet. In order to meet the zoning–cost restrictions each rectangle must remain as such with the exception of one protrusion which could be cut *from* it and added as a wing, closed-in porch, or whatever is preferred. Instruct the children to think of the number and kinds of rooms they will need and where they might be located. Consider the outside in terms of view, privacy, and sunlight. They may draw a single red line for an interior wall, a heavy blue line for a window, a triple blue line for glass doors, and a heavy black line for a solid door. Allow the edges of the

123

paper to serve as the outside walls. Discuss average sizes of rooms in terms of the approximate scale. (Do not let the technique interfere with the imagination.) Each room may be labeled as to its use. Those who have time might want to add diagrams for furniture and fixtures. Keep the floor plans for the second period.

At another time distribute the smaller rectangles. These will be modified to fit the front side dimensions of the floor plans. Have the pupils locate doors and windows on these shapes, in reference to their floor plans, and develop these as front views of the exteriors of the houses. The roof lines may be altered by trimming and adding. Use colored paper and pencils to provide textural variance to these exteriors. Discuss the textures that can be contrasted between roof, windows, doors, and walls. When these are completed, each person may add his unique contribution to the lot designated on the large format. At another time equally individual landscaping might be added.

124

The Objective
Individuality as well as intelligent conformity.

The Situation

Materials

Stimulation

Procedure

Area Three
Visual Organizational Learning

The situations in this area are intended to lead to the formation of concepts about visual arrangement and expression while working with various art media.

The concepts are not intended as theories apart from feeling and expression; responses to these art learning situations involve reliance on both the rational and irrational.

In addition to seeing, feeling, and thinking about what he is doing with art media, a child can learn something about the inherent properties of these media.

The concepts then, in concert with these media, become a means of developing an ability to express ideas and feelings in visual rather than only verbal ways.

A more acute visual sensitivity toward art forms and qualities in the environment could result from manipulation of art media.

Area Three is ultimately concerned with developing in many children a capacity for response to *visual* qualities, and, simultaneously, discovering and encouraging a minority of potential artists.

The Visual Components of Art

Some art problems can consist of pure (nonpictorial) design.

14 Problems of this kind involve the interaction of visual *elements* and *principles*.

Often these components are mere verbal abstractions, but when they are separated from subject matter they may become more understandable.

It is also possible to isolate only one or two elements and one or two principles so they can be better seen and understood.

Further, by learning about these components of art, children might become able to see relationships between them and many varieties of visible (physical) reality.

The Objective

Ability to arrange the visual components of art in various ways.

The Situation (No. 1)

Similar shapes in changing formats. Modify two or three sets of similar shapes to correspond to the proportions of two or three different formats.

Materials

From 12″ × 18″ manila paper, cut three formats for each person in the following sizes: 12″ × 12″, 9″ × 12″, and 6″ × 18″. Provide each child with crayons or tempera. Limit either medium to one color of their choice.

Stimulation

Distribute the 9″ × 12″ sheets and the necessary media. Use the term *format*. Describe it as an area in which ideas, shapes, lines, and colors are to be contained. For this experience, ask the children to invent four or five *shapes* that can be "caged" in this format. The shapes are just shapes—there is no need for subject matter. There is a special problem though. All edges of the format are to be touched by a shape at least once. This is not to say that one shape touches all four edges. Some shapes, not all, should touch other shapes. All will not be floating separately from each other. And, each shape must be somewhat different from the others; they may appear to be "cousins" though they are cousins of different sizes. Review the problem. Emphasize the importance of fitting (designing) the shapes into the format.

Procedure

Problems in *design* involve adherence to certain limitations that give structure and credence to the specific situation. This statement should not be misinterpreted to mean that there are "rules for art." Do, however, encourage consideration of the limitations inherent in a particular problem. Observe each child at work.

When most of the pupils have finished, distribute a second format of different *proportions*. Those who have yet to finish the first design may pause to listen to instructions for the second problem. Instruct the children to draw the same shapes from the first format on the second one, making whatever changes are necessary to "fit" them into position according to the limitations originally prescribed. (Review if necessary.) Discuss possible modifications. Which shapes will have to be made "fatter" to fill in an area? Which might have to be "stretched"? Continue with the same color in order to focus more effectively on the visual quality of *shape* in relation to the *proportions* of the format. Once again help the children relate to the structure of the problem as they work. For those who seem capable and express interest, introduce the third format of different proportions. The colored shapes, though modified to fit the new area, and other limitations remain constant.

Relate the underlying concept of this design problem to other visual arrangements. Such discussion might center on furniture that "fits nicely" in rooms, flowers in relation to a vase, and figures that have been adapted to a format (not necessarily touching the edges but nonetheless fitting in a painting).

The Objective
Ability to arrange the visual components of art in various ways.

The Situation (No. 2)
Relating unrelated shapes. Establish two entirely different *nonobjective* shapes. From these, develop several "hybrid" shapes that may eventually unify in a total design.

Materials
Provide everyone with a 12" × 18" sheet of manila paper or newsprint, a sheet of thin colored (tonal) paper, scissors, and rubber cement or paste.

Stimulation
Ask the children to think of objects or animals that are quite different from one another in appearance. Discuss the visual quality of *shape* rather than color or texture in ascertaining specific differences. Elicit from them possible imaginative combinations of shapes; for example, in what kinds of *shapes* would an elephant-horse "hybrid" emerge? What kinds of shapes would emerge from several combinations of a book and a pencil sharpener? Think of other "opposite" shapes and possible "hybrids" that might be made by borrowing and combining parts from each.

Procedure
Have each child choose a color of tonal paper. Distribute the other materials. Review the concept of *shape* as a component of the visual arts. Focus on shapes, again, as things in themselves. Instruct the children to cut, without any preliminary drawing, a "pleasing" nonobjective shape from the colored paper. If you prefer, specify minimum and maximum sizes. Examine the visual characteristics of these nonobjective shapes. Which ones are fluid or soft? Which are hard or jagged?

From the remaining colored paper ask them to cut a shape that is entirely different in character and appearance from the first one. Try cutting more than one "opposite" shape; share opinions among the group as to which pair is most different. Have each child place his two shapes at opposite ends of the manila format.

From the remaining colored paper ask the children to cut several different shapes that *share* the characteristics of each of the two original opposites. Encourage a variety of sizes among these "brothers," "cousins," and more distant "relatives" of the two opposite shapes. Some children might prefer to work from left to right (as they are learning to read) or from right to left (as left-handed children often do). Have each child place each new shape, in its proper relationship to the one from which it was derived, in a horizontal row across the format. Ideally, the shape in the middle of the row should have visible characteristics of both of the opposites. Those nearer the left and right might more closely resemble those opposites.

When most of the children have a good sampling, focus for a moment on the proportions of the format. Invite the children to modify, if they wish, the *proportions* (keeping the format rectangular) before they arrange the shapes. Adhere all of the shapes to this format in a random design, not in a row. Encourage the children to "hide" those shapes that do not "get along" with others underneath those that are more compatible. Place shapes near all four edges. Examine the composition for *variety* and *unity*.

The Objective
Ability to arrange the visual components of art in various ways.

The Situation (No. 3)
Flat formats with "space" and "depth." Treat the surface of the paper as actual "flat" space and virtual "depth" by varying the arrangement of achromatic (noncolored) lines.

Materials
Everyone should have two identical manila paper *formats.* Provide scissors, paste, crayons, and an ample supply of neutral-colored tonal or construction paper. Have available a reproduction of a *nonobjective* and a *realistic* painting. (See Chapter Seven for examples.)

Stimulation
Show a blank piece of paper. Indicate that an artist (a painter) looks upon such a surface as a format or a space into which he organizes ideas and feelings visually. Some artists look upon a blank space for what it actually is, a flat surface with four boundaries. Focus on an example of nonobjective painting or *cubism* that conforms to this flat quality. Many other painters, from the past and present, however, develop pictures that give the feeling of having so much "depth" that one can almost walk into them. Focus upon one of these examples. The four edges still serve as boundaries but the surface gives way to a "virtual space," a pretended space where the eye can wander from a *foreground* through a *middleground* to a

background without departing from the surface. Give a sheet of paper and the other materials to each person.

Procedure
Instruct the group to cut some reasonably thin strips (lines) from the neutral-colored paper. Keep the thinness constant but vary the lengths. (Some children might prefer to execute this problem with crayon directly on the format.) With these lines, solve the following problem: divide the format into fifteen unequal spaces with lines that touch but do not overlap. Some of the lines may be curved (via crayons). When completed, the space of the format will have a different "feeling" and appearance but it should retain its actual flatness.

Distribute the second format. On this one ask the children to use separate lines, of varying widths and lengths, in such a way that they never touch one another and do instead give a feeling of "depth," as if some were far away, others up close. Discuss some of the ways of achieving this effect. Consider the position of the lines (high or low) on the format, the relationship of sizes (proportions of large and small), and the relative position of one in reference to another (closeness and distance). Encourage the children to arrange the lines in such a way that the eye is led "into" the format and back again to the surface. Remind them to use a variety of sizes in order to achieve this effect of "depth in space." You might indicate that this is an "artistic" space exploration, one that has been of concern to man for centuries.

Compare the two designs. Generalize from these nonobjective designs to some of the group's recent pictorial work. Cite relationships. Discuss different ways of treating space in future pictures.

The Objective
Ability to arrange the visual components of art in various ways.

The Situation (No. 4)
Pictorial or nonpictorial textural composi-

130

tion. Use simulated textures from magazines to develop a composition.

Materials

Ask the group to bring several discarded pictorial magazines. Provide everyone with a background format of 12″ × 18″ white construction paper (which he may alter), scissors, rubber cement, and a sharpened Blackie pencil.

Stimulation

Distribute the magazines. Invite the children to turn them upside down and tear out any page that has a *black and white* photograph that contains surfaces they can almost "feel." Discuss actual *texture* in relation to those photographs that show *simulated* textures. Indicate that just as some paintings or pictures produce an illusion of depth and distance others do something similar with texture; they produce illusionary surface qualities. These surfaces possess a "pretend" (simulated) texture. After tearing, cut swatches of implied texture from these photographs of cake frosting, carpets, straw, hair, silk, concrete, pebbles, tile, and other surfaces.

Procedure

Distribute the other art materials. From the cuttings select some large swatches of variant texture. Hold them side by side. Discuss textural *contrast* as it occurs through a gradation that is composed of a succession of grains from tiny or smooth to large and rough. Define *pattern*, such as plaid cloth, as something that occurs on a larger scale. Some patterns when reduced in scale might give a feeling of texture. The windows of a skyscraper appear as large rectangular patterns; on a photograph greatly reduced in size the same windows might be graded down to simulate texture instead.

Ask the children to sort their simulated textures according to a smooth-rough gradation. They will, of course, have contrasts of light and dark as well. The variable of color has, however, been eliminated so they may focus better on implied texture.

From these swatches the children may cut simple shapes which may be adhered to the background paper in form of a "pure" design. Or, if they prefer, they may cut "subject matter" shapes from the swatches. If they employ subject matter, however, remind them that they are to make their own shapes from textures which were intended as something else in the original photographs. In other words, they should make their own shape for a head of hair from a texture alien to it, not from one originally used as hair in an advertisement. If they were to make a house they would not make one from a photograph of a house. Stress textural contrast and the use of a variety of textures. Allow some of the original format to show through in order to prevent "busyness." Rest the eye with an occasional "quiet interval." Allow overlapping.

When complete, some children might try to reproduce some of the textures with a pencil. Encourage them to incorporate hand-made textures such as these when they work on future compositions.

The Objective

Ability to arrange the visual components of art in various ways.

The Situation (No. 5)

Variety and unity—a checkerboard transformed. Use a unified, monotonous checkerboard pattern as a point of departure for a design which maintains unity while attaining variety.

Materials

From 1″ strips of black and red paper, cut enough squares to provide everyone with eight of each color. In addition, each pupil will need a 4″-square format of manila paper, scissors, colored chalk or pastels, and rubber cement.

Stimulation

Distribute the colored squares and square formats. Invite the children to set up the obvious—checkerboards. Look at these, however, as something other than formats for a game. Look at them instead as *designs.* Criticize the visual properties of the "boards." In doing so, ask the children to describe what they see in terms of shape and color. Identify *shape* and *color* as elements of art (more specifically of

131

visual art). Discuss the manner in which these elements have been arranged. Indicate that elements are arranged, either intentionally or not, in accord with certain *principles* of art. One of these principles is that of *unity*. What might this mean? Does the checkerboard as a design possess visual unity? Why? Another principle is that of *variety*. What visual variety, if any, is evident in this design? What is the opposite of variety? Monotony? Focus on the colors. Notice that there are only two (referring to black as a "color" for purposes of this discussion). Each color is repeated in the same shade. Look at the shapes. Any variety here? None. You might indicate that every design and work of art has to have *variety* and *unity*. Accordingly, there has to be just the "right amount" of each, or one "principle" will overpower the other and affect the total design or painting.

Procedure

Distribute the other art materials. Invite the children to modify the existing checkerboards. They are to use all of the red and black squares, cutting, reshaping, and reassembling them in a less monotonous pattern. They are in effect introducing variety of shape and pattern. Allow little or no white to show through. Add colored chalk to the original red and black in order to inject variety of color. Try several combinations of modified shape and color arrangements. Stop before disunity occurs!

Whenever a child has a satisfactory arrangement, have him slide some rubber cement (on a thin strip of paper) under the shapes and secure them in place. (In reference to the objectives of Chapter Thirteen, notice the variant responses.) Ask the children to identify other things or places they have seen that would benefit from an injection of variety. Discuss variety as it is treated in music. Also identify its necessary partner, unity, as it occurs in their surroundings and in music. If possible, examine some of their previous visual work from a unity–variety frame of reference.

The Objective

Ability to arrange the visual components of art in various ways.

The Situation (No. 6)

Equal spaces—opposite colors. Use complementary colors in identical *total* amounts distributed among varying shapes.

Materials

There will be need for an assorted color pack of 9" × 12" construction paper, tempera in primary colors, small round brushes, plastic egg crates, partially filled water containers, and paintcloths. For demonstration have a white background (a movie screen or white posterboard) and a larger sheet of colored paper.

Stimulation

Place the white background where it will be easily seen by everyone. Hold a sheet of orange paper, cut in a diamond shape, in front of it. Ask the children to focus intently upon it for about thirty seconds. Remove the paper from the white background but invite them to continue gazing at the same area. What do they see? Those who were able to concentrate, barring any vision disorder, should have seen a faint blue diamond shape. Ask the children to look elsewhere in the room. Some will retain the afterimage for several seconds and will be able to locate it nearly anywhere. Indicate that one's own system of vision enables him to see the opposite or near complement of the color he saw on the paper. Have each child choose a color from among the smaller sheets. Distribute the remainder of the art materials.

Procedure

Ask each person to tear a small hole in a scrap of writing paper and place that sheet over the colored paper. Have him look at the colored shape revealed by the hole for several seconds, transfer his vision to another area of the writing paper, and describe the color he sees. The afterimage of red should appear as blue-green (depending on the actual red-orange content of the construction paper), and that of purple as light yellow.

Ask each person to select a tempera color, or select two and mix them as one (in the egg crates) that corresponds to the *complementary* color seen in the afterimage. Have him divide the space of the colored paper format with shapes, painted directly on that surface, which contain the complement. They are to paint some shapes that are large enough to "go off" the edges. These painted shapes should occupy about the same number of square inches as the remaining space, which contains the original paper color. The figure (painted areas) should be equal in total area to that of the ground (original surface). The child paints only *half* the paper but in a variety of shapes.

When a child is finished, he should have difficulty determining which color represents the original surface. The figure and ground should be interchangeable. Notice what happens along the edges of the complementary colors (many tend to vibrate). Have the group look at all of the shapes of one color and then switch attention to the others. Which shapes appear brighter? Which duller? Discuss the *effect* of one color on the other. Look for examples of complementary colors in the environment.

The Objective
Ability to arrange the visual components of art in various ways.

The Situation (No. 7)
Color dominance, balance, and rhythm. Develop three situations that involve experiments in color interaction.

Materials
Obtain several assorted color tissue packs. This material will be used on three separate formats of 12" × 18" heavy white paper. The tissue may be adhered with rubber cement or with thinned white glue applied with ¾" flat bristle brushes (which should be washed immediately after use) on the format first or through the thin tissue. The latter method causes the paper to wrinkle thereby producing a textural bonus (or, to some, "a mess"). Some children might need scissors.

Stimulation
The colors themselves are exciting. Each of the following three problems, which you will probably prefer to develop at separate times, are also challenges in themselves. Prior to the distribution of materials and in reference to each problem discuss such pertinent design concepts as dominance, balance, and rhythm. All problems will involve the development of "areas" of color rather than combinations of well-articulated shapes. Area is used here to describe nebulous masses of color that are likely to occur as the tissue is torn or cut and adhered in ways to achieve *color* effects.

Procedure
Because the materials and alternative methods of adhering remain constant, the three problems will be described herein.

Two equal areas of color dominance: Have the children use at least six of the tissue paper colors. They may cut or tear and arrange them spontaneously. Some might prefer to brush glue directly onto the format and lay the tissue over the sticky surface. Or they may place the tissue over a dry surface and adhere it by forcing the thinned white glue through it with a brush. Direct their perception toward the mixture of colors that occurs when the transparent layers overlay. As they are adhering the various sizes of tissue shapes, ask them to develop at least *two color areas* that will emerge from the total sea of color as dominant. These two areas should "hold" the design together yet not "jump" away from the rest of the format. Discuss ways of achieving dominance after the children have had opportunity to get acquainted with the medium. Scrutinize the designs in order to check the communication of *dominance*.

Color balance: Use a minimum of five colors of varying intensity. Try to use them in amounts that balance one another. For example, a small amount of intense orange might have the equivalent strength of a large area of light brown. Once again avoid subject matter and fill the format (no white showing) with random areas of overlapping colored tissue. Compare color balance to such familiar uses as a man's red tie and gray suit, a turquoise pillow and a tan carpet, and other combinations. Control intensity.

A rhythmic-directional color composition: Use three chief colors that take the eye on three different paths amidst other colors throughout the format. Encourage the children to repeat some of the three chief colors in the *negative space* and some of the negative space colors in the rhythmic, directional colors (otherwise crisp, flaglike designs might emerge). Upon

133

completion, ask other children to locate the color routes.

The Objective

Ability to arrange the visual components of art in various ways.

The Situation (No. 8)

Design games. Explore several brief problems of visual organization.

Materials

From a 1"-wide stripe of gray construction paper, cut enough squares to provide everyone with twelve. From a 1¼"-wide strip provide everyone with twelve triangles. Some efficient helpers might do the cutting. Package the shapes in individual envelopes. Each person will need a 9" × 12" manila paper format.

Stimulation

Approach this as a design game. Each game will have rules. The outcomes are likely to be just as varied as those in many games. The outcomes are not predictable. Art and games have this in common. Distribute the formats and envelopes. Invite the children to open their envelopes. The contents might arouse some curiosity.

Procedure

Symmetrical arrangement: Discuss the meaning of *balance.* Further, identify *symmetry* as one kind of balance. Instruct the group to "imagine" a straight line that cuts through the middle of the *format* from top to bottom. Using this imaginary line as an axis, they may develop a design (using the mobile triangles and squares) that fills most of the area and remains the same on each side. Use the format in either a horizontal or vertical position. Develop *nonobjective* designs. Allow enough time for all to finish. Review the concept of symmetry as the work is being done.

An asymmetrical conversion: When all have finished, introduce the next problem. Maintain much of the initial symmetrical design but by moving only five squares and five triangles convert that design into one that is *asymmetrical.* Discuss asymmetry as another kind of balance.

Study the design to determine which shapes could be moved most effectively. Once the ten pieces are removed, they are not to be returned to the original position. Continue to occupy most of the format. Check the arrangement for tension. When complete ask each child to remove one square or triangle that might destroy the entire balance.

Rhythmic arrangement: Remove all the shapes. Have the children use all twenty-four pieces to form a *pattern.* Make the necessary analogies to patterns that appear in fabrics and wallpaper. This arrangement should *not* possess any area of dominance.

A design with an area of dominance: Once again remove all the shapes. Have each child develop a design, using all of the pieces, wherein three squares and two triangles dominate one area of the composition and still maintain *unity* with the other pieces. Since the compositions cannot be displayed, encourage the children to walk about the room and observe the variant solutions.

When the problems are finished, return the pieces to the envelopes. Invite the children to invent other games involving principles of design.

The Objective

Ability to arrange the visual components of art in various ways.

The Situation (No. 9)

Part–whole rearrangement: nature form. Develop an *abstract* design wherein two shapes, one derived from the whole and one from a part of a nature form, exert dominance.

Materials

Prior to this situation ask the group to bring *complete* examples of small organic nature forms. Photographs might suffice as substitutes for those who are unable to collect actual specimens. Provide everyone with black and white tempera, a plastic egg crate in which to mix several shades of gray, a small round brush, a partially filled water container, a paintcloth, and an 11" × 14" sheet of posterboard or heavy white paper.

Ask several children to identify the nature forms they have brought. Several children may share one form, if they prefer. Instruct them to hold the object against the light of a window and squint while looking at it. Reduce the object to one "solid shape" via this induced silhouette. Ask them to turn the object in several positions while looking at it in this manner. Select a favorite silhouette.

Procedure

On writing paper with an ordinary pencil, the children are to draw a few of these solid shapes representative of the most pleasing silhouettes exhibited by the nature form. Focus again on the form. Look at some of the inner shapes and details. These would include scales on a fish (hopefully from a photograph of one), the segmented shapes within a turtle's back, the petals of a flower or any part from any other whole. Ask the children to draw some of the inner shapes (parts of the whole) in solid form. Compare the parts to the wholes. In what way do they repeat each other? In what way, other than size, do they differ?

Distribute the art materials. Describe the problem as follows. Each child is to paint (using thick tempera of gray, white, or black) one of the parts from the nature form on a large scale in a position of prominence on the format. Fill in the shape, making it solid. Use a similar procedure in painting the shape of the whole nature form, but draw it *smaller* than the part. In other words, reverse the actual size relationships.

At this point each child has two shapes on the format. No color will be used. Instead, he may continue with various *values*. The two shapes extracted from the nature form are to remain as the dominant shapes in the format. All of the format is to be filled in with *other* shapes to be invented without further reference to the nature form. The problem is that of incorporating "new" shapes, which are essentially nonobjective, with those that are *abstract* in that they have been taken from the nature form. Some shapes should touch others. Some may "grow" off the format edges. Discuss contrast of light and dark as a means of attaining dominance. Also paint in the spaces that remain between the shapes. Develop an exhibition of the completed designs in association with the nature forms that provided their nascence.

The Objective

Ability to arrange the visual components of art in various ways.

The Situation (No. 10)

Unification of diversities into one design. Select two photographs that are different in visual character and modify them into a unified design on one format.

Materials

Use discarded pictorial magazines (an excellent art material source). From these the children are to find two photographs that are similar in size but entirely different in subject matter and character. Instruct them to select a black and white pair or a colored pair. Provide tempera (primary and secondary colors plus black and white in plastic ketchup dispensers), plastic egg crates into which monitors may dispense the desired colors, small round brushes, partially filled water containers (for cleaning brushes between colors, not for thinning the paint), paintcloths, 12" × 18" manila paper, scissors, and white glue. Have them mount and trim the two photographs on the manila paper before the introduction of the problem. The pictures may be mounted upside down or sideways in relation to one another.

Stimulation

Distribute the previously mounted pairs of photographs. Ask those whose photos are not already disoriented in the mounted positions to turn them upside down. Ask them to try to "erase" the subject matter from the pictures and to look at them as areas of dark and light (in shades or in colors). Look at edges as if they were lines. Look for variation of *line* in one photograph as compared to the other. Look for variation in *shape* and *texture*. Now that these two diversities share the same format what could be done to bring about visual compatibility (*unity*)?

Procedure

Discuss the possible approaches, then distribute the necessary materials. Referring to

135

ideas advanced in the discussion, encourage the children to look at a shape in one photograph, and, by painting directly on the surface, echo it or *parts* of it in an appropriate area in the opposite photograph. Borrow "edges" (lines), shapes, textures, and values (or colors) from one photograph and incorporate these into the other and vice versa. In making these visual transplants, allow well over half of the original surface of the photographs to show through. Introduce change only when it seems effective.

If the tempera bubbles or slides, have the children brush back and forth until the surface is dulled, or wait until a partially covered area is dry and add a second coat. Keep the temperas thick and *opaque*.

Encourage those who are using colors to mix them to correspond to those in the photographs by adding the *complement* to dull a color, and black or white to darken a shade or make it lighter. As they work, remind them to maintain the original boundary lines made by the edges of the photographs. Retain some identity of each section but alter each to the degree that the two photographs become unified. Try a similar approach at another time with some of their previous paintings.

136

The Objective
Ability to arrange the visual components of
art in various ways.

The Situation

Materials

Stimulation

Procedure

137

Art Media and Processes

15

The examination of art media and development of rudimentary skills in using these media are unique aspects of art education.

These media serve as a means of visual expression but are not necessarily central to it.

The various media are subservient to people who are sensitive enough to have something to express.

Some media, used separately or mixed, possess inherent properties which in themselves might incite ideas and feelings.

Children who have been introduced to these media are likely to recognize in what ways these inherent properties hold potential for certain kinds of personally compatible expression.

They might learn to ask what one medium can do, as controlled by them, that another medium cannot do. A more intelligent choice and perception could result.

The Objective
Familiarity with a variety of art media and processes.

The Situation (No. 1)
Wax crayon versatility. Discover many ways of using crayons as a medium for visual expression.

Materials
Provide each child with large crayons in a minimum of eight colors, scissors, and three sheets of 12" ✕ 18" paper, one manila and two newsprint.

Stimulation
Very often the medium most familiar to chil-
dren is taken for granted as an ordinary plaything. Distribute the crayons. Invite the children to examine these as new "drawing and coloring tools." Distribute the paper. Discuss the visible and tactile properties of the crayons.

Procedure
Ask the children to feel the exposed area of a crayon. Identify the "slickness" as a waxy substance that holds the *pigment* in a solid state. Examine the point. What kind of mark does it make? (Most children have, of course, discovered this through self-initiated manipulation of the medium, but not all have *realized* the potential of such marks.) Invite the children to make dots and lines. Ask them to cut small

rectangles from the manila sheet and develop small designs made of the two simple kinds of markings.

Have each child cut a larger rectangle from the manila paper, and color in several areas, each somewhat larger than a postage stamp, by rubbing the points of the crayons more vigorously on the paper. Use at least eight different colors. Ask them to rub the areas until they shine. When they have finished, have them close their eyes and feel the actual *texture* produced by the medium and their vigor. Ask them to focus on the heavily colored areas and apply a different color on top of at least five of them. Determine which colors hide the colors underneath and which ones blend. Encourage the children to use the remaining manila paper for further experimentation.

Use the newsprint. Ask the children to peel somewhat over half of the paper from the sides of the crayon. (For those who are predisposed not to "ruin" their crayons in this way, provide a few crayon remnants.) Ask them to use the crayons on the *sides*, applying varying degrees of pressure, twisting them, and making long, swirling gestures by running them across the page. In what way are these applications different from those made with the point? In what different kind of subject matter might both methods of application be combined? Separated?

Use the other sheet of newsprint for some crayon rubbings. Have the children look about the room for visibly textured surfaces. Instruct them to put the newsprint over the surface and rub the crayon, again on its side, *over* the paper thereby registering the texture from underneath. Encourage them to hold the newsprint stationary and "capture" the texture by applying more than one color over the same area. Fill the format. Review the processes. What can be done with crayons that cannot be done with cut paper? With watercolors?

The Objective
Familiarity with a variety of art media and processes.

The Situation (No. 2)
Crayon and watercolors: the best of each combined. Combine the resisting properties of wax crayons with the flowing, transparent properties of watercolors.

Materials
Provide everyone with a 9″ × 12″ and a 12″ × 18″ sheet of heavy white construction paper, a soft round brush (medium size), pan watercolors, a partially filled water container, a paintcloth, and large wax crayons.

Stimulation
Ask the children to think of things that shed water (ducks, raincoats, etc.). Why do some surfaces resist water? Is there an art *medium* that sheds water? Distribute the small sheets of paper.

Procedure
Distribute the crayons after the children have identified them as the medium most likely to resist water. And, in keeping with the discussion, what art medium is most fluid? Distribute the watercolors and necessary accoutrements.

Before the children attempt anything pictorial, guide them through some experiments that will enable them to identify the basic properties of these media as they accrue when combined. Divide the crayons into "warm" colors (reds, yellows, oranges) and "cool" colors (blues, greens, and some purples). On the left of the small sheet instruct the children to draw some light lines and some heavy, waxy lines with the warm colors. Near the same locale they may draw two open rectangles, one with light lines the other with heavy waxy lines. Then they may draw two solid rectangles, one filled in heavily and the other lightly. Repeat the two sets of lines, open shapes, and solid shapes with the cool colors on the right side of the practice sheet.

Review the preparation of watercolors. Have the children moisten each cake of paint with a few drops of clean water. Rinse the brush to make sure that whoever used it last cleaned it. Discuss the importance of applying the watercolors with quick strokes. Discourage the "windshield wiper" approach whereby several back and forth strokes muddy the colors and roughen the paper. Encourage the children to mix colors by quickly dropping one stroke of another color over the first one while the former is still wet.

139

Focus on the warm and cool sections of crayon. Remind the children that there will be no need to paint "in" and "around" these wax lines and shapes as the water should not adhere to them. Before applying paint, moisten the entire sheet with clear water. Then paint *over* everything with rapid, smooth flowing brush strokes of *thin* (well-watered) watercolor that will *contrast* with the crayon colors (cool over warm).

Examine the results. Notice that the watercolors partly hid the lightly waxed areas. The heavily waxed areas resisted better although some drops of water dried over them (discourage removal of these "natural" marks). Also notice the color contrasts (even though the watercolors are not as bright as they were while wet). Discuss the possible subject matter application. Think of *objects* made of crayon and surrounding *areas* made of watercolor. Distribute the larger sheets for such an exploration.

The Objective

Familiarity with a variety of art media and processes.

The Situation (No. 3)

Paper, torn and cut, opaque and transparent. Use various papers for establishing shapes and areas in a picture or design. (This problem may be extended into two situations.)

Materials

In all there will be need for assorted colors of tonal (*opaque*) and tissue (*transparent*) paper. Each type is available in assorted color packs. One pack of each for every four children should suffice. Save the larger scraps for future use. For each child provide white glue (thinned with water), ¾" flat glue brushes (to be washed immediately after use), scissors, and white background paper for mounting.

Stimulation

For younger children the tonal paper lends itself best to pictorial work whereas the tissue is best adapted to *nonobjective* composition. In introducing the materials, stress the elements of *shape* and *color* as attributes of each. Indicate that pencils and crayons can be used effectively to make lines but these papers, by contrast, are not easy to use in that manner. Discuss the notion of drawing and designing with cut and torn paper. Approaches to introducing each of these media will be treated separately under procedure.

Procedure

Tonal paper: After distributing all of the materials, ask each child to hold a sheet of the paper in front of him. Discuss its opacity. Ask the children to think of objects that could be represented best by tearing the paper (clouds, foliage and other more nebulously defined shapes). Then ask them to think of objects that could be represented best by cutting the paper. What objects could be shown by combining both approaches? (The human figure—and, by this approach, "stickmen" are unlikely to emerge.) Encourage the children to develop a picture by tearing and cutting. Fill most of the background paper in order to avoid a "postage stamp" distribution of small cut and torn pieces over a vast whiteness. Natural colors may be overlooked in favor of fantastic colors, such as yellow for clouds and purple for people. Cut and torn papers lend themselves to fantasy. Encourage the children to use the inherent properties of shape by tearing and cutting *directly* without any preliminary drawing. Think in terms of shapes rather than lines.

Tissue paper: Scrutinize its obvious transparency. Have the children try cutting and tearing some random shapes of tissue and experiment in adhering them to the background sheet. Which method is most effective? Most clumsy? Encourage them to discover the most natural way to use the tissue. Avoid forcing the medium into a role it cannot play (or one beyond the skills of the children). Invite them to cut or tear the tissue into a variety of shapes that are just shapes and not symbols for objects. Overlap two contrasting shapes to obtain a third shape in the area where two meet. What other art medium provides a third shape by overlapping two? What other art medium has crisp edges and is transparent? Discover these unique properties of tissue. Utilize them in subsequent expressions that demand such visual qualities.

The Objective

Familiarity with a variety of art media and processes.

The Situation (No. 4)

Colors that blend but do not run: pastels. Blend and mix colors with a medium that is particularly adaptable for such use.

Materials

Provide everyone with a sheet of 18" × 24" oatmeal paper and a set of good quality pastels. Avoid using brittle, pale chalkboard colors. Obtain two pressurized cans of *fixative* for future use with pastels. (Read the instructions.) Cover the table or desk tops and the vulnerable parts of the children.

Stimulation

Invite the children to look at the sky. Ask some of them to describe the variations of light and dark, bright and dull, that occur therein. Have them squint while looking at several objects within the room. Can they detect different shades of one color within the same shape? Indicate that you have an art *medium* that is particularly useful in showing these differences of light and dark within an area and shape. Also, it can be used to show how certain colors blend into other colors. Ask them to cite examples of color blending which they might have observed in nature (sunsets, rainbows, etc.).

Procedure

Distribute the materials. Have each child choose a color he prefers. Have him "fly" over the large sheet of paper with the pastel stick and allow it to "land" anywhere on the *format* except the exact center or next to an edge. Once he has "landed" he is to color in an area equivalent in size to one hand (but not in that shape).

Examine the colored area. Is it light or dark? Bright or dull? What *color* would be most likely to *blend* in with it if the two colors were placed side by side? Have the child think about colors and try one by surrounding the original color area with a concentric band of the new color, equivalent to the approximate width of a hand. Ask whether he was able to bring some of the second color into the first, and vice versa, without making either color "muddy." Have him

look at the second color and select another one that might blend nicely into it. Repeat the analysis and subsequent color-blending application until much of the format is filled.

In the peripheral spaces, suggest that the child add a color that blends with the one it is about to surround, but *within it* try to show a variance from dark to light by gradually blending white.

Examine the results. If the completed practice sheets resemble lopsided archery targets, with well-articulated rings of color, there is some indication that blending did not occur. Indicate, however, that these were merely practice sheets. At another time (of their own choosing if you prefer) they may select a new sheet of paper and use pastels in a picture or design that requires blending of light and dark within one color area or a gradual change of one color into another. In what way do pastels differ from cut paper? From watercolors?

The Objective

Familiarity with a variety of art media and processes.

The Situation (No. 5)

Tempera paint, from wet to dry. Become acquainted with different uses of this readily available medium.

Materials

Tempera is available in powder, liquid, and paste form. Powdered tempera should be mixed according to instructions (add water but maintain opacity). Also, it is often necessary to add wintergreen oil as a preservative if the mixed amount is to be used over a period of several days. Liquid tempera is more convenient and costly. High quality temperas (most expensive) are also available in tubes. These colors can be thinned by the children just before application. Dispense liquid temperas from nonbreakable, airtight, plastic containers. Each child should have a plastic egg crate into which the colors can be dispensed and eventually combined for the mixing of "new" colors. Use flat ¾" bristle brushes with long handles. Large, soft, round bristle brushes are also useful. Provide paintcloths and shirts, partly filled

141

water containers, and 18" × 24" heavy white or gray bogus paper for each person. Use any workable horizontal or vertical surface that is protected and to which the paper can be easily attached.

Stimulation

Distribute the materials. Let the medium take over as a stimulus in itself. The child should make a painting rather than a picture. He should load the brush with an ample amount of tempera and brush it in alternate directions as far as it will go. Examine the results of this first contact on the paper. Does the area near the center seem opaque? What happened to the tempera as the brush began to run dry? Does the white show through these dry brush strokes? Why?

Procedures

As the children continue with their painting, encourage them to mix colors by adding one to another directly on the paper while the first is still moist. Does tempera blend as easily as watercolor? Why not? Dip one corner of the brush in one color, the other in another color, and apply the two simultaneously. Do the combined colors remain separate or do they run together like watercolors? If they do run together, this could be an indication that the tempera is too thin. Practice mixing colors in the egg crates.

As the children explore the surface, encourage them to apply a second color of tempera over a completely dry area. Does it completely hide the first color or does it remoisten it and mix in with it thus producing a third or muddy shade? Does the color change as it dries? As more of the paint dries, instruct the children to dip the brush in contrasting color, wipe it partially dry on the paintcloth, and drag it over a dry painted area. Notice the tracks produced by the nearly dry brush. Allow the tracks to fade away gradually until they appear to blend in with the color on which they are superimposed. Identify this as a *dry brush* technique. In a sense, since temperas dry so quickly and defy smooth blending, this method can be a substitute for shading. Moreover, the dry brush approach produces *simulated* texture. Temperas themselves produce an *actual* texture if applied thickly upon a rigid surface. (Thick temperas on thin surfaces flake

off.) Let the brushstrokes show. Let the end product appear as an opaque painting.

The Objective

Familiarity with a variety of art media and processes.

The Situation (No. 6)

Clay, as volume and as surface. Experiment with ceramic-moist clay in order to discover its pliable three-dimensional properties.

Materials

Obtain some red firing ceramic-moist clay (twenty-five pounds in an airtight plastic bag). Provide each person with a masonite palette (see page 112), a water container, some paper towels, and a ³⁄₄-pound ball of clay. Have each pupil bring a large paper sack. Keep the apportioned amounts of clay moist until distributed. Have on hand a variety of marking tools such as spools, thimbles, large nails, and other small objects.

Stimulation

Distribute the balls of clay in the paper sacks —one per person. The children are not to look into the sacks. They are allowed only to *touch* the contents.

Procedure

Request that they put both hands in the bag and fashion the clay into an object that is pleasant to hold in either or both hands. (Encourage "thoughtlessness.") Keep the clay in one piece but do not attempt to make it representative of any object. It is nonfunctional. Without peeking, they may squeeze it, turn it, transfer it from one hand to another, develop a volume that "feels" interesting, introduce some "ins" and "outs" and possibly some voids (openings) that pass entirely through the clay. When the object feels comfortable while held in any of a variety of positions, remove it from the bag. Dip the fingertips lightly into the water and smooth out any cracks or unsightly nodules. Allow the tool (finger) marks to remain— avoid giving clay a "slick" appearance. The object may be viewed from several directions. There is no need for a specific top or bottom.

142

It should tend to "float" in any position in which it is placed. Discuss clay as a "volume." What advantages would it offer in symbolizing a human figure?

If the children are not too enamored of these, flatten them, on moistened palettes, into slabs about ³/₈" thick. Encourage them to create flat shapes from the former volumes. Add water to keep the clay moist and pliable.

Distribute the marking tools. Encourage the children to produce actual (tactile) textures on the surface of the clay. If they close their eyes when the various tools are repeatedly pressed into the surface of the clay, they can organize a textural design by touch alone. They should use at least three different tools or one tool in three different ways. When the surface has been completely modified have them place the forms in a vertical position and bend, roll, or fold the clay until the textured areas face outward on what is once again a free-standing three-dimensional structure. Observe the effects of light and shadow as they play upon this surface.

If any child wants to keep the final experimental product, wrap it in a moist towel and allow it to dry very slowly. Eliminate all cracks by rubbing in additional moist clay *before* it is set aside for drying. What happens to clay when it dries? Return the remaining clay, remoistened and "re-balled," to the airtight bag so that it may be used again.

The Objective
Familiarity with a variety of art media and processes.

The Situation (No. 7)
Brayer painting. Recognize the contributions of a tool, in conjunction with a medium, while involved with a visual organization.

Materials
Provide everyone with sufficient floor or wall space and a 4' length (or more) of hard-surfaced white butcher paper (available in economical rolls). Use cookie tins as palettes for rolling inks and paints. Each person should have a rubber *brayer* and a tube of black or brown water-base block printing ink. Liquid tempera, with thin white glue added, may be used as a substitute for the thicker block printing ink.

Stimulation
Appeal to the cultural fondness for magnitude. Hold up one of the large formats. By contrast hold beside it a small watercolor brush. How many would care to paint on such a large format with such a small brush? (Some patient ones might!) Introduce the brayer as a more likely implement (for them) for such an endeavor. Demonstrate the preparation and application of the medium. Squeeze two or three inches of thick ink from the tube onto the palette. Roll the ink out with repeated back and forth motions of the brayer. Sprinkle a few drops of water on the mass of ink. Continue rolling until the inked surface resembles the texture of an orange peel. Load the brayer by rolling it through two or more revolutions and apply the ink or glue-tempera directly to the format. Use the edges of the brayer for linear effects. Add water and ink to the palette frequently. Have them choose between black and brown ink. (Eliminate color as a variable so they can better focus on the use of the tool instead.)

Procedure
Allot sufficient space to each pupil, and distribute the materials. If the children can think of the brayer as a drawing-painting tool, they will be able to use it in reference to any subject matter they choose. As they work, remind them to make modifications in the shapes they draw as necessitated by the peculiarities of the brayer. Again, do not force the tool (as the conveyor of the medium) into a role it cannot perform. Rather, exploit the *capacities* of the brayer. Utilize the wide strokes, the straight edges, and the long thin lines it is capable of making. The children can discover what the brayer permits in the way of marking on paper that brushes and pencils do not. Feel free to distort subject matter in consideration of these marks.

Some children might be more concerned about the limitations of the brayer than elated over its possibilities. Such variant outcomes are to be expected. Do, however, encourage a second attempt at another time. Give them opportunity to test out a variety of material

143

approaches so they will be able to make more effective choices when they select their own media and develop their own problems in the future. The brayers and palettes may be cleaned with water. Hang, do not stack, the wet masterpieces. "Park" the rubber brayers on the protrusions provided rather than with the roller contacting a surface. Clean with water.

The Objective
Familiarity with a variety of art media and processes.

The Situation (No. 8)
Relief casting: "ins" in clay, "outs" in plaster. Become familiar with one of the rudimentary casting processes.

Materials
Have the children bring shallow boxes and lids (about 4" × 7" × 2") and small objects that could be pressed into clay to make a design (nuts, bolts, spools, combs, etc.). Each person should be given about a pound of ceramic-moist clay.

Acquire a 100-pound sack of moulding plaster (inexpensive and delivered by nearly any lumber yard). Obtain a two- or three-quart-capacity flexible rubber or plastic mixing bowl and rubber gloves. Have a pail of water nearby for rinsing, as residue plaster should not be poured down a conventional drain. Do *not* mix the plaster until later because it hardens quickly. Mix the plaster just before pouring time as follows: Fill the mixing bowl halfway with water and *add* an approximate equal volume of plaster to it (until a mound of plaster arises like a volcano). With glove-enshrouded hands mix the plaster into the water until a "milk-shake" consistency is attained. Pour the substance into the box lids to a depth of one-half inch. A two-quart mixture should fill several. The plaster generates heat as it solidifies. Wait one hour, however, before peeling the clay and box lid from the plaster cast. Rinse the plaster after overnight drying.

Cover the working areas with newspapers. Set up a "pouring station" for the completed clay works.

Stimulation
Indicate that they are going to have opportunity to do some "reverse" thinking and designing. How many have ever made a footprint in the mud? Describe its visual properties. What would happen if plaster were poured into the footprint? Would it be "art"? Hardly. But this technique, relief casting, can be adapted for designing. The shapes that are scooped from clay will protrude; the areas of clay that are built up will be indented in the plaster. Distribute all of the materials.

Procedure
Press the moist clay into the box lid until it fills the entire area to a depth of one-half inch. Smooth the surface with the fingers. Make the clay surface three-dimensional by pressing in and pulling out shapes and lines (in awareness of the reverse outcome). Since this design is within a format, remind the children to develop an area of *dominance*. And, to attain some visual *unity,* encourage them to repeat some tool marks elsewhere in the composition. Cluster some of the marks. Roll some of the clay and press it back onto the surface. Allow portions of the original surface to remain untouched, thereby providing an occasional restful interval between heavily textured shapes and areas. The children should turn these designs in several directions as they organize the tool marks and textures. Try combining several tool marks in one area. Press, roll, and twist some of these implements.

Have the completed clay work deposited at the pouring station. Pour six at a time to a depth of one-half inch. Jiggle the boxes up and down to eliminate air bubbles. An hour later peel away the clay, clean and moisten it, and return it to the plastic bag. Examine the visual quality of the relief casts.

The Objective
Familiarity with a variety of art media and processes.

The Situation (No. 9)
Paper construction from construction paper. Use the three-dimensional properties of paper.

144

Materials

Use 12" × 18" gray construction paper (avoid color). Provide everyone with scissors, a ruler, white glue, paper clips (for provision of temporary support while glued joints dry), and a cardboard surface that may serve as a desk covering.

Stimulation

Distribute the construction paper. Ask what it is. What does the term construction imply? Look at the present two-dimensional state of the paper. What could be done to give it three-dimensional status? Elicit several possibilities.

Procedure

Distribute the other materials. Present a three-dimensional design problem. Unlike the cast relief problem, this one is entirely in the round. Have each child develop a *nonobjective* design that possesses several different "sides." Moreover, each side should have a point of interest (*dominance*). There will be no "front" or "back." In that this design is self-supporting and made of only one sheet of paper (which may be cut and reassembled) the following approaches to construction might be reviewed.

For scoring, instead of folding the paper, "draw" a line on it with one open scissors blade, guided by a ruler, with just enough pressure to break the surface fibres of the paper. Fold *away* from this scored line in order to produce a crisp edge. Some children might like to place several of these scored folds close together, on alternate sides of the paper in order to produce an accordion effect. It is also possible, though somewhat more difficult, to produce curved folds by "drawing" a curved line with a scissors blade tip. Several of these placed some distance apart will provide the surface with an additional *bas relief* quality.

Construct cones by cutting half-circle shapes and pulling them downward, tightly against a table edge, in order to weaken the fibres on one side of the paper, which, as a consequence may be easily rolled and glued into a conical form. Cylinders may be fashioned in a similar way by using a basic rectangular shape.

Slotted joints can be used to facilitate the actual construction of the independent forms. Before the shapes are joined, however, they should show some textural variance. Introduce

patterns of light and dark by cutting half circles, "V" shapes, and others that can be pushed in or folded out in areas where they will *enhance* the surface. With all surface treatment or decoration consider moderation: do not destroy the over-all rhythm and structure of the form by unsightly details.

The paper can be rolled, bent, curled, twisted, and joined in a variety of ways. Use all of the original paper. Exploit its potential for self-support and rigidity. Check the free-standing designs from all sides and under different sources of light. Eventually apply these skills to the construction of expressive and symbolic art forms. The medium and skills are only means for composition and expression.

The Objective

Familiarity with a variety of art media and processes.

The Situation (No. 10)

The collective potential of pens, pencils, and people. Experiment with these ordinary media in terms of line, light, and shade. Recognize the distinct contributions of each.

Materials

Everyone will need two sheets of 9" × 12" white drawing paper, an HB pencil, and a pen (ballpoint, fountain, or detachable tip with holder). Ask the children to bring a total of about two dozen medium-size boxes in a variety of shapes and volumes (round, octagonal, square). Have them covered with white tempera or paper. Arrange them at a visible elevation in two clusters, each resembling a "cityscape," at opposite ends of the room. Make sure each cluster has a source of light coming mainly from above and one side.

Stimulation

Introduce the word *chiaroscuro*. Discuss its meaning in reference to the handling of light and dark in drawing and painting. Have the children seat themselves so either one of the illuminated clusters of volumes is visible. Have them squint at the objects and pick out the flow of light and shadow upon and among the individual objects. Have some of them show

145

where the darkest and the lightest areas are located. Where do they see *abrupt* differences between light and dark? (Edges defined by corners where planes meet.) Where do they see a *gradual* change from light to dark? (On rounded surfaces.) Tell them that they will have opportunity to make two drawings based partly upon what they see (the illuminated volumes) and partly upon what they imagine. One drawing will be executed with pencil, and the other, containing similar subject matter, will be executed with pen and ink.

Procedure

Distribute the paper and pencils. The children are to rearrange, on paper, any of the forms in the clusters. Moreover, each form, or combination of forms, can be changed into a building which in turn could be a component of an imaginary city, past, present, or future. You might suggest that they first make an outline sketch of the general arrangement of shapes. Then, in reference to the actual objects, turn the flat shapes into "volumes" by shading with the pencil. Assign areas of light and dark within each shape. Allow the white of the paper to represent the lightest area. Exaggerate the darks. Also try to indicate the diffusion of *cast* shadows. Maintain simplicity. Try to obtain a wide range of values from the pencils.

Put the pencil sketches aside and at a convenient time approach a similar problem with pen and ink. Have the children suggest ways of showing a gradual change in value with this medium. Differences in pressure have little effect. Discuss the possibility of starting with solid areas of ink and fading away by opening up areas with crisscrossing lines that become more widely spaced and eventually culminate in unattached lines against the bare paper. Give the illusion of volume and shadow. Ascertain which medium is better for making lines, shading, and volume. Compare the media and the two drawings.

146

The Objective
Familiarity with a variety of art media and processes.

The Situation

Materials

Stimulation

Procedure

147

One Medium Explored: Watercolor

16

A child who is familiar with the properties and limitations of a variety of art media is more likely to be able to select from them one in particular that best suits his own interests, abilities, and personality.

The investigation of a single medium also gives equilibrium to an art education which otherwise might overemphasize a variety-of-materials approach.

Accordingly, and whenever possible, opportunity should be provided for experimentation with a medium of personal preference.

Through such an approach, art education should enable a child to attain at least a modicum of personal satisfaction with that particular medium.

(The following suggested situations concerning experimentation with watercolors are intended to be mainly exemplary of this objective. Similar probing on a more personal but guided basis could occur in reference to any one of the other media introduced elsewhere.)

The Objective
Frequent experimentation with one particular art medium.

The Situation (No. 1)
Watercolors: see how they run. Become acquainted with the inherent fluidity of the medium.

Materials
Each child should have a large round brush, a set of pan watercolors containing only the primary colors (large cakes), two sheets of 12" × 18" white construction paper, a partly filled nonbreakable water container, and a paintcloth for drying fingers after squeezing brushes. Work on impervious surfaces.

Stimulation
Inquire as to how many children have ever painted on a *wet* surface. Most will be accustomed to working on ordinary dry paper with dry or wet *media*. Give each child one sheet of paper, a clean brush, and water. Indicate that they are about to use watercolors—with particular emphasis on the *water*. Water, in this instance, comes first and color second. Their working surface should be made level. From the containers each may pour a small puddle of water in the center of the *format,* then spread the water, with the clean brushes, over the entire surface of the paper. Encourage the use of swift, light, long strokes.

Procedure

Distribute the paintcloths and watercolor sets. Instruct them to squeeze a few drops of water on each of the three large colored cakes. Check the moistened paper. Add more water if the dampness has subsided. The paper should be thoroughly wet but free of any standing puddles.

Each child should dip a brush into the water, then into one of the colors, and then onto the paper. He should deftly distribute the color in an area somewhat larger than a hand. Then he should squeeze the brush with his fingers *over* the paintcloth and dip into the water again and into the same color. This time have him paint a smaller area somewhere else on the format, squeeze the remaining color from the brush into the cloth, and wipe the brush on the cloth *afterwards* just before changing colors. With the clean brush he can dip into the water again and then into a second color. This color could be used in two or more areas next to the initially established areas. The colors should come close enough so that they mingle as a result of the wet paper, which serves as a carrier. After cleaning his brush and dipping it into the water, he may try a third color, distributing it between the areas already painted. Between dips into the water the excess drops of this third color may be squeezed over some of the still moist areas of the first two colors. Ask the children to notice what happens to the colors when they mix. What happens to the color areas where the edges touch and mingle? Are there still only three colors? What does the wet paper contribute?

Distribute and wet the second sheets of paper. Have the children again apply three colors in areas of varying size, using one color in several areas before switching. While the paper is still moist it should be lifted and held in vertical position. Observe and discuss the results. To what future use might this knowledge be applied? In what way might these results be valuable in themselves?

The Objective

Frequent experimentation with one particular art medium.

The Situation (No. 2)

Water and color: to see through. Recognize the transparent properties of watercolors.

Materials

Supply each child with a watercolor set that contains three large cakes of primary colors; an inexpensive ¾″ flat soft-bristled, long-handled brush, one sheet of 12″ × 18″ white construction paper, a nonbreakable water container, and a paintcloth. For demonstration, have some swatches of colored tissue paper. Store the cleaned brushes with the bristles up.

Stimulation

Against a white background, partly overlap two colors (perhaps blue and yellow) of tissue to produce a third. Ask the group why the two overlapping colors produce green. Introduce the word *transparent*. What other art medium is transparent? Discuss watercolors as a transparent medium. Distribute the sets and brushes. Examine the cakes of paint. Is it possible to see through them? In use then, what causes the transparency? Distribute the water and paper.

Procedure

Discuss the water as a vehicle (carrier) for the color (*pigment*). In addition to carrying the color, water also introduces the quality of transparency. This time the paper will remain dry. As before, however, the color will be wet.

Remind the children that the brush must first contain water so the color may be carried across the paper. Also, if the brush is dipped into water first and the paint cake second, the water in the container will remain clean for subsequent dipping (providing the excess paint is squeezed from the brush onto the paintcloth between immersions). With these bits of procedural advice in mind, introduce the problem.

With the flat brush each child is to distribute several 1″-to-2″-wide curved or straight bands of *one* color in several directions throughout the *format*. After cleaning the brush between colors (by squeezing first and wiping it on the cloth second), he is to repeat the procedure, applying a series of transparent bands composed of a second primary color crossing over *some* of the initial bands. If the second color is sufficiently transparent, some of the first color should show through, producing a third hue. If the third hue does not appear, this is probably an indication that the second color contained

149

too much pigment and not enough water. Watch the children as they work and advise accordingly.

Suggest the sparse use of a third primary color, to be applied in a similar transparent manner. In addition to merely using a medium they are also building a *design*. Perhaps the third color could be placed in strategic areas to lead the eye about the format. This third primary color looks best painted over bands that have not previously been overlapped. Why? It seems that three colors (as exemplified by three overlapping bands) produce a muddy, gray tone. Encourage the children to keep the colors pure and to allow some of the white of the format to show through for "sparkle." Focus especially on the areas where the colors cross over. Strive for transparency in subsequent watercolor paintings.

The Objective
Frequent experimentation with one particular art medium.

The Situation (No. 3)
Water as color and paper as white. In addition to the fluidity and transparency of the medium, recognize the contribution of the white surface of the paper.

Materials
Use the materials described in the immediately preceding situation.

Stimulation
On the basis of their previous experience, ask the group in what way they can obtain black by mixing watercolors. (By combining the three primaries or relying on a black pigment.) In what way can they obtain white since there is no cake of white in the set? What material, aside from the watercolors themselves, is white? Discuss the surface of the paper as a contributor of "white and light" to this artistic process.

Procedure
Develop a system whereby the materials can be efficiently distributed and collected. Present the problem upon their receipt of the materials (or at any moment you consider appropriate).

Review their previous experiences with watercolors. How many have used watercolor to produce thin lines? Why not? Establish the concept of watercolor as a medium which permits a more natural application of area, mass, and shape whether on a wet or a dry surface. During the current problem the group will continue to acknowledge area, mass, and shape but will in addition pay attention to the dry white paper as a device that separates some colors and provides a luster throughout the painting.

Have each child make shapes of single and mixed colors that ultimately occupy about 90 per cent of the format but seldom touch one another. Most are to be separated by varying amounts of white paper. Paint on a *dry* surface. The shapes may be established *directly* by the natural configuration of the brush bristles and direction of stroke. At this time discourage outlining and the subsequent filling in of shapes.

Some of these simple, directly painted shapes should contain mixed colors. If the colors are to be mixed on the paper one has to be brushed over another while the first one is still wet. Colors can also be mixed in the compartments in the box lids. In these compartments colors may be added to a previously deposited puddle of water. With either approach, discourage the addition of a wet color over one that has already dried on the paper.

As the children work, ask them to focus on the white spaces between the colored shapes. Encourage them to build a rhythm of white which appears and reappears throughout. Upon completion (in addition to cleaning the brushes, paint cakes, and pans) ask them to imagine how their paintings would appear if *no* white permeated the format. Some might be interested in an experiment of this kind.

The Objective
Frequent experimentation with one particular art medium.

The Situation (No. 4)
Light and white from water and paper. In addition to recognizing paper as a mediator

between shapes, recognize water as a means of reducing *value* within shapes.

Materials

Introduce pan watercolors that contain primary colors, secondary colors, and black. Each child will need a pencil and some writing paper.

Stimulation

With pencil and paper, each child should draw an outline of a long, narrow rectangle (about 1" × 5"). Within this rectangle he should show the range of *value* (light and dark) permitted by the interaction of the pencil and the light surface of the paper. He can begin at one end with a heavy application of pressure and gradually diminish until the pencil barely touches the paper near the other end. Examine the results. Discuss the range of light and dark in terms of the pencil, the paper, and the control over both. How would one obtain similar results with a different medium, namely, watercolors? Distribute the materials.

Procedure

Ask the children to moisten the cake of black paint with a few drops of water. While the cake is becoming softer, each may fold and tear the white sheet of paper in halves, placing one of the formats lengthwise on his working surface. With a clean brush (always), apply water from the bottom edge upward to slightly less than half of the format. From the dry top edge, downward, begin painting with a brush first dipped in water but containing a fully saturated load of black pigment. The top horizontal inch or so should be as black as the watercolors will permit. Upon completion and as rapidly as possible, squeeze the brush over the paintcloth, dip the brush in water and again into the black, this time with proportionately *less* pigment and *more* water, and apply some deft horizontal strokes that slightly overlap the heavier black above and go below an inch or more. Repeat this process quickly, using more water and less paint as the moist regions of the format are reached. The very bottom inch should be slightly tinted or composed of the original white of the paper. If the child works quickly and slightly overlaps each series of strokes, he should see a *transition,* downward,

from black to several grays to white. In order to avoid "layer cakes," watch the children as they work and help them understand the problem. Upon completion some might benefit from a second experience with a reverse approach; ascend from the white paper and use less water and more pigment. Remind the children to squeeze the brush onto the paintcloth *before* dipping it into the water just prior to each addition of pigment. Keep the water clean.

Focus on one of the dry sheets. Remove the curl if there is any. Of what might this dark to light space remind them? Many will read it as a sky. Encourage the children to populate the space with appropriate subject matter in different values of black. Have at least three values represented in the objects. Discuss *contrast* as a visual necessity. If puddles occur within the superimposed subject matter shapes, instruct the children to dry the brushes and touch the puddled area lightly, directing the water upward into the dry bristles. Remind them to control values by changing the proportionate amount of water and pigment.

The Objective

Frequent experimentation with one particular art medium.

The Situation (No. 5)

Watercolors with many values and few strokes. Use the medium as economically as possible in direct response to subject matter (trees in foliage).

Materials

Obtain an inexpensive 18" × 24" sheet of Upson board (from any lumberyard) for each pupil. This will serve as a drawing board for outside sketching and painting. Attach 12" × 18" white construction paper (or 11" × 16" inexpensive textured watercolor paper) with thumbtacks or four short strips of masking tape. Have the children bring jars with lids and a heavy paper bag in which these, the watercolor sets, paintcloths, and brushes may be carried. Choose a sunny day and an outdoor area that has a variety of trees in foliage.

151

Stimulation

The opportunity to learn while outdoors is stimulating for most children. The problem is also challenging. You might prefer to describe it before going out in search of possible solutions.

Procedure

Ask the group to name a game in which a *low* score is desirable. Introduce the concept of economy. Each child will have a chance to choose one tree as his own to interpret through watercolor. In making this visual interpretation he is to try to show the general shape and growth pattern of the tree; an elm should be discerned as an elm, an oak as an oak, a fan palm as a fan palm, and so on. Within this readily discerned shape he should try to include from three to five values of each color involved. He need not concern himself with any other area or object around the tree. Before picking up a brush he should spend a few minutes in *looking* at the tree, examining the skeletal growth, beginning with the trunk as it emerges from the ground on up through the smallest twigs. Observe the changes in *dimension* and *value*. Examine the foliage by squinting at it. Where is it most dense (almost *opaque*)? Before painting, the child should pick out clumps or clusters of light, middle, and dark *values* within the foliage. All of these observations are to culminate in a watercolor painting that has no more than twenty-five or thirty individual brushstrokes. The brushstrokes should be discernable; they should not "melt" into trees that resemble sucker shapes.

When the children are situated outdoors, briefly review the problem. They may work from light values to dark values or vice versa (as long as the brush is squeezed dry each time before it is dipped in the persistently clean water). Most will benefit from an outline drawing in a light-blue tint, made with the corner of the brush. Also, most might find it easier to paint the foliage first and let the trunk and branches "grow" into it. Otherwise, if they first establish a series of dark branches, the transparent greens will not hide their presence. They should paint the foliage from the inside of the tree outward, as the branches actually grow. Encourage acute observation of value contrasts and an economical use of the medium.

The Objective

Frequent experimentation with one particular art medium.

The Situation (No. 6)

Shapes first, lines last. Emphasize the natural inclination of watercolor toward mass and shape with little reliance on linear definition while painting human figures.

Materials

Provide everyone with the watercolor equipment (listed in No. 4) and 12" × 18" white construction paper. In addition to the large flat brush, each pupil will need a small round one. Have some of the pupils bring costumes that can be worn during three brief poses.

Stimulation

Each child will have a chance to utilize watercolors for the interpretation of limbs and growth somewhat different from that associated with trees (previous situation). Clear a sturdy table upon which the models may stand. Use at least three models in varying costumes and poses. Ask the children to look at the models, examine the action of the pose and the effect of light and dark on their clothing, and paint something about them *after* the pose has been completed. After all, the unpaid models should not be deprived of the opportunity to paint.

Observe the models as suggested. Ask the children to find several shades of one *hue* in an area of a skirt or shirt. Seek the action that underlies the clothing. As the children observe, they should think in terms of watercolor. How can such a fluid medium be adapted to interpret a human form? Remind them that with the flat brush, on dry paper, watercolor is best used to show *shapes*. These shapes will "bend." The fluid quality of watercolor lends itself to the portrayal of action if the shapes are not restricted first by an outline drawing.

Procedure

Have the materials ready for use immediately after the observation session. Invite the children to paint a full-length figure, from memory, based upon any one of the poses and costumes

152

they found interesting. As with the tree paintings encourage them to make a terse visual statement, limiting the total number of strokes but including more than one value within each color area. The cowboy's blue dungarees may consist of three different blues. Avoid any preliminary drawing. The shapes need not follow the exact contours of arms, legs, and heads. Instead, encourage the children to indicate merely the presence and action of these parts with flat brushstrokes of appropriate color value. (Upon completion, you might indicate, they can add lines that define edges, features, and details with the point of the small brush dipped in a darker color.) If they remember a bent leg or an arched back from the pose ask them to bend these parts even more with quick strokes of the flat brush. Make the figures as relaxed and fluid as the watercolors. Avoid stiff, cut-paper poses.

For the present do not include any background details around the figure. Focus mainly on the inherent properties of watercolor in relation to the human form. When the shapes which denote the action and general color values of the figure have dried, the children may proceed with linear details. Very often a line that denotes an edge of a shape, for example, a leg, will come *inside* the area of color which may freely "spill" beyond it. Lines should not be restricted outlines that merely echo the color shapes; though subordinate to color and shape, they too should be free. Try painting other shapes in future subjects accordingly.

The Objective
Frequent experimentation with one particular art medium.

The Situation (No. 7)
A *highlight watercolor sketch*. Utilize the white of the paper in achieving a luminous quality. Refer to an actual outdoor scene.

Materials
Attach 12" × 18" white construction paper to the Upson boards and carry the usual watercolor equipment (including a water jar with a lid) in individual heavy paper bags. In addition provide each person with a white wax crayon. Develop this activity, outdoors, on a sunny day.

Stimulation
Draw some thick and thin lines with the white crayon on a sheet of white paper. Dip a flat brush in water and then onto one of the premoistened cakes of dark watercolor (the usual procedure). Brush the transparent color across the heavy white wax lines. Demonstrate the *resisting* properties of the wax. Indicate that the white crayon enables one to preserve some of the original white of the paper. (Rubber cement would also suffice but it is difficult to control.)

Invite the children to hold their hands in a position whereby the light strikes them from one side. Notice that the light illuminates several edges nearest the source. Think now in terms of watercolor and white paper. Since there is no white pigment in the watercolor sets, remind them that highlights, such as those just observed, must be indicated by preserving white lines and shapes from the original surface of the paper itself. By first drawing all observed highlights with crayon much of this original white will be reserved for future highlights which will not be destroyed by the application of watercolors. Mature artists can control these white spaces and allow for the "behavior" of the medium. By reserving white in advance with wax, the children might at least develop the habit of allowing the white to show through where it should. (In atmospheric landscapes this is less essential.)

Procedure
Select an outdoor setting that contains manmade forms, nature forms, or both. Ask the children to look only at the areas that are illuminated by the sun. Try to focus upon the rhythms produced by these light areas. Record those that are visible, on the basis of personal perception, with a heavy application of white crayon. Hold the paper horizontally, near eye level, to check the thickness of the application. Devote most of the time to this particular observation and application of crayon. Those children who have time may apply the watercolors with quick simple strokes to the shapes representing the *objects* initially highlighted with crayon. As they work, ask them to squint

153

at the objects in the scene and then at their own paintings, looking for a correspondence of "sparkle," light, and dark. Do not be concerned about perspective or proportion among the objects depicted.

Those children who do not have time for an outdoor application of watercolor may finish at another time indoors. Limit the time for the watercolor phase of the problem. Dwell mainly on the preservation of highlights. Encourage some children to dispense with the crayon on subsequent tries. Notice how mature artists such as Homer, Cézanne, Marin, Wyeth, Kingman, and others incorporate the white of the paper in their watercolor paintings.

The Objective
Frequent experimentation with one particular art medium.

The Situation (No. 8)
Watercolors as atmosphere. Extend outdoor subject matter beyond the usual sunny day approach by using watercolors to depict a variety of weather conditions.

Materials
Introduce everyone to a *textured* watercolor paper. Order 16" × 22" half sheets of student-grade paper, and reduce these to 11" ×16". Even though the painting will be done indoors, it would be helpful to attach these sheets, which tend to curl, to the previously ordered 18" × 24" Upson boards. Use thumbtacks or masking tape. Use pan watercolor sets that contain seven or eight colors. There will be need for the 3/4" flat brushes and the small round ones that come to a point when wet. The usual water containers and paintcloths may be retained.

Stimulation
Develop this situation on a rainy day. Ask the children which art medium they would choose to paint an outdoor scene that was immersed in rain or fog. Cut paper? Why not? Watercolors? Why? Inquire as to how many have ever painted an outdoor scene which depicted such weather. Indicate that they will have an opportunity to do just that.

Procedure
Distribute the materials and attach the textured watercolor paper to the boards. Focus on the rough texture of this paper as compared to the smooth surface of construction paper.

Since they are going to try to depict the visual qualities of rain and fog on paper, which approach, wet on wet or wet on dry, would be more effective? On the basis of their assumed correct response suggest the following procedure.

Ask them to invent a landscape that has three "grounds," *back, middle,* and *fore.* Soak the paper thoroughly by pouring a puddle and distributing it over the entire format with a large clean brush. The upper area of the format might be more heavily moistened than the remainder. While the paper is in a very wet state, have the children record the sky (by mixing and mingling colors and values appropriate to it and them) and those objects that would appear in the *background.* Though the paper is wet, they should still dip the brush in water and use little pigment because the distant objects are obscured during rainy and foggy weather. If the shapes turn into "caterpillars," the children should wait until the upper area is less moist.

As the format becomes *damp,* encourage them to populate the *middleground* of the landscape. What objects might they find midway between themselves and the distance? Represent these by slightly increasing the pigment content in the brush. These objects will appear somewhat brighter and darker though still soft edged and subdued.

When the format is almost *dry,* instruct the children to establish the larger, more vivid objects located in the *foreground.* Many of these objects will overlap the previously established landscape. *Less* water and *more* pigment in the brush should permit this coverage. Lines and small details may be superimposed last of all with the small pointed brush. The work should be done quickly and in accord with the drying time of the paper. Do not add water or go back over objects when they have dried. Check the results from a distance. Strive for depth as well as control of values. Why would a reverse of the above procedure be difficult?

The Objective

Frequent experimentation with one particular art medium.

The Situation (No. 9)

Watercolor and manmade objects. Reconcile the frequent rigidity and solidity of manmade objects, as subject matter, with the transparency and fluidity of watercolor.

Materials

Use the materials recommended in the immediately preceding situation. Cut the 16" × 22" sheets of textured watercolor paper in half.

Stimulation

Review some of the previous watercolor explorations. Discuss some of the problems experienced. Underline the importance of reacting to subject matter in *terms of the medium* as well as the children's own interest. Not all media are as appropriate as others for certain subjects. At times, however, it is somewhat of a challenge to adapt a seemingly inappropriate medium to specific subject matter. Watercolors, as learned, tend to be transparent and fluid. They are not easily contained. By contrast, manmade forms, buildings, automobiles, signs, and telephone poles are solid and compact. Ask the children to think of other manmade forms that might be of interest to them as subject matter in any kind of painting, regardless of the medium. The problem will be that of adapting these subjects to the medium. The medium will be predominant, the subject matter subordinate.

Procedure

Distribute the materials. Notice once again the coarse texture of the paper. How might it be best utilized by a wet-on-wet or a wet-on-dry method of application? Indicate that flooded watercolors might fill in all the white spaces of the textured surface whereas a wet-on-dry application would allow glints of white to show through the paint. Encourage the latter approach.

Any manmade objects may be used as subject matter. A few preliminary lines might be helpful. These may be established by using water, tinted lightly with blue, and painted with the tip of the small brush. Avoid pencils. The lines should be approximate, not restric-

tive. Each child should think about what is most important in the picture and place these objects in a position of *dominance*. Also consider *contrast* of size, *color,* and *value* as a means of attaining dominance.

The medium is paramount. Most children will probably work best by first establishing the lighter values. It is conceivable that dark values could overlap these lighter values, when dry, whereas it would be impossible, with watercolors, to go over a dark color with a light one. When possible, areas that are to contain future light-colored shapes, such as an automobile in front of a dark building, should be left white.

Vary the values within the same objects. A red building might possess a light red with yellow added on the sunny side and a darker red with some purple added on the shady side. If a green building is next to the shady side a thin wash of light green could be placed over the darker red (when the red is dry) to reflect that hue into the other building. Encourage repetition and mixture of watercolors. Keep them transparent. Allow white edges (with or without crayon use) to show as highlights. Do not worry about a few runs. Add lines and internal details last.

The Objective

Frequent experimentation with one particular art medium.

The Situation (No. 10)

Watercolor and nature forms. Develop an imaginary but recognizable landscape painting in consideration of the attributes of watercolor and visual unity.

Materials

Use the materials recommended in the two preceding situations.

Stimulation

Ask the group to imagine an outdoor scene. Exclude all manmade objects. Ask the children to describe what they "see" in an "order of transparency." What, within the image, for example, is *most transparent?* (In most instances the sky.) What might be next in a scale of transparency? (Possibly water and various

155

kinds of foliage.) Where in nature, in their images in particular, do we find objects that are *opaque*? (Hills, rock formations, tree trunks, etc.)

Now, how can these varieties of transparency be reconciled with the transparency exemplified by the medium, watercolor? (Reemphasize the role of the medium as the *foremost* reality in painting. A painting is composed of *symbols* for a landscape through the medium; *actual* sky, wood, and rocks are not present.)

Procedure

On the basis of their previous experiences, discuss possible solutions to the above problem. One has to think of watercolor first and sky second. Watercolor is the actuality; sky is the point of departure. Many children would probably do well to paint the sky first, because in terms of transparency it is most consistent with the medium. Moreover, it ordinarily occupies a large area of the format. Discourage compositions that are exactly half sky and half land.

Objects that are of middle transparency might be next in order of placement. Momentarily suspend discussion and distribute the materials. Have the children transfer their images of landscapes to new percepts on paper with a few thin, light blue lines. For the present ask them to paint in the areas and shapes that are of middle transparency. Many of these areas and shapes will have middle and perhaps even dark values. (Darker colors can be applied *thinly* and still retain transparency.) They will, however, have open spaces (reflections in water, spaces within foliage) which allow much of the white paper or the color they overlap to show through.

Check the work as of the moment. Review the discussion about objects that are by nature opaque. How many were able to allow some glints of white to show through in areas of thin and middle transparency? Try to preserve this quality in the nearly opaque areas as well. Show that more of the white grain within the texture will be preserved if brushes (either flat or round) are held with the handle almost level with the paper, the bristles resting mainly on their sides. Control the ratio of pigment to water when loading the brush. The problem is that of making convincing solid shapes yet maintaining *unity* through the medium with subject matter that is *different* in degrees of transparency. If a choice is involved a "thin, watery" rock is *artistically* preferable to one that appears heavy enough to sink into the page. Look for exceptions to all of the preceding suggestions concerning the use of watercolors. Experiment beyond the suggestions.

156

The Objective
Frequent experimentation with one particular art medium.

The Situation

Materials

Stimulation

Procedure

157

Expression of Ideas and Feelings through Art

17

The expression of ideas and feelings is embodied in the *content* of a work of art.

A child can learn to express himself artistically through visual ordering and by using art media.

Content, composition, and media all can be effectively combined. In arriving at this synthesis an art experience becomes satisfactory if it succeeds as a visual rather than a verbal expression.

Much of our education is devoted to the latter.

The visual process provides each person with another way of examining and expressing his present ideas, attitudes, and feelings.

The Objective

Expression through art of ideas, attitudes, and feelings.

The Situation (No. 1)

Changing lines, changing feelings. Depict subject matter in different ways, using the same number of lines each time.

Materials

Provide each person with seven white pipe cleaners and a 9″ × 12″ or 12″ × 18″ sheet of black construction paper. Have a long-arm stapler available.

Stimulation

Review any previous experience that relates lines to feelings. Draw a variety of *nonobjective*

lines on the board. Remind the children that although these lines have no relationship to *subject matter,* they can still express feelings. Pupils will now have opportunity to express feelings, as possibly echoed by these lines, in relation to a specific subject. Instead of using chalk, they will use movable lines—pipe cleaners. Demonstrate the versatility and flexibility of a pipe cleaner as a line. Distribute the materials. Use the black paper as a *format* or *background.* Instruct each child to "draw" a face by bending and subsequently placing the pipe-cleaner lines on the format.

Procedure

Examine these "faces" for their possible expressive features. Some might, of course, be expressionless. After studying the possible expressive properties, ask each child to "erase" parts of the "face" by removing some of the "lines." He may then refashion and replace each line in an effort to modify the original expression. Provide sufficient time for repeated modification of and experimentation with different facial expressions. Maintain the limitation of line (seven pipe cleaners). Indicate that many artists, especially those who live in Japan, use the most economical means possible in expressing their ideas and feelings.

At another time or immediately following the preceding experiment, provide each child with two formats and two sets of pipe cleaners. He is to choose a "living" subject such as an insect or a flower. On one format he could arrange the lines to depict, for example, a delicate flower. On the other format, using an identical number of lines, he could depict a flower quite different in character, perhaps a man-eating plant. A similar approach could be employed with insects, based upon actuality or an extended imagination.

If they like, the children may staple into a permanent position some of the designs with which they are satisfied. Develop an exhibition that demonstrates the expressive potentials of something as simple as a line, even with the complete absence of color. Some children might be interested in employing this flexible medium in *nonobjective* designs similar to those encountered in the stimulation. The chief advantage of pipe cleaners, in this instance, is that they enable you to demonstrate how a predetermined number of originally identical lines can be modified to connote an endless number of expressions. Use pipe cleaners in other problems of a related nature.

The Objective

Expression through art of ideas, attitudes, and feelings.

The Situation (No. 2)

Using common senses. Respond to various stimuli through the sense of smell, touch, or sound. Give "visual expression" to these responses with a medium of personal choice. (This problem may be developed in one or three situations.)

Materials

Establish an easily accessible supply table which contains tempera, watercolors, colored paper, a variety of formats, and the necessary brushes, tools, adherents, and containers for these various media. Prior to this experience have the children bring some paper grocery bags and a variety of small things that have either unique aromas or textures or both (various foods and objects). Tape record some noises, or have a means of contriving sounds which are familiar yet out of context (a bird, a falling object, a siren, a door slamming, a squeak, etc.).

Stimulation

About what do poets write? About what do musicians compose? About what do painters paint? List some stimuli. Further, do poets and musicians respond only to what they hear? Do painters respond only to what they see? Why or why not? Poetry and music are concerned mainly with sound (Chapter Five). Painting is a *visual* art form. Is it possible for painters and other artists to respond effectively through several senses (their eyes, ears, and noses) rather than the one which relates closely to their kind of art? Tell the children that they are about to respond to a variety of things through the senses of smell, touch, and sound but *not* sight. With an art medium of their choice they are to try to paint (or paste) and show in a *visual* way their *reactions* to what they encounter through any *one* of the senses employed. There will be no attempt to draw the appearance of the object to which they are responding. React to and visualize the *feeling* associated with *one* of the following:

To smell: Pass around (or have the children pass by) a bag that contains an object of aromatic significance (lilacs, an old catcher's mitt), which can be sniffed but not seen. No peeking or touching allowed. Encourage them to close their eyes and lips and try to form an image of what the aroma might help conjure.

To touch: Have several textural objects and surfaces in paper bags with openings just large enough to permit entry of the hand. Each person should reach inside, touch, and respond accordingly.

To hear: Ask the children to remain at their seats and close their eyes. Remind them that their problem is that of visualizing something

159

they cannot see. Introduce the recorded or contrived sounds. Again ask them to respond with images.

Discuss some of the associations derived from these various sensory stimuli. How many children were able to think beyond the objects, and imagine events as a result of the sensory contact? For example, did a pile of sawdust elicit an image of a pile of sawdust or did it lead to the image of a carpenter, a stable, or a circus? Discourage "literal" portrayals.

Procedure

Each child, after choosing a medium, may proceed with the visualization of *one* of these nonvisual experiences. Perhaps you might prefer to develop three situations from one sensory exposure at a time.

The Objective

Expression through art of ideas, attitudes, and feelings.

The Situation (No. 3)

The simultaneous expression of opposites. Within the confines of one *format,* give visual expression to feelings or ideas that are opposite in character.

Materials

Either hold the medium constant or establish a supply table with a variety of materials. Colored chalk, used on 18" × 24" oatmeal paper, is a medium which many could use in a reasonably effective way. Some excellent thin sheets of fadeproof colored paper are also available for those who would prefer to cut, tear, and adhere. If chalk is used, spray the completed work according to instructions stated on the pressurized *fixative* containers.

Stimulation

Tell the children that for many centuries artists have expressed in their sculpture and painting a concern for things that are opposite to one another. In the sixteenth century the Italian Michelangelo sculptured two figures, "Day" and "Night," which adorn the same tomb. Each is different in character from the other. An American painter, Adolph Gottlieb, has included lines and shapes that are quite opposite one another in visual character within the same *nonobjective* painting. Very often the upper part of the format contains rounded shapes while the lower part contains a frenzy of lines and color. Somehow he made the two differences compatible. Ask your group to list opposites of interest to them that might serve as a point of departure for a different kind of picture or painting. Such opposites as happy–sad, hot–cold, quiet–noisy, friendly–angry, war–peace, and healthy–ill might be listed.

Procedure

The "opposites" may be expressed in the form of a picture, which shows *symbols* for actual objects, or a *nonobjective composition,* which shows *shape, line, color,* and *texture* instead.

Discuss (or review) the role of color, devoid of shape or subject matter, as an expressive force. Which color, for example, is likely to connote "war" and which, by contrast, "peace"? You might encourage a child who relies on subject matter to use an unusual color that might express the feeling he would like to communicate. Encourage exaggeration. Actually hold sheets of contrasting colors side by side for purposes of assessment. Demonstrate how the expressive properties of some colors change according to the influence of the neighboring colors. Pink, for example, might look warm next to a blue sheet and suddenly appear cool when viewed next to a red-orange sheet. One cannot neatly assign "cool" and "warm" to colors without considering their neighbors. Also review the influence of kinds and positions of lines as another visually expressive force.

Because color is such a predominant expressive element the fadeproof sheets of intense color would be appropriate. As much as possible, however, permit a choice of medium commensurate with individual abilities and prior experiences. Ask the children to find other opposite objects, ideas, or events that are compatible. Relate the principles of *contrast* and *unity* to this experience.

160

The Objective

Expression through art of ideas, attitudes, and feelings.

The Situation (No. 4)

A change of view; a change in expression. Through *two* situations investigate the change in expressive quality (*content*) that is likely to occur by showing different views of related *subject matter*. Change the "what" rather than the "how."

Materials

Tempera would probably be the most versatile medium. Develop a system whereby supplies for tempera painting can be easily distributed and collected. Each person should have a plastic egg crate for containing and mixing the three primary colors plus black and white, with some reservoirs of water. Provide large and small brushes, paintcloths, and 18" × 24" sheets of white construction or heavy gray bogus paper.

Stimulation

Ask the group to think of an object that is big enough to contain themselves either upon it or in it. List their responses, which might include a playground swing, an automobile, a housetop, a hilltop, a mountain, a skyscraper, or an orbiting space capsule. Ask them to think about the object or place in terms of tempera paint. Ask what significant visual features are present. Their task is that of painting a "portrait" of the automobile, hill, or building of their choice.

Procedure

Distribute the supplies. Remind those children who have not painted for some time that they may make, if they prefer, a preliminary sketch on the large format with blue-tinted water and a brush. Some might prefer to paint directly without any preliminary line drawing. Also remind them of the *opaque* properties of this medium. Proceed accordingly. Save the completed paintings as a departure for the next situation, to be developed at another convenient time as follows:

Have the children examine their completed object or place portraits. Ask them, through the imagination, to stand upon (the hilltop) or go inside what they have painted (the automobile or building). What might they see from such a position? Discuss the possible subject matter that could ensue from these variant vistas. Develop a list of some object–view relationships.

Ask the children in what ways the *expressive* qualities of the views, as seen from the original places or objects, might differ from those qualities evident in the objects themselves. For example, a view from a forlorn, weatherbeaten building might include a vast, pleasant seascape or an entangled, colorful junkyard that seems to burst with energy. Let the object depicted in the first painting serve as a stimulus for the imaginary subject of a second picture.

In art, one frequently encounters the statement, "it is not *what* you paint that is so important, but *how* you paint it." The emphasis in this situation is in opposition to that statement. At times *what* a person paints can change the meaning and quality of an expression. An emphasis on the *what* might also lead him away from trite, borrowed subject matter. Look for departures from habits and stereotypes.

The Objective

Expression through art of ideas, attitudes, and feelings.

The Situation (No. 5)

A miniature stage design. Become acquainted with a three-dimensional mode of visual expression.

Materials

Ask each person to bring a cardboard box about 10" × 16" × 8". Provide a variety of fadeproof papers and construction papers in sizes from small scraps on up to 18" × 24". You will also need posterboard, cardboard, cardboard tubing, and tempera. Provide paper clips (for temporary holding only), white glue, thread (for suspending objects), pointed scissors, and an occasional stapler (with abundant ammunition). Pipe cleaners may be used as armatures upon which colors can be "draped" to indicate the presence of people. The main emphasis, however, will be on the *stage* design, not costumes. Read or play a recording

161

of a dramatic episode of general interest to your group.

Stimulation

Inquire as to how many have seen a stage production. Discuss the *visual* aspects of such a production. Arrive, through this discussion, at the problem of creating a proper mood for the verbal presentation by means of expressive visual properties. Read or play the recording. Ask the children to listen with their eyes closed. In this way they can form images and design scenery as the words and sounds issue forth. Keep the image-design private. It may be revealed in due time through the miniature stage sets.

Procedure

Determine how many children would prefer to design a miniature stage set for an episode other than the one they all heard. Some might prefer to design a set for a production of their own origin. Others might design a stage set and get an idea from it for a play. Encourage diversity of approach. Moreover, some might work in groups of two or three on one design.

Distribute the boxes. The top and one *side* should be removed. First the large areas should be considered—the two ends, the back, and the floor. These may be covered with colors of paper that are appropriate to the mood or *content* expressed by the episode. If the large color areas are to be treated with various values, textures, or streaking of any kind, these modifications should be made *before* large pieces are glued over the raw cardboard. The remaining standing objects can be cut from cardboard, in simple flat shapes, and enhanced by the appropriate medium.

Focus on the overhead areas of the stage. Strings or threads may be stretched across the top opening. From these, other shapes such as tree foliage or stalactites could be suspended. Although this set is but a model for a stage design, remind the children of the need to exaggerate the intensity of colors and thickness of line so each would be highly visible even to those in the back rows of the theatre. A stage design is but one more expressive art form. Many painters, among them Picasso, Berman, and Dali, have designed stage scenery. Let the imagination become evident in what is to an extent a three-dimensional fantasy-picture.

The Objective

Expression through art of ideas, attitudes, and feelings.

The Situation (No. 6)

An important personal event. Develop for a "personal calendar" a visual page that depicts a day of special significance.

Materials

Remind the group of the possibility of using mixed media as possible means of expression. Or, in concert with your group, decide upon a common medium such as pastels or crayon that would be adequate for all. Use (and modify) 12" × 18" or 18" × 24" formats of heavy white or oatmeal paper.

Stimulation

What do illustrations on calendars usually depict? List some of the frequent seasonal and scenic themes that seem to persist. Ask the children what day or event, aside from their own birthdays or national holidays, is of special *personal* significance. Ask them to reflect on the possibility. If you like, list some of their answers. For some it might be the first day (or the last) of each school year. Others might enjoy special family gatherings or secret meetings with a gang of friends. Some preferences might be more general. Some painters, for example, have visualized such themes as "A Summer Night" or "March Wind." The advent of a season might also be a more general yet recurring event to which some might look forward.

Procedure

Before distributing materials, discuss the meaning of the term *symbol*. What "visual marks" could the children make that would stand for and somehow communicate to others the date or event of significance? Isolate the theme "Summer Night" as a point for discussion. Elicit some ideas for expressing this event. Some of these might evolve from different scenes based upon experiences in actual places —a view from the roof of a tall building, or a moonlit lake as viewed from a summer camp. Discuss less "scenic" ways of visualizing the event. What entities might be associated with it? A perusal might indicate the presence of a

162

moon, a drop of moisture on a blade of grass, a lawn chair, a moth, or a firefly. What colors might they think of? Some might respond in terms of dark cool swatches. You might suggest that individual shapes could be placed amid appropriate colors in order to form an arrangement or *design* rather than a picture that shows things in a logical relationship. Encourage fantasy.

After determining what event or date is of personal importance some might do well to make a list of things that could be portrayed visually in terms of shape, line, and color. Encourage those who are inclined to work more spontaneously to pick up their materials and get the feeling or idea on paper before it "gets away." It is also conceivable that many might record an event with streaks of color (a cold March wind) free of any objects. Allow for a latitude of visual expression.

This experience also allows for introspection. A corresponding activity usually occurs through theme writing at a verbal level. Give the children the opportunity to visualize as well. Exhibit the results in a "group calendar" of personal events and preferences. Such a calendar could be highly imaginative by contrast to the usual visual diet.

The Objective

Expression through art of ideas, attitudes, and feelings.

The Situation (No. 7)

A visual vocabulary book. Develops a visual vocabulary which consists of a variety of representational subject matter.

Materials

Provide everyone with several sheets of 9" × 12" white drawing paper and a 2B or 4B drawing pencil. Some may prefer to reduce these sheets by half. Have a stapler available for general use.

Stimulation

What is a vocabulary? How many thousand words does a person have in his own reading, speaking, and writing vocabularies? How many know at least three hundred French or Spanish words? Introduce the concept of a *visual vocabulary*—the ability to make a reasonably representational drawing of something. Have each child make a list of objects he has had frequent occasion to draw in the past few years. He might underline those with which he is usually satisfied. Also, he should list the subjects with which he is most *dis*satisfied. On a separate page he should list subject matter that he would like to learn to draw if he could (and many can learn).

Procedure

Each child will have an opportunity to start a visual vocabulary book, one which will not have a specific ending but will continue to develop as long as he is interested. After the children have examined their three lists, distribute the materials and have them start the book by drawing three objects with which they are satisfied and three (or more) with which they are displeased. They may mark each page accordingly. Do not offer any advice at this time. Allow these drawings to serve as assessments of their current through limited visual vocabularies. Staple the pages together, collect them, and keep them for future reference. Ask the children to check three or more objects from their "would like to learn" lists. Suggest that they investigate these objects in actuality (or through good facsimiles) before the next art learning situation. Meanwhile develop or add to your own visual file on the basis of these interests.

At another time distribute the same drawing materials and encourage the children to add to their visual vocabularies. Some children may prefer to draw from actual objects within the room. Provide reference materials for others. Add these pages to those previously contained in their books. From time to time redistribute the books and examine the contents. Have the children select subjects they think can be improved upon in a second or third drawing. Encourage observation. Children who possess normal physical and mental capacities can probably learn to draw in a representational manner. This is not to say that their work will be highly interpretive or artistic but it can become more coherent, at least to them. Devote time to the acquisition of this kind of vocabulary as well as to the more usual pursuit of a verbal one. Pass the book on, with fre-

163

quent editing en route, from grade to grade as a cumulative record of visual learning.

The Objective

Expression through art of ideas, attitudes, and feelings.

The Situation (No. 8)

A great idea or a historic event visualized. Develop a symbolic visualization of a significant but more remote event.

Materials

Use the thin colored tonal or fadeproof papers, a heavier construction paper for a mounting surface, rubber cement, scissors, and any linear medium for additional details and lettering. Limit the medium in this instance to permit a more intense focus on the historic idea or event. Collect problem-related examples from magazines (such as Container Corporation of American advertisements).

Stimulation

On the basis of their prior experience, discuss with your group some events of historic significance. Ask them to think of visual properties that could be brought together to "symbolize" rather than to merely "make a picture" of a particular event. For example, Leif Ericsson's discovery might include such visual entities as striped sails (not necessarily attached to ships), viking helmets, rhythms of waves, indications of a land mass, a shield and spear, and numerous other motifs related to the event. Such symbols could be arranged on a *format* in defiance of gravity, actual location, and proportion. The general visual "flavor" could be that of discovery by a unique group (the Vikings), but there will be no picture-making process.

Some children might appreciate another approach. Read aloud some familiar quotations. In what way could these be visualized without drawing a scene? Some children might prefer to incorporate lettering of the quotation into their visualization. If so, how would their usual way of lettering have to be modified to capture the flavor of the quotation? Would the letters be long, thin, slanted, thick, or bulbous?

(On the board letter the word "fast" in the usual lower-case manuscript style and contrast that with lettering composed of severely slanted capitals to demonstrate how the style of lettering can add feeling.) Display some of the examples of great ideas symbolized. Some children might use only modified letters amid appropriate shapes or areas of color to get their feeling about the quotation across. Once again, encourage diversity.

Procedure

Let each child pick up his own materials when he decides what idea to use. Help him in distilling the essence of the idea (as exemplified by a quotation) or the historical event. He might first choose an appropriate color. From the sheet of color he might then cut one of the more significant shapes. This shape could serve as a nucleus for others that might be less important.

As the children work, review some of the aspects of nonverbal communication (Chapter Four). Try to exhibit each of the completed visualizations. Upon completion have each person letter the name of his chosen event on a small card. Redistribute these cards at random and ask the children to unite the card with the appropriate symbolization. Also look for the *dominant* visual feature in each. Look for a synthesis of *content* and *composition,* in other words, getting the "flavor" of the idea across in an artistic way.

The Objective

Expression through art of ideas, attitudes, and feelings.

The Situation (No. 9)

A three-dimensional symbol for a world fair. During several sessions develop a model for a symbol that relates to a theme and also meets a utilitarian need.

Materials

Use thin cardboard, construction paper, and sheet balsa wood. Provide sloyd knives, scissors, a cardboard cover for cutting on desk tops, white glue, thin colored paper (assorted),

164

pins, and paper clips. Also reserve shelf space for storage of unfinished work.

Stimulation

Discuss the concept of a world fair. Review some of the more recent international expositions. Invite the children to assume that the next one will be held near their own locale. Review some of the *symbols* around which some of the previous fairs were organized (sphere and pylon, space needle, unisphere). Of what purpose are such symbols? List some possibilities. Ask for suggestions of themes that might provide an organizing basis for the local fair. Ask each person to think of a theme and, accordingly, design a three-dimensional model of a symbol that could be seen from any part of the fair ground. For those who would rather abide by an established theme offer them one; "world peace" might be interesting. Acquaint them with the available materials. (Review the safety procedures concerning the use of sharp tools.)

Procedure

Some children might be able to work in consideration of a scale of approximately one inch equals ten feet. (This need not be mandatory.) Some might also prefer to draw some preliminary plans. If so, remind them of the two-dimensional limitation of such an approach. Encourage them to draw elevations of each "side" if differences are likely to occur in that way. Two views might suffice for some. Others will prefer to execute their ideas directly with the intended materials. Encourage both approaches.

For those who grasp the problem and seem able to go beyond it, introduce an additional condition. This symbol could have a function other than its thematic communication in that it could be a highly visible sign post indicating the location of exhibitions from different nations. Since it is already to be visible from any place in the area it could also point the way to these other important features. Existing symbols such as flags from actual nations could be incorporated with the larger original symbol. However, if the theme "world peace" is elected as something to symbolize, you might encourage the children to think of something other than the ordinary bird-and-twig

approach, or at least use the bird in an imaginative way.

As a follow-up problem, with the same media or with clay, some children might design a three-dimensional symbol that somehow summarizes the unique attributes of their actual community. It is possible that some children will be able to express their ideas more effectively through these three-dimensional approaches than by flat symbolization. Determine which pupils seem to benefit from such an experience. Try to develop a display area, such as a well-lighted and appropriately covered table, that will provide an adequate setting for the array of symbols.

The Objective

Expression through art of ideas, attitudes, and feelings.

The Situation (No. 10)

A visual message to another country. Develop a drawing or painting exemplary of a regional aspect of our culture.

Materials

Use conte crayons or 2B pencils on heavy white drawing paper or tempera on white construction or gray bogus paper. Provide *fixative* for the completed drawings and the necessary equipment for tempera painting.

Stimulation

Pose a question: If a visitor from another country were to be guided by you through this locale, what would you be sure he saw? Which sites or events are most important to you? List some. Identify a visitor from a specific country. Ask the children (on the basis of their social studies) if knowledge of his origin would make any difference in regard to what might be included on a local tour. Why or why not?

Because a foreign visitor is not present, offer the following alternative. Ask the children to draw or paint, in an interpretive way, something about their region or something in which they strongly believe or are interested in that would be of possible interest to a foreign visitor. Suggest that it might be possible to

165

actually send some of their drawings and paintings to a foreign country. Moreover, it might be further possible for them to see some work by persons of their own age from other countries. (The National Art Education Association and the American National Red Cross are co-sponsors of the International School Art Program, which facilitates the shipment of school art to other nations and offers exhibitions of our own and foreign school art for circulation here. Call your local Red Cross chapter for brochures and other information regarding the eligibility of your age group for entry and for the possible scheduling of an exhibition of foreign work for local viewing. Filmstrips are also available.)

Procedure

Distribute the chosen drawing or painting materials. Ask the children to make *dominant* in their compositions the thing they most value in their immediate lives and region. Emphasize the importance of showing something unique by including more than the usual details of certain objects and events. Some children might do on-the-spot sketching as an adjunct of this situation. Occasionally ask them to switch viewpoints and look at their work in progress (as much as possible) from the viewpoint of a foreign observer from a culture of which they have some knowledge. What might his impressions be? In consideration of the latter, discourage the portrayal of such unexpressive sterotypes as postcard copies, ducks on ponds, sleeping fishermen, or anonymous heavily-rouged cheerleaders jumping up and down. Invite the children to scrutinize the worth of their lives in reference to their own regions. Enable them to visualize, as artistically as possible, events which they have experienced directly. Through this art learning situation they have opportunity to consider their own locale in reference to possible reactions elsewhere in the world. Regionalism such as this is a kind of universal thinking. Encourage the children to develop an "artistic Care package" with this in mind.

The Objective
Expression through art of ideas, attitudes, and feelings.

The Situation

Materials

Stimulation

Procedure

167

Form in Art

18

There are many forms of art—performing, literary, musical, visual.

Form should not be misconstrued as something which is solely three-dimensional (a volume).

Within each of these art forms there are more forms; each has unique structural properties.

In the visual arts many of these forms can be developed through any one of a variety of possible art media.

Although a classroom *mural* may be executed with temperas cut paper, or pastels, these media would be employed in further reference to the unique properties and demands of the mural as a particular form of art. A mural is not merely a "large picture."

The Objective

Production of evidence of sensitivity toward form in art.

The Situation (No. 1)

Additive sculpture: planes and volumes. In at least two situations, become acquainted with the construction and modeling approaches of additive *sculpture*, with emphasis on sculpture as a *form* of art, not a *medium*.

Materials

For the construction approach, provide everyone with scissors and a variety of sizes of rectangles cut with a paper cutter from medium-weight cardboard (tablet backs and cardboards from laundered shirts). The sizes of the rectangles could range from 1½" × 2½" to 3" × 4". For the modeling approach, use ceramic-moist clay, one pound per person.

Stimulation

The natural evolvement of the shape by way of these two diverse additive approaches will in itself be interesting. Discuss briefly the concept of *additive* sculpture as a *form* of visual art different from carving (subtractive) and painting (which is flat). Ask the children, however, what a *three-dimensional* form of art such as sculpture shares with music. (Time, as one has to walk around and see, rather than hear, different parts before going on to the next.)

Procedure

Construction from planes: Distribute the scissors and about eighteen rectangles to each person. Identify them as "planes." The problem will be that of joining all of their planes together, without using any glue or tape, to make something that stands by itself. Subject matter need not enter in, though for some it may. The children are not to fold the cards, which will be used again, but they may cut slots in each and join them accordingly. Ask them to try to bring the planes together to make a total structure that is as wide *or* as high as their ideas, the number of cards, and the nonglued joints permit. At another time explore the expressive possibilities of this art form. For now, and also in subsequent tries, enjoy the play of light and shadow on the various planes as an expression of visual worth and interest in itself.

Solid volume modeling: As soon as possible after the above situation provide everyone with one pound of moist clay. Discuss the concept of solid volume as contrasted to flat planes and hollow spaces. Indicate that clay is but one *medium* that can be used to make solid art forms. Have the children pull off portions and stick them back on to the clay until all of the original ball has been taken apart and re-arranged. The final object should be something other than a ball even if no subject is evident. What should be in evidence is a feeling for *modeling*, the organization of a three-dimensional sculptural form by means of pressing separate pieces into a new totality. Remind the children to press each addition tightly into the total unit. Add moisture as cracks appear. Allow these objects to dry slowly. If they fall apart, the indication is that they were not properly jointed. Remoisten the clay and try again. How do these two approaches compare to carving? To drawing?

The Objective
Production of evidence of sensitivity toward form in art.

The Situation (No. 2)
"Pure" painting. Develop a situation whereby *painting*, as another form of art, can be contrasted to *illustration*.

Materials
Provide working space that will accommodate an 18" × 24" sheet of manila or white butcher paper for each child. Everyone should have a long-handled brush, tempera in the three primary colors plus white, a plastic egg crate, water for cleaning between colors, and a paintcloth. Have several well-illustrated books available for visual reference.

Stimulation
Examine some of the book illustrations with the group. Elicit descriptions of the apparent visual qualities. (Mainly the containment of color in crisply defined shapes with and without outlines.) What are they called? Pictures? If they are pictures, are they the same as paintings? Why not? (They are reduced in size and printed by the thousands. Also, the paint and the idea both have been used to conform to a special task, that of telling a story already established in printed words. As a consequence, these pictures are referred to as *illustrations*.) Tell the children that they will have an opportunity to paint, not for illustration, but for the sake of painting. Painting is a special form of art that can be used to convey an idea or a feeling that is personal. Pictures also can be *paintings* when they do not try to "hide" the fact that they were made with paint (regardless of what kind of painting *medium* is used). Paintings, however, need not be pictures.

Procedure
Distribute the materials. Encourage the children while using the paint to be as much like painters as possible. If they are using subject matter, they should allow the shapes to emerge as direct actions of the brush rather than force the large brush into a small cramped shape that will be filled in smoothly without a trace of a brushmark or arm movement.

Some children might appreciate an approach that requires no previous intent. Many *contemporary* painters work in this way. (See *abstract expressionism, tachisme.*) Encourage those who would benefit from such an approach to "interact" with the brush, paint, and *format*.

Regardless of approach, emphasize that one attribute of painting is that of color mixing. This form of art allows for a combination of colors, in a *fluid* state, which may intermingle in unique ways. Encourage the children to mix colors by employing a *wet-on-wet* approach

169

directly on the format as well as in the compartments of their egg crates. Use some thick applications (*impasto*). After all, paint is the only medium applied by a *brush;* use it! Accordingly, let the children try dragging a nearly *dry brush* over an area of contrasting color thereby producing varying textures. Many children (depending on their backgrounds) insist on making paint look "slick" or "neat." Remind them that the brush is a legitimate tool, the "tracks" of which are an honest part of any painting. Let these tracks show. A close scrutiny of pictorial works by Hals and Rembrandt shows evidence of a recognition of paint *and* brush qualities. Encourage the children to turn their work in different positions as they work. Focus on color repetition as well as mixing. Seek rhythm in the repetitions of brushstrokes as events in themselves. Repeat some shapes yet introduce a sufficient variety to maintain visual interest. React in terms of *paint* and arrangement!

The Objective

Production of evidence of sensitivity toward form in art.

The Situation (No. 3)

Functional ceramics. Produce a form of art that relates design quality to utility.

Materials

Rely once again on ceramic-moist clay. Since the products should be sent out for firing and possible glazing (an inexpensive service quite readily available), be sure the clay is free of air bubbles and foreign particles. Provide everyone with water containers, small orange-stick tools, and a masonite palette upon which to work. Set aside an area where the clay products may dry slowly and safely. Have the children collect spoons, broken hack saw blades, and other devices that could be used for shaping and for producing texture.

Stimulation

Each form of art seems to serve a certain purpose. Even paintings, often to be enjoyed just as things in themselves serve a purpose in enabling people to respond in a way different from their ordinary approach to objects which are usually made for specific functions (like autos or refrigerators or toys). Ceramic art forms differ from paintings in that often they are made for a specific function. Like all genuine art forms, however, useful ceramic objects are made in further consideration of *design* or appearance. Similar to sculpture, many are also expressive of ideas or feelings. Expression, though, is often absent and instead replaced by an intent to decorate.

Suggest that each child think of a small useful object, other than an ashtray, that he could make of clay. Further indicate that this object will be fired in a kiln and become permanently hard. It will, as a result, become usable. List some of the possibilities.

Procedure

Distribute the clay. Each child should think of the general volume of his object. If it is mainly vertical (a bud or flower vase), he might roll clay into lengths as thick as a large pencil and coil them upward. (Demonstrate this.) Subsequent rolls can be attached to the ends of those preceding. The inner and outer walls may be smoothed with the thumb and some additional clay and moisture. Eliminate all cracks. Use the orange stick for a final shaping. View the object from all sides.

For an object that is shallow and horizontal, the child can establish an over-all volume by pressing the clay into the cup of a hand or on the palette and pinching out any necessary depression. Spoons and looped wires are useful for scooping. This shallow form can be turned upside down and further refined. Encourage honesty in establishing volumes. A pencil holder should not emulate a baby shoe, a mint dish should not appear as a turtle with a hole in its back. Allow these art *forms* to follow the intended *function.* We might refer to them as functional art *forms.*

Employ the tools for incised decorative lines and textures that enhance but do not overpower or detract from the forms. Discuss the purpose of *decoration.* Some forms possess sufficient visual clarity in themselves; decoration is unnecessary. Cover the finished products with a damp cloth and allow them to dry slowly before firing.

170

The Objective

Production of evidence of sensitivity toward form in art.

The Situation (No. 4)

Combines: a recent art form. By contrast to some of the most ancient art forms, ceramics and paintings, become acquainted with a new visual form.

Materials

For each person obtain a sheet of heavy white posterboard or corrugated cardboard (about 16″ × 20″). Each person should have tempera in the primary colors, black, and white and the equipment necessary to apply it. Have white glue available for adhering small, lightweight, discarded three-dimensional objects which each child has collected. These may include lids of all kinds, corks, drainplugs, plastic toys, old pencils and erasers—any little treasure that can be glued to a cardboard surface.

Stimulation

Briefly review painting and ceramics as forms of visual art that have been produced for centuries. Indicate that at this time the children will have a chance to explore a form of art which is referred to as a *combine* (a joining of non-art objects with paint—a mingling of untraditional materials with a traditional medium). In a sense this new form represents an attempt to break away from the more familiar ways of producing art. Some of the artists who make combines think this particular form of art has more to do with the times in which we live than do the traditional forms. Some recent efforts include stuffed goats and automobile tires combined with oil paint on what is otherwise a flat though very large format. Not everyone agrees as to the validity of the combine as an art form, but most critics recognize it as a rather daring kind of experimentation. Combines are expressive to some people, amusing to others; some find them to be well composed and many think they are chaotic.

Distribute the materials. Everyone should have at least three small three-dimensional objects. Encourage the children to relax and enjoy a visual experiment.

Procedure

Encourage each child to compare the sizes of his objects with the format. If the objects appear "lost," he can reduce the size of the cardboard. When the size relationship (*proportion*) of objects and format is reconciled, he should glue the objects in position. Encourage *asymmetrical* arrangement. The objects may be arranged to represent *subject matter* or they may be used as *shape, color,* and *texture.*

Examine the objects for predominant color. The child can then mix some tempera colors that correspond to colors in the objects, repeating these colors, strategically, somewhere on the cardboard format. What else can be done to attain *unity* between the non-art objects and the remainder of the format? Some children might introduce lines and shapes that echo the lines and shapes in the objects. They should not, however, paint over the objects themselves. The brush can be used to produce textures and patterns that are compatible with textures and patterns in the objects. Conversely, opposite colors and textures might produce a *contrast* that could be successful in relating the three-dimensional objects to the flat format. Exhibit and examine the completed combines for their visual and possibly expressive worth. Are they unified forms or chaotic fads?

The Objective

Production of evidence of sensitivity toward form in art.

The Situation (No. 5)

Murals: size, sequence, and scope. Recognize the mural as a unique form among the visual arts.

Materials

Project a set of color slides or a color film that pertains to a specific locale, community, or event therein that would be of interest to your group. Reserve some bulletin board space (3′ × 7′ or more) within the room. Cover this with white butcher paper. Provide each person with assorted colors of fadeproof colored paper, chalk or crayon, scissors, and white glue. Have some straight pins available for a temporary

171

arrangement of individual shapes on the mural *format*.

Stimulation

Review the movie or slide series as an art form that shows a series of events going on in time and many objects from different viewpoints. Indicate that there is one other visual art form that attempts to do some of these things but in a different way. Any hunches? Identify *mural* as a form that shows many events occurring at different times and many objects that are in different places, all within the same format. A mural is different from a film because it is always visible and it does not move. Moreover, it conforms to a wall as a part of a building. Often, in addition to communicating a message, it is intended to make the *architecture* more visually pleasing. Some present-day murals are mainly decorative. The older murals were also informative. The children will have opportunity to do two things, namely, to add visual interest to their room and to communicate an idea. Ask them to view the film and extract from it the visual features they think did most to signify whatever was depicted. To familiarize them with the *medium*, distribute the materials prior to the viewing.

Procedure

Handle the responses in any way you and they prefer. Make a list of possible visual ingredients that will appear in the mural or let each develop in private his salient visual extract from the film. From the latter method more duplication of *subject matter* will occur but the *content* of each idea will probably vary. Moreover, these duplications tend to indicate what was of significance to the children.

Before developing these symbolic shapes, discuss the location and shape of the mural *format*. Consider the surrounding *colors* and *textures*. Encourage the children to keep the "objects" they make "flat" because the mural is a part of a flat wall. De-emphasize *chiaroscuro* and *perspective*. (Many will attend to this de-emphasis without intending to.) Remind them that actual proportions and distances between objects in both time and space is of little consequence. A mural (unlike a painting) can absorb these differences as an over-all decorative–communicative form of art.

Decide what object each child is to make.

The object may be cut from several sheets of paper, reassembled, and given additional color and detail by means of chalk or crayon. As the objects are completed, have each child pin his to the format. When consensus is gained as to the final *composition*, attach the objects permanently. Appoint some children to add color and texture to the original butcher paper (*negative space*) that shows between the cut-paper objects. Evaluate the total in relation to the intent and the wall around it. Why is a mural not merely a big picture? Not an illustration?

The Objective

Production of evidence of sensitivity toward form in art.

The Situation (No. 6)

Collage: another twentieth-century art form. Develop a visual expression with reliance on adhered *textures* and *patterns*.

Materials

Prior to this situation develop a collection of lightweight textures and swatches of thin, patterned material that can be easily glued to a cardboard format. As much as possible limit the collection to "actual" textures (burlap, shingles, different kinds of paper and cloth, wrappers, etc.) but include some "simulated" textures from magazine advertisements (carpets, cake, suds, wood, stone, etc.). Use discarded posters and corrugated cardboard for individual formats. Provide white glue, scissors, and a stapler.

Stimulation

Select and hold in view some of the more highly visible textures. Encourage the children to look at each texture in terms of its possible expressive qualities. Of what might a torn piece of tar paper remind them? A sheet of corrugated paper with the ribbing exposed? A simulated (photographed) texture depicting a slick sheet of formica? A bit of simulated chrome? Many children will be able to assign these varied "surfaces" to the points of origin. Some will recognize other expressive qualities. Reverse the point of discussion. Ask the chil-

172

dren to think of different environments which they have visited in terms of "textural traits" found in each. If they were able to visit a certain place and cut swatches of textures from it what would these findings communicate? An ice cream fountain, for example, might include leatherette, a slick counter covering, chrome trim, crumpled napkins, twisted straws, a patterned menu (with a possible addition of color added by occasional drops of melted flavors), white starched cloth, surfaces that reflect a fluorescent glow, asphalt tile, decals on glass, and so on. Ask the children to identify other environments according to textural traits and surface patterns.

Procedure

Introduce the term *collage*. Reintroduce Picasso and Schwitters as artists of this century who helped develop this form of art. Indicate how they incorporated everyday materials into an artistic form of expression. The collage is one more departure from traditional form.

Invite the children to think out an environment in terms of texture and, in turn, find textures in the collection that correspond to the environment. Cut each swatch in a simple shape so as not to detract from the surface itself. Some textures might best communicate the chosen environment if the edges are torn rather than cut. Some shapes might be more rounded than angular. Encourage the children to cover most of the format and in doing so give the eye an occasional respite by introducing "plain" areas between otherwise busy patterns and textures.

If both actual and simulated textures are used in the same format, a problem in unity arises. Encourage an expression based mainly on one or the other. Attach some of the actual textures with staples. Add weights to some until the glue dries. Emphasize texture and pattern relationships more than line, shape, and color relationships. Develop an environmental exhibition based upon the results. At another time you and they might enjoy going on a "texture tour" of a specific environment.

The Objective

Production of evidence of sensitivity toward form in art.

The Situation (No. 7)

Drawing as "pure" line and contour. Approach drawing from the standpoint of "inventing" lines that are in themselves significant.

Materials

For the *contour* approach everyone should have a 12" × 18" sheet of newsprint and a ballpoint pen. The "pure" line approach can be developed through any number of materials that make unique lines. Among these would be medium-weight cardboard cut into trapezoid shapes about 2" × 4". The four edges of these shapes can be pressed into a pad of several damp paper towels soaked with black ink or thinned tempera. A unique line is made by stamping the inked edge on a sheet of newsprint. Each person should have an 18" × 24" drawing board (cut from Upson board obtainable from any lumberyard) and thumbtacks. Provide a model or a visible still-life arrangement, or go outdoors for reference to actuality.

Stimulation

Drawing, in all of its variety, is possibly one of the oldest of visual art forms. Some artists, you might indicate, think that drawing is basic to all of the visual arts. There are many approaches to drawing. Some artists emphasize the quality of the *lines* themselves rather than the object they are looking at while drawing. Some artists just draw lines without attempting to relate them to a visible subject. Lines such as these are referred to as "pure." Another use of lines, *always* in reference to objects, is *contour* drawing. This act resembles batting a baseball; one looks at the object but not at the tool or the paper on which he draws. Let the children try either or both approaches.

Procedure

Pure approach: Use the inked pads and cardboard trapezoids. Try a few practice lines by pressing an edge on the moist pad and immediately stamping it on newsprint. Focus on the referent object (model, still life, trees) and stamp its general proportion and shape with this "tool." Notice that curves have to be indicated by many-faceted straight lines, which give the illusion of curves (similar to extending an octagon into a circle by adding several shorter straight lines). Also notice that the lines

173

themselves have a unique character apart from the referent object. Experiment with the tool in order to vary the *width* of the lines. Stamp hard and stamp soft to vary the lightness and darkness of each line and the expressive qualities, which can range from fragility to boldness. The lines, in other words, take precedence over the object. But do not ignore the visual attributes of the object.

Contour approach: Focus on the nearest part of the object. Determine where that part of the object might be located on the *format*. Put the ballpoint pen at that position. Look away from the paper and pretend that the point is touching every ridge within and every edge "around" the object. Try to "feel" the object from afar. Look at the paper only to start a new journey. Do not be concerned about actual proportions. Notice instead the sensitive quality of the thin, continuous line. Seek details. Draw often. Why is drawing a different form of visual art from painting? From collage?

The Objective

Production of evidence of sensitivity toward form in art.

The Situation (No. 8)

Drawing: pictorial line as a symbol for edges. Recognize line as a manmade invention and a substitute for edges in drawing.

Materials

Provide everyone with a 2B drawing pencil, a 12" × 18" sheet of newsprint, and a sheet of white drawing or manila paper of comparable size. Have someone be prepared to assume a costumed pose for a period of fifteen minutes.

Stimulation

Distribute the pencils and newsprint. Have each child draw, with one continuous line, a life-size profile of a face from the hairline to the chin. Allow sufficient time for all to finish. Ask them to describe what they see on the paper. What do they "read" from it? Many might describe it as a "face." Others might see it for what it is—a line. Ask them to look at

this line as if it described something to the left of it (if the nose protrudes to the left, and vice versa if it does not). In other words, the line which reads as "nose" now dips *inward* and so on. Turn the paper and view this line in a horizontal position with the nose protruding downward. Ask them to view this line as if it were the edge of some mountains underneath it. Let them shade in the area in order to achieve this effect. In consideration of this exercise, just what does a line represent in drawing? Enable them, through the exercise and discussion, to recognize line as a manmade invention by which he depicts edges. The singular line they just drew could be confusing, however, because it did not continue on around to define an entire shape. (Have them complete the entire outline of the head.) Even when the entire head is outlined it fails to describe adequately. (Have them add some internal details, an eye, ear, mouth, and hair.) The interior lines, as symbols for other edges do much to complete the "message." These lines, which attempt to describe objects accurately, may be referred to as pictorial lines. These lines, in a sense, are servants to the objects they try to describe. They may flow and vary from thick to thin, but as lines in themselves they are not as dominant as those referred to as "pure." These lines are more descriptive of the *object*.

Procedure

Distribute the drawing paper and pose the model. Ask the children to look at the model for a few minutes before drawing. Do they see any *actual* lines on the model? Do they not see *edges* of folds and features and shapes instead? Their problem is to draw, with lines, substitutes for these edges. Encourage them to look at the model through this "line for edge" frame of reference. Appreciate line as a rather wonderful invention which is ordinarily taken for granted.

As for *proportion*, instruct them to perform some "visual long division"; they may divide the head into different parts of the body in order to determine equivalent size relations. En route, encourage them to draw some lines that run from head to toe rather than to compartmentalize several separate shapes. Work from the general to the particular, all with pictorial line. Avoid shading until another time.

174

The Objective

Production of evidence of sensitivity toward form in art.

The Situation (No. 9)

Subtractive sculpture. Become acquainted with an ancient form of art which requires a unique kind of manipulation and conceptualization.

Materials

Have everyone bring empty, rinsed milk cartons in one-quart sizes. From any lumberyard order a bag of molding plaster and a bag of vermiculite (a lightweight insulation product). Obtain a large flexible mixing bowl and rubber gloves. Don the latter and devote about a half hour to mixing and pouring the following ingredients into the cartons, which should be assembled upon a covered surface. Half fill the bowl with water and add equal amounts of plaster and vermiculite to it until a sizable mound forms above the surface. Mix these semi-thick ingredients by hand and fill each carton within an inch from the sawed-off tops. The material will solidify within a few minutes, but do not peel off the cartons for at least an hour. Do not dispose of or rinse off excess plaster in the sink. Use dull knives, old hacksaw blades, rasps, and files for sculpture tools (have on hand a stiff brush to clean the latter). Provide adequate covering for working surfaces.

Stimulation

Distribute the solidified blocks. Have the children peel the coverings. What do sculptors do? Until the invention of welding, they carved in stone and wood. Many still work in this traditional form. Focus on the solid, rectangular objects. Observe the texture produced by the vermiculite. (This additive also decreases the weight when the product is completely dry.) In discussing traditional sculpture, emphasize the process of *subtraction*. Once something is removed from this block it cannot be replaced. There is no "erasing." Moreover, several sides have to be considered, not just one as in a drawing. One cut affects the whole block. The sculptor must "think around corners."

Procedure

Distribute the sculpture tools. Since little of the original surface will show on the final piece, let the children get acquainted with the tools and block by making some small scoops and cuts. Follow a similar approach when work actually commences–nibble rather than gulp, or tragedy will follow in the form of a fractured block.

Freedom from subject matter might enable many to become better acquainted with the subtractive process. Suggest the following procedure: First, decide whether the sculpture will be horizontal or vertical in position (though this intent may change upon completion). Second, subtract sections that vary in size from all four of the sides. Third, eliminate at least two (or all) of the four corner edges. Fourth, preserve at least a square half-inch of each of all six of the original sides and ends (to prevent a complete dwindling of the form).

As the children cut away small amounts at a time, encourage them to observe the indentations and emerging protrusions. Notice how the light creates shadows. Some might prefer to "tunnel" through, creating voids that integrate the air around the sculpture with its interior. Turn the objects continually. Near completion look at them as if one line could lead the eye from area to area and pass *around* the entire form without being interrupted. Compare the attributes and limitations of subtractive to those of additive sculpture.

The Objective

Production of evidence of sensitivity toward form in art.

The Situation (No. 10)

Printmaking: woodcuts. Recognize relief printing, as exemplified by woodcuts, as one aspect of the *form* of printmaking.

Materials

From a lumberyard order some 1" × 6" soft white ponderosa pine in lengths sufficient to provide everyone with a sawed piece about 8" long. Obtain some block-cutting tools which retain sharpness and thus are easier to use. Some have interchangeable blades. Obtain *water*-base block printing ink (tubes), rubber

175

brayers, cookie sheets (to be used as palettes), thin paper for printing, brushes, and black liquid ink. Allow space for drying the sticky prints. Try to obtain reproductions of the following woodcuts: Feininger's "Lehnstadt," Frasconi's "Self-Portrait," Kirchner's "Portrait of the Dealer," Heckel's "Portrait of a Man," Schmidt-Rottluff's "Melancholia," or Nolde's "Prophet."

Stimulation

Have each child place a coin on his desk. Be prepared to lend pennies. Introduce the palette, block printing ink, and brayer. Squeeze some ink on the palette and "grind" it with the brayer until it assumes a texture comparable to an orange peel. Ask the children what would happen if they inked a coin, placed paper on top of it, and rubbed it. Which parts would "print"? (The raised parts, because the shallow parts would not be touched by the inked brayer.) In what way would the relief (raised parts) appear in printed form in relation to the actual coin? (In reverse.) Present a block of wood. What would happen if it were inked in its present state? Try it. "Grind" more ink. Add a few drops of water. Place thin paper *over* the inked wood and rub it quickly with the ball of the hand. Peel it diagonally from corner to corner. The result should be that of a black rectangle with some evidence of faint pattern produced by the wood grain.

Select a gouge. Push it away from you. Never hold the block with the other hand in front of the oncoming gouge. Steady the block with the other hand behind the tool. Cut with the grain. Make another print, then clean your hands. Notice that the part which was cut away does *not* print. Only the *original* surface of the wood holds ink. Clean the brayer and palette with water. Damp clean the block with moist paper towels.

Procedure

Distribute the wood, brushes, *liquid* ink, and cutting tools. Ask the children to make their original surfaces black by coating them with the fast-drying *liquid* ink. Now, as they experiment with different tools and expose the white of the wood beneath the black surfaces, they will get a "preview" of an actual print in terms of light and dark. (Remind them, however, of the inevitable reversal.)

Encourage them to combine tool marks into patterns and textures. As much as possible, cut with the grain using the gouge-type tools. Use flat blades for the minimal crossgrain cuts. Allow some sections of the original black to remain untouched. Incise some lines. Invite the children to follow the rhythm of the wood grain and develop designs accordingly. Knots can provide visual cues for subsequent shapes and rhythms. Have the children print as described above. Look at some examples of woodcuts. Generalize from these and the actual experience during a future exploration of this form of art.

176

The Objective
Production of evidence of sensitivity toward
form in art.

The Situation

Materials

Stimulation

Procedure

177

Summary and Suggestions

Much of the foregoing is based upon the idea that the meaning of art as a dimension of human experience can be partly realized in elementary art education. This incipient realization can occur in the form of a series of discoveries—discoveries preceded by effective exploration.

Effective exploration usually involves reasonably defined goals. The objectives emphasized throughout attempt to identify and "map" possible goals which can be attained in the early phases of art learning. They emerge as clear intentions as to what can be learned. The many situations related to these intended objectives are but intervals of ongoing journeys directed toward these very goals.

The presence of objectives need not preclude discoveries which can be made inductively en route. Alert exploration will improve the map, which will at best be only partly accurate because of the everchanging terrain. Nor does a well-mapped exploration into the domain of art restrict those so engaged to singular, identical discoveries upon arrival at major points of realization; art is such that many possible discoveries await each participant. The situations herein have been developed with this open-ended kind of discovery in mind.

Further, each situation is directed toward the formation of concepts in and about art. Each concept gained can contribute to a continued effective exploration. Or each concept can, like art, be enjoyed in and for itself. And, akin to the over-all goal of general education, concepts of oneself in relation to one's natural and cultural environment can emerge as another

aspect of art learning. Though not providing the only way, concepts do, after all, provide people with a way of realizing relationships. Accordingly, this book suggests a way to learn about art, not the only way.

This summary of intentions appears idealistic: by presenting a wide range of the art learning situations embodied herein, the teacher can be assured that art concepts will follow. Hardly. As implied by the blank space at the end of each chapter, each teacher, in consideration of a unique group of children, will have to develop additional situations. This involvement can become a kind of open-ended discovery for the teacher as well as the children. Moreover, each of the suggested situations in this book will have to be modified when it is actually presented, according to the uniqueness of the children and the teacher. In addition to the content, the procedure, as it appears in the written development of each situation, also can be modified.

To reiterate, the teacher is invited to examine and re-examine the sixteen objectives from which the situations emanate. Each objective and each situation should be subjected to further scrutiny as an aspect of effective exploration. This task will be more difficult to pursue when a series of successes result from the implemented situations. Scrutiny is more likely to occur, however, when a situation results in a general failure! Yet, the occasional failure of a situation does not in itself warrant an immediate rejection of either it or of the related objective. Instead, a frequent referral to the suggestions in Chapter Two, "Organizing and Evaluating Art Learning," can be helpful

178

with regard to the outcomes of each presentation. The situation and the performances of the children and the teacher all are subject to appraisal.

Much of the success of any of these situations depends on factors extraneous to this publication. It is quite apparent that a teacher must possess considerable knowledge about himself, children, their art, their learning processes, their culture, and, of course, the content of art. This knowledge must be accompanied by refined attitudes, abilities of organization, and communication. One cannot romantically assume that many children throughout the span of the elementary grades will automatically find their own way in art. To counter this assumption an attempt has been made herein to organize and inject *art content* into elementary art education. Content and method have merged. Yet in the process of this merger this book hardly purports to be all-inclusive. It is more practical than theoretical, but not exclusively so, for how could theory and practice be separated and retain any meaning?

Accordingly, in order to give additional meaning to all of the preceding and in turn strengthen one's background in respect to learning theory, practical method, and art content, the following books are recommended for further reading. These recommendations are allocated according to the organization of this publication. A diversity of viewpoints will be discovered among them. Much material for the development of potential insights on the part of the elementary teacher can be found in them.

FOR FURTHER READING

ART EDUCATION, LEARNING PROCESSES, AND ORGANIZATIONAL CONSIDERATIONS

Barkan, Manuel. *Through Art to Creativity*. New York: Allyn and Bacon, Inc., 1960.

Bruner, Jerome S. *On Knowing: Essays for the Left Hand*. Cambridge: The Belknap Press of Harvard University Press, 1963.

Conant, Howard. *Art Education*. Washington, D.C.: The Center for Applied Research, Inc., 1964.

Harris, Dale B. *Children's Drawings as Measures of Intellectual Maturity*. New York: Harcourt, Brace, and World, Inc., 1963, Part One.

Krathwohl, David R., Benjamin S. Bloom, and Bertram B. Masia. *Taxonomy of Educational Objectives: Handbook II: Affective Domain*. New York: David McKay Co., Inc., 1964.

Lowenfeld, Viktor, and W. Lambert Brittain. *Creative and Mental Growth*, 4th ed. New York: The Macmillan Co., 1964, Chapters 1-8.

McFee, June K. *Preparation for Art*. Belmont: Wadsworth Publishing Co., Inc., 1961, Part Two.

Merritt, Helen. *Guiding Free Expression in Children's Art*. New York: Holt, Rinehart & Winston, 1964.

Wachowiak, Frank, and Theodore Ramsay. *Emphasis: Art*. Scranton, Pa.: International Textbook Co., 1965, Chapters 1—5.

AREA ONE: VISUAL PERCEPTUAL LEARNING

Arnheim, Rudolph. *Art and Visual Perception*. Berkeley: University of California Press, 1954.

Birren, Faber. *Color: A Survey in Words and Pictures*. Hyde Park, N.Y.: University Books Inc., 1963.

Blake, Peter. *God's Own Junkyard, the planned deterioration of America's landscape*. New York: Holt, Rinehart & Winston, 1964.

Canaday, John. *Keys to Art*. New York: Tudor Publishing Co., 1962.

Copplestone, Trewin. *Modern Art Movements*. New York: Marboro Books, 1962.

Elsen, Albert E. *Purposes of Art*. New York: Holt, Rinehart & Winston, Inc., 1962.

Gombrich, E. H. *Art and Illusion*. Pantheon Books, 1960.

Goodrich, Lloyd, and John I. H. Bauer. *American Art of Our Century*. New York: Frederick A. Praeger, 1961.

Hubbard, Guy, and Ivan E. Johnson. *Instructor Modern Art Series*. Danville, N.Y.: F. A. Owen Co., 1962.

McFee, June K. *Preparation for Art*. Belmont, Calif.: Wadsworth Publishing Co., Inc., 1961, Chapters 3 and 4.

Nairn, Ian. *The American Landscape, A Critical View*. New York: Random House, 1965.

Read, Herbert. *A Concise History of Modern Painting*. New York: Frederick A. Praeger, 1959.

Read, Herbert. *A Concise History of Modern Sculpture*. New York: Frederick A. Praeger, 1964.

Reusch, Jurgen, and Weldon Kees. *Nonverbal Communication*. Berkeley: University of California Press, 1956.

Vernon, M. D. *The Psychology of Perception*. Baltimore: Penguin Books, Inc., 1962.

Whitney, Elwood, ed. *Symbology: The Use of Symbols in Visual Communication*. New York: Hastings House, 1960.

AREA TWO: DEVELOPING ART-RELATED BEHAVIOR

Berger, René. *The Language of Art*. London: Thames and Hudson, 1963.

Bruner, Jerome S. *On Knowing: Essays for the Left Hand*. Cambridge: The Belknap Press of Harvard University Press, 1963, Part One.

Contemporary American Painting and Sculpture, Urbana: University of Illinois Press, 1965.

Gotshalk, D. W. *Art and the Social Order*. New York: Dover, 1962, Parts One and Three.

Koestler, Arthur. *The Act of Creation*. London: Hutchinson of London, 1964.

Langer, Susanne K. *Problems of Art*. New York: Charles Scribner's Sons, 1957.

Lowenfeld, Viktor, and W. Lambert Brittain. *Creative and Mental Growth*, 4th ed. New York: The Macmillan Co., 1964, Chapters 1—8.

McDonald, Frederick J. *Educational Psychology*, 2nd ed. Belmont, Calif.; Wadsworth Publishing Co., Inc., 1965.

McFee, June K. *Preparation for Art*. Belmont, Calif.: Wadsworth Publishing Co., Inc., 1961, Chapters 2, 6, and 7.

National Cultural Center. *Creative America*. Washington, D.C.: Ridge Press, Inc., 1962.

Parnes, Sidney J., and Harold F. Harding, eds. *A Source Book for Creative Thinking*. New York: Charles Scribner's Sons, 1962.

Shahn, Ben. *The Shape of Content*. New York: Vintage Books, 1960.

Stolnitz, Jerome. *Aesthetics and Philosophy of Art Criticism: A Critical Introduction*. Boston: Houghton Mifflin Co., 1960.

AREA THREE: VISUAL ORGANIZATIONAL LEARNING

Anderson, Donald M. *Elements of Design*. New York: Holt, Rinehart & Winston, 1961.

Andrews, Michael F. *Creative Printmaking*. Englewood Cliffs, N.J.: Prentice-Hall, Inc., 1964.

Bach, Robert O., ed. *Communication, The Art of Understanding and Being Understood*. New York: Hastings House, Publishers, 1963.

Blanch, Arnold. *Methods and Techniques for Gouache Painting (Opaque Water Color)*. New York: American Artists Group, 1946.

Chaet, Bernard. *Artists at Work*. Cambridge: Webb Books Inc., 1960.

Collier, Alan Graham. *Form, Space and Vision*. Englewood Cliffs, N.J.: Prentice Hall, Inc., 1964.

Faulkner, Ray, Edwin Ziegfeld, and Gerald Hill. *Art Today*, rev. ed. New York: Holt, Rinehart, & Winston, 1963.

Halprin, Lawrence. *Cities*. New York: Reinhold Publishing Corp., 1963.

Hogarth, Paul. *Creative Pencil Drawing*. New York: Watson-Guptill Publications, Inc. 1964.

Itten, Johannes. *The Art of Color*. New York: Reinhold Publishing Corp., 1961.

Itten, Johannes. *Design and Form, The Basic Course at the Bauhaus*. New York: Reinhold Publishing Corp., 1963.

Krevitsky, Nik. *Batik: Art and Craft*. New York: Reinhold Publishing Corp., 1964.

McFee, June K. *Preparation for Art*. Belmont, Calif.: Wadsworth Publishing Co., Inc., 1961, Chapter 11.

Moseley, Spencer, Pauline Johnson, and Hazel Koenig. *Crafts Design, An Illustrated Guide*. Belmont, Calif.: Wadsworth Publishing Co., Inc., 1961.

Neutra, Richard. *Life and Shape*. New York: Appleton-Century-Crofts, 1962.

Pollack, Peter. *The Picture History of Photography*. New York: Harry N. Abrams, Inc., 1958.

Röttger, Ernst. *Creative Clay Design*. New York: Reinhold Publishing Corp., 1962.

Röttger, Ernst. *Creative Paper Design*. New York: Reinhold Publishing Corp., 1963.

Sachs, Paul J. *Modern Prints and Drawings*. New York: Alfred A. Knopf, 1954.

Wachowiak, Frank, and Theodore Ramsey. *Emphasis: Art*. Scranton, Pa.: International Textbook Co., 1965, Chapter 6.

SUMMARY AND SUGGESTIONS